INSIGHTS

General Editor: Clive Bloom, Senior Lecturer in English, Middlesex Polytechnic

Editorial Board: Clive Bloom, Brian Docherty, Gary Day, Lesley Bloom and Hazel Day

Insights brings to academics, students and general readers the very best contemporary criticism on neglected literary and cultural areas. It consists of anthologies, each containing original contributions by advanced scholars and experts. Each contribution concentrates on a study of a particular work, author or genre in its artistic, historical and cultural context.

Published titles

Clive Bloom (*editor*)
JACOBEAN POETRY AND PROSE: Rhetoric, Representation and the Popular Imagination
TWENTIETH-CENTURY SUSPENSE: The Thriller Comes of Age
SPY THRILLERS: From Buchan to le Carré

Clive Bloom, Brian Docherty, Jane Gibb and Keith Shand (*editors*)
NINETEENTH-CENTURY SUSPENSE: From Poe to Conan Doyle

Gary Day (*editor*)
READINGS IN POPULAR CULTURE: Trivial Pursuits?

Gary Day and Clive Bloom (*editors*)
PERSPECTIVES ON PORNOGRAPHY: Sexuality in Film and Literature

Brian Docherty (*editor*)
AMERICAN CRIME FICTION: Studies in the Genre
AMERICAN HORROR FICTION: From Brockden Brown to
  Stephen King

Rhys Garnett and R. J. Ellis (*editors*)
SCIENCE FICTION ROOTS AND BRANCHES: Contemporary
  Critical Approaches

Robert Giddings (*editor*)
LITERATURE AND IMPERIALISM

Robert Giddings, Keith Selby and Chris Wensley
SCREENING THE NOVEL: The Theory and Practice of Literary
  Dramatization

Graham Holderness (*editor*)
THE POLITICS OF THEATRE AND DRAMA

Paul Hyland and Neil Sammells (*editors*)
IRISH WRITING: Exile and Subversion

Adrian Page (*editor*)
THE DEATH OF THE PLAYWRIGHT? Modern British Drama
and Literary Theory

Jeffrey Walsh and James Aulich (*editors*)
VIETNAM IMAGES: War and Representation

Gina Wisker (*editor*)
BLACK WOMEN'S WRITING

WRITING
3

DATE DUE

OC 7 '94			
MR 14 '97			

Black Women's Writing

Edited by

GINA WISKER

Senior Lecturer in English
Anglia Polytechnic, Cambridge

St. Martin's Press   New York

formation, write:
ice Division,
'5 Fifth Avenue,
. 10010

ites of America in 1993

; Kong

ISBN 0-312-06864-6

Library of Congress Cataloging-in-Publication Data
Black women's writing / edited by Gina Wisker.
        p.   cm.—(Insights)
    Includes index.
    ISBN 0-312-06864-6
    1. Literature—Black authors—History and criticism.
  2. Literature, modern—20th century—Women authors—History and
  criticism.   3. Literature, modern—20th century—History and
criticism.   I. Wisker, Gina, 1951–   II. Series: Insights (New
York, N.Y.)
PN841.B57   1993
809'.89287—dc20   91–24257
                                                          CIP

Contents

Acknowledgements

Acknowledgements are due to a number of publishers, and through them their authors, for permission to print extracts from several works:

Methuen and Ntozake Shange, for the extracts from *For Colored Girls Who Have Considered Suicide When the Rainbow is Enuf;*

Oldcastle Books and Claudia Tate, for the extracts from *Black Women Writers at Work;*

The Women's Press Ltd and Joan Riley, for the extracts from *The Unbelonging;*

Virago Press and Laurette Ngcobo, for the extracts from *Let It Be Told;*

Karnak House and Grace Nichols, for the extracts from *I Is A Long Memoried Woman;*

Bogle L' Ouverture and Valerie Bloom, for the extracts from 'Trench Town Shock', 'Longsight Market' and 'Yuh Hear Bout?';

The Women's Press and Amanda Hopkinson, for the extracts from 'Lovers and Comrades';

New Beacon Books and Lorna Goodison, for the extracts from 'I Am Becoming My Mother';

Zed Books and Merle Collins, for the extracts from *Because the Dawn Breaks* (London: Karia, 1985);

Zed Books, for the extracts by Helena Joseph and Christine Davies, published in *Words Unchained: Language and Revolution,* ed. Chris Searle (London: Zed Books, 1984).

Acknowledgements are also due to the many students whose comments formal and informal, written and spoken in groups and individually, have helped form arguments in the chapters which explore the studying, reading and discussing of Black women's writing. Among others: Julie Palmer, Lynn Morgan, Sandra Young, Jagdish Singh, Adarsh Grewal, Ann Young, Lisa Wares, Helen Jones, Gillian Banks, Stephanie Margetts, Ann Turnbull, Lyn Evans, Christine Bruley, Anna O'Neill, Samantha Maton, Elizabeth Turnbull and the group she represents.

Personally, I should like to thank Alistair Wisker for his support and advice during the editing of the book, the many babysitters who persuaded my two sons to let me get on with it, Brian Docherty and Clive Bloom for editorial help, and Sarah Dann and Frances Arnold for their enthusiasm and support over publishing the book, from start to finish.

GINA WISKER

Notes on the Contributors

Eva Lennox Birch is a lecturer at Manchester Polytechnic in the Humanities department and has a book in preparation on Black women's writing, with the working title of *A Coat of Many Colours.*

Sara Chetin teaches literature and is the Director of the Academic Advising programme at Richmond College, London. She has a BA Hons from the University of California, Berkeley, in French literature, a Licence de Lettres Modernes from the Sorbonne, Paris, and is currently completing her PhD on 'The Concept of Female Subjectivity in African Literature' at the University of Kent. She has given papers and published articles on African literature in *Kunapipi, Wasafiri* and the *Journal of Commonwealth Literature.*

Dorothy Driver is a Senior Lecturer in the English department at the University of Cape Town, South Africa. She has published various essays on writing by South African women. She is also South African correspondent for the *Journal of Commonwealth Literature* where she publishes an annual bibliography and survey of the year's work in South African literature and literary criticism. Her book *Pauline Smith and the Crisis of Daughterhood* was published in 1990.

Gabriele Griffin teaches literature at Nene College, Northampton. Her research interests include lesbian writing and the work of contemporary women's theatre groups. She has publications in process including *Lesbian Images in Twentieth-Century Women's Writing* (1991) and, with E. F. Aston, *Stage Left: Women's Theatre Groups in Interview* (1991). She and Dr Aston are also editing plays for the Women's Theatre Group for Sheffield Academic Press.

Christine Hall is working on her PhD on Toni Morrison at Nottingham University and teaches locally in adult education. She has published articles on Black women's writing in *Overhere.*

Elaine Jordan teaches in the Department of Literature, at Essex University where she directs the MA in 'Women's Writing'. She has published widely, including a book on Tennyson (1989).

Jackie Roy has just completed her MA at Leeds University and has recently published a work of fiction entitled *Soul Daddy* (1989).

Gina Wisker teaches literature at Anglia Polytechnic, Cambridge, runs the College Access course and teaches on the women's studies MA and short course. Gina has a PhD in contemporary English and American fiction from Nottingham University. She has published articles on contemporary writing and on Black women's writing in *Overhere, Literature Teaching Politics, Gen* and *Ideas and Production*, and has contributed essays to other *Insights* volumes.

Bruce Woodcock teaches English literature at Hull University. He has written on John Fowles in *Male Mythologies: John Fowles and Masculinity* (1984), on Tony Harrison and Thom Gunn, as well as articles on Caribbean literature.

1

Introduction. Black and White: Voices, Writers and Readers

GINA WISKER

Look at you. You black, you pore, you ugly, you a woman. Goddam, he say, you nothing at all . . . .

I'm pore, I'm black, I may be ugly and I can't cook, a voice say to everything listening. But I'm here.

Amen, say Shug. Amen, Amen.[1]

Celie's assertion of identity and worth as a Black woman in *The Color Purple* is a revolutionary step for a woman who has been crushed under the triple burden of her race, class and gender. Alice Walker's creation of the semi-literate, letter-writing Celie is itself a radical intervention in terms of the writing, speaking and reading practices in the context of which Black women's writing is received in the literary and academic world. *The Color Purple* appears on numerous student syllabuses from degree level to A level, to WEA and Extra-Mural Board classes. It is a popular contemporary classic of Black women's writing.

It is because of this popularity, and because of issues the study and reading of the book raises about typicality, reading and publishing practices, that it seems useful to begin this collection of essays with some discussion of the production, content and reception of *The Color Purple*.

Even the rather embarrassing Spielberg film version, starring Whoopie Goldberg, has been useful in introducing many readers to that broad, varied and fruitful field of writing from which this novel springs. But the novel itself raises many questions about writing practices, publishing practices and reading practices. It also raises questions about how far a single book, from one cultural intersection

– Afro-American women's writing – can be said to represent the breadth and variety of the field of Black women's writing, which springs from so many very different cultures. It also raises significant questions about how the largely white literary establishment *can* read and teach these works.

The Color Purple itself, while perhaps initially in danger of being the token text by a Black woman on a syllabus or an individual's reading list, raises other key questions about Black women's writing and its reception. The novel asserts itself to be a personal testimony, it uses both dialect and 'literary' style and revives that traditional form, the epistolary novel, whose roots lie as far back as other work on gender and class-based assault, specifically Richardson's eighteenth-century *Clarissa* and *Pamela*. Its woman-centredness has caused uproar among Black males who see this indictment of gender-based brutality as an undermining of the combined effort against racism.

Alice Walker's *The Color Purple* is a novel which focuses on the testimony of an individual, establishing her identity through giving it voice. It uses the dialect and colloqualisms of local speech, rather than the greater anonymity of 'established' literary prose. And it focuses with a specifically political intent on a woman-identified relationship as a positive and creative move towards self-recognition and establishment of self-worth, as stated in the introductory quotation. This relationship is largely ignored, defused, coyly avoided in the film. If, as much critical comment suggests, many groups of Black lesbians find it particularly difficult to come out, this film would only reinforce that difficulty.

For many of us *The Color Purple* will be the first novel we read by a Black woman writer, at least consciously, and the first of such novels, then, which causes us to think in relation to Black women's writing, about contextual and cultural reading practices, testifying, autobiography, the use of dialect and the representations within and effects of a book which deliberately focuses on relationships between Black men and women. There are other, technical concerns with the novel, largely centred round its use of a Utopian, magical ending, which use of the magical and of Utopian closure are actually frequently met in writing by Black women from a number of different cultures.

These issues of message, political view and form are central to our reading of Black women's writing from a variety of very different cultures, including Black British women's writing, and it is for this reason that discussion of *The Color Purple* provides an appropriate introduction to this collection of essays.

Cora Kaplan positions *The Color Purple* as seminal in that it offers a

> paradigm of change through the agency of black women and a fictional celebration of their capacity to assess and affect the social relations in which they find themselves. An ability to survive the brutal exploitation of their bodies and their labour, by both the dominant culture and their own world of social relations.[2]

Alice Walker herself argues that in her writing she creates models of alternatives which reverse the stereotyped versions of Black women's lives that history has passed down to us, if we, both black and white, have any image at all of Black women's lives in history, for they are signally *un*represented in literary texts and art. Fiction is a creative and revolutionary model for change; it enables expression of experience and as representation of some of the possible atlernatives and solutions to problems in Black women's lives. Walker says, 'When I write . . . I try to make models for myself, I project other ways of seeing.'[3] When Toni Morrison and Maya Angelou argue that they need to discover and define a history, find ways to describe the variety of experience in order to recognise and explore expression of culture and identity: 'I think my whole program as a writer is to deal with history just so I know where I am';[4] and: 'To bear witness to a history that is unrecorded, untaught, in mainstream education, and to enlighten our people.'[5]

Writing is a political act of breaking silence, and writing for Black women from the diversity of backgrounds discussed in this collection of essays bears witness to a variety of histories both individual and more broadly cultural. For some, for Afro-American women in particular, in comparison with the more historically oral traditions, such as that of Africa, there is already a fairly well-established literary tradition within which to write, and in the context of which to be studied. Zora Neale Hurston – the precursor of Alice Walker, Maya Angelou, Toni Morrison, Paule Marshall, Audre Lorde and other Afro-American women writers – has had her work studied as well as read for pleasure for several years. When Black women's writing comes on to the syllabus it is more likely to be from the Afro-American tradition than from Africa, South Africa or the Caribbean, and less still is it likely to be from Black British women's writing.

One of the aims of this collection is to introduce readers, teachers and students alike to some of the range of writing by Black women, and to continue the interest of those of us who have enjoyed the work of the Black women writers we have read, and who would like to read about others as well as those we love. Another aim is to bring into the open some of the tensions and difficulties of its publication and, more centrally, of its reception in the largely white literary establishment, the academic as opposed to the widely popular (and much of this writing has a widely popular following) context of the actual reading and studying of Black women's writing by white or mixed-race teaching groups.

As Audre Lorde puts it, writing is empowerment for others to speak out, step out and value their lives. It provides testimony of their experience as both individuals and members of a community. For us as readers examining the reading experience, it provides enlightenment, self-awareness, a recognition which is not always personally pleasant, and great enjoyment. Recognition and expression of difference is essentially creative: 'In our work and in our living we must recognise that difference is a reason for celebration and growth, rather than a reason for destruction'.[6]

This collection is a celebration of (some of) the diversity of Black women's writing and of the fraught and immensely fruitful experience of reading, discussing, enjoying and valuing it.

The writing of more and more Black women becomes available to readers, students and teachers daily as publishers recognise the popularity of this wide range of works. The Open University has recently adopted Toni Morrison's *Song of Solomon* for its new literature course, which will ensure that the work of Morrison, at least, reaches an extremely wide audience here in Britain.

The range of writing by Black women is diverse and comes to us from such a wide variety of cultures that it would be arrogant to suggest that a short critical work could cover the field, and we would be crazy to attempt to do so. This book provides insights into Black women's writing through a set of specially commissioned essays each of which focuses on the work of specific writers. We have confined ourselves to writers from Africa and South Africa, from America, the Caribbean and from Britain, though several of these categories overlap.

Afro-American writing is considered here in essays by Elaine Jordan on Toni Morrison, by Gina Wisker on Toni Morrison and Alice Walker, and by Christine Hall on Alice Walker. Ntsozake

Shange's choreopoem *For Colored Girls who Have Considered Suicide when the Rainbow is Enuf* is one of three texts considered in a teaching context by Gabriele Griffin, and Gabriele also looks at *The Unbelonging* by Joan Riley, a Black British writer and *I is a Long Memoried Woman* by Grace Nichols, a Caribbean-British writer. Sara Chetin considers the work of African writer Ama Ata Aidoo, while Dorothy Driver concentrates specifically on Bessie Head among South African women writers.

Bruce Woodcock provides a far-reaching and critically useful introduction to the range of poetry being written by women in the Caribbean, while some of the focus of this Introduction is to look at some of the same writers, such as Grace Nichols, who are also Black British women writers, having settled in England. Jackie Roy, herself a Black British woman, concentrates on the experience of studying literature in higher education and on the production, publication and reception of texts by Black women, including herself.

This specifically reading/teaching/student-centred approach is one which runs throughout the collection of essays. The initial spur to the collection arose out of that very relationship of white readers and students and teachers to texts by Black women writers which is discussed in several of the essays. Those of us who are white academics are conscious that this poses a problem in our reading and teaching of texts from other cultural configurations and this collection openly confronts and addresses that problem, without pretending to solve it. As readers who enjoy Black women's writing and teachers who wish many varied examples of Black women's writing to become a normal part of the literary syllabus, we felt that discussing the texts, partly through the focus of our own teaching and the comments of our white or mixed student groups, was a way of acknowledging the difficulties and of finding ways of reading and studying the texts represented here. It is only by looking closely and honestly at the difficulties and the joys of reading Black women's writing – in the majority of cases here, particularly for the white feminist – that we can develop self-aware, culturally contextual, critical reading techniques and, while we might argue that there is no overt racism in our feminist classrooms, perhaps some of the blunders of any covert racism can be avoided.

One very important element in our reading, teaching and studying of Black women's writing is that of ensuring the recognition of cultural and historical context. It is only through ensuring that these texts, as any others, are read in context that the kind of essentialism which surrounds and validates the works of the 'great tradition' and its canon can be undermined and the difference and worth of works hitherto ignored or marginalised be properly acknowledged and read from a basis of something more than ignorance. Cora Kaplan argues:

> Unless we are actually specialist on the area from which these foreign anglophone literatures come, and teaching them in that context, our more than usually fragmented and partial knowledge of the history, politics and culture in which they were produced and originally read, frequently leads us into teaching and thinking about these texts through an unintentionally imperialist lense, conflating their progressive politics with our own agendas, interpreting their versions of humanism through the historical evolution of our own.[7]

For those of us, Black and white, who do not come from the various cultural contexts out of which Afro-American, African, Caribbean and Black British writing spring, it is important that the diverse 'otherness' of these texts always be recognised and their contexts understood as far as possible, in order that we may grow nearer to an appreciation of their intention and achievement.

We need to know of the cultural context of writing, and also of the background and development of the forms of expression used. The particular significance of the autobiography is one such form of writing. The autobiographical mode is of particular importance to people who have been silenced hitherto. Historically, slave narratives were counted as both proof of identity and testimony to lived individual experience. Maya Angelou's five-part (so far) fictional autobiography is a fine example of the mode, as is Buchi Emecheta's *Head Above Water* and, earlier, Zora Neale Hurston's essays, *Dust Tracks on a Road* and *I Love Myself when I am Laughing*. Eva Birch comments on reading and teaching both African and Afro-American autobiographical works, noting how students can engage with the personal testimony and desire to investigate the cultural context from which these works spring.

Eva Birch asks questions about the universality of women's preoccupations in autobiographies, how racial awareness shapes self-definition and how this relates to the concept of class and of gender socialisation. Finally, she asks questions which reappear in this collection of essays: about how teachers and students, as readers, relate to the issues raised in the autobiographies and how they could evaluate these texts as literature. *Head Above Water* deals with the 'burden of motherhood' as *Dust Tracks* does not, but both texts raise the issues of how a contemporary group of students in Britain can relate to the very different lives portrayed in these autobiographies from different cultures. Particular issues were raised because of the seemingly contradictory attitude of Hurston who wished to celebrate her Blackness and her race without drowning the individual in the community, arguing that the lives of Black people are so diversified that 'there is no possible classification too catholic that it will cover us all'.[8] This kind of statement can actually be found in a host of writings by Black women from different cultures who wish to assert that difference, find an identity within it. In *Charting the Journey: Writings by Black and Third World Women*[9] the editorial group state that their collection deliberately represents differences and debates among Black women in Britain:

> These differences are themselves reflective of the divisions amongst the various constituencies of Black women. Indeed, though our starting point has been to stress the historical link between us of colonialism and imperialism, we have also been concerned to reflect the divisions and contradictions amongst us. Contradictions that may themselves be the result of historical legacy, or are increasingly generated and reproduced by the contemporary circumstances in which we find ourselves.[10]

Autobiography causes readers to think about representativeness, as Eva Birch's essay testifies. It also raises questions about the self-fictionalising techniques and about the status of autobiography as a literary form.

Elsewhere the literary commonplace of a first-person narrator takes on a new significance against the vital assertion of *name* and identity. Alice Walker uses this form of testimony in *The Temple of my Familiar*, discussed in Gina Wisker's chapter (Chapter 5) and mentioned briefly in Christine Hall's chapter on Alice Walker (Chapter 6). Here Miss Lissie's narrative encompasses different selves throughout race history, each embodied in a photograph of her as different woman, each recalled in narratives. She testifies to slave-ship crossings, echoing a number of voices, and goes back as far as mythic history when women were the cause and source of creativity and power. The personal voice ensures a sense of authenticity, makes

history, individuality and the relationship with the racial group
plausible and palpable.

The empowerment of the autobiographical statement is also evident in poetry, discussed in essays here. Grace Nichols's *I is a Long
Memoried Woman*, considered both in Bruce Woodcock's chapter on
Caribbean woman poets (Chapter 4) and in Gabriele Griffin's chapter
on teaching a variety of texts from different cultural contexts (Chapter
2), explores the issue of identity and the description of individual
identity set against a broader background. Grace Nichols deals in
depth with the experience of women under slavery. The slave legacy
is spoken *through* the voice of an unknown Black woman who charts
her journey from capture in Africa by other Black people to her life
as a slave in the Caribbean where she worked in the sugar-cane
fields and was made the white man's mistress, forced into bearing
his children. Gabriele points out the alignment of this poem with an
oral tradition and argues convincingly that Grace Nichols is writing
the body, embodying the identity the Black woman achieves in tune
with her body, in the body of the text, itself little-scored and affected
by punctuation and the formal constrictions conventionally placed
on layout and expression. Gabriele's essay uses the work of Kristeva
and theories about writing the body to provide extremely useful
insights into ways of radically reading and studying work by Black
women writers.

The history of Black women's writing and publishing in Africa
does not go as far back as that of the Afro-American woman, but the
African woman has traditionally been the repository of oral folktales;
in Western Africa the female folktale teller was/is known as a *griot*.
The Black woman storyteller as carrier of history is a figure who
reappears in Alice Walker's work, particularly *Meridian*, discussed in
this collection by Christine Hall (Chapter 6). She illustrates how the
moment of liberation comes for Meridian when she realises she is
not to be a revolutionary leader but 'a recorder of the past, not in the
detached impersonal manner of the eye behind the camera, but as an
engaged performer, a repository of songs and stories'. This vital role
places the Black woman artist centre-stage in establishing and continuing a nascent literary tradition. Alice Walker's own *In Search of
Our Mothers' Gardens*[11] testifies to the many ways in which creative
Black women in the past had their creativity repressed or channelled
into lost, transient or devalued forms, female forms. The woman
who grows the beautiful garden or who cooks wonderful meals
finds her work transient. The woman who actually carries the oral

literature with her is, however, a part of history. Her creativity and her literary and artistic abilities are channelled through the community; they make her generic, historical.

In the work of Bessie Head, discussed here by Dorothy Driver (Chapter 10), the issue of oral and written literature is again central. Here the woman in South Africa is the voice of the community as she carries its stories and songs. Dorothy Driver argues that the effect of this in Head's texts, as in Ellen Kuzweyo's *Call Me Woman* and others is to involve the reader more thoroughly:

> Head's representation of the storyteller and storytelling involves a refusal both of the authorial authority and the authorial creative function that typically mark the literary text.
> ... one consequence is an invitation to the reader to share in the dramatic conflict around which the story pivots.

The Black woman in Grace Nichols's poem *I is a Long Memoried Woman* embodies for the reader her personal expression, but like Miss Lissie's *In the Temple of My Familiar* it also signifies different but similar expressions by other Black woman. Lauretta Ngcobo in *Let it be Told*[12] points out that the writing of Black British women is often not strictly individually personal, but represents a collectivity of individual personal voices:

> Few of our writings are strictly personal in the subjective sense of encompassing individual exploits. Rather they reflect a collective subject, the common experience of Blackwomen reaching, reflecting and capturing different shades and depths and heights of moods.[13]

The testimony in Grace Nichols's *I Is . . .* is other than celebratory; it can be deeply shocking in its revelations of the brutality of experience lived under slavery when a mother might strangle her infants to save them from being sold into slavery. This horror has to be named, to be lived with but never forgotten, as also when dramatised in Toni Morrison's *Beloved*, discussed here in both Elaine Jordan's and Gina Wisker's chapters (7 and 5).

Testimony and naming are signally important for everyone but perhaps particularly for victimised or marginalised groups of individuals. One other of Gabriele Griffin's chosen texts, Joan Riley's *The Unbelonging*, is considered in her chapter in terms of its depiction of a search for self-identity (Chapter 2). *The Unbelonging* actually broke new ground in terms of publishing, as it was the first book by a Black British woman writer to be published by a major feminist publishing house. Barbara Burford, the author of many poems and novels, including the controversial *The Threshing Floor*, gave voice to her feelings about Black women's writing, publishing and reception in an article in *Spare Rib*. She notes that the writing of Black British women is distinct from that of, for example Afro-American writers, and that Black British women readers wish to see in their reading a life they can recognise – 'Yes, I am interested in the lives and realities of Black people living in other cultures, but I am reluctant to have their lives read into the record as *my* reality'[14] – despite a 'commonality' of experience, to some extent. She argues that those controlling the media seek to control a consensus about what reality is and so if Black women's experiences are only minimally (if at all) represented in print, they are largely wiped from the perception of people in Britain and elsewhere. Barbara Burford's arguments ring very true; she finds that publishers demand a certain kind of writing for publication today, a 'little black pain undressed'[15] as she calls it, quoting Grace Nichols: a tale testifying to the pains of being Black. While there is much autobiography produced by Black women writers, Burford argues that this itself can be a limitation, that there is a staggering arrogance in the assumption that this is all Black women writers *can* produce: 'the racism implicit in the presumption that we are somehow not "sophisticated" enough for fiction or fantasy is staggering'.[16] She argues that, until there are Black women working in publishing and criticism, there will only be a filter on the representation of Black women's experiences and their fictions; an avoidably misleading filter. Burford urges the writing and publishing of a variety of fictions for the variety of Black women readers and for those interested in learning of the variety of these experiences. Above all, she insists that this current interest in Black women's writing must not be a fad: 'as blackwomen writing and being published in Britain today we have to make sure that, this time, we do not remain a liberal fad, that we are not merchandised and commercialised into obsolescence'.[17]

Burford's novel *The Threshing Floor*[18] is testimony to her determination to write out of and represent the variety of Black experience. Its central mixed-race, lesbian relationship provoked many confused responses. The whole issue of a mixed-race relationship stands to some extent as a figure for the confusing position of the immigrant, who settles in the host country and becomes part of it and its communities but retains her own community and her own racial identity, her own difference. This is a difficult unity to manage without feeling schizophrenic, perhaps, and it is discussed at length also by the many writers who have recently put together collections of writing by Black women in Britain: Lauretta Ngcobo,[19] Shabnam Grewal, Jackie Kay[20] and so on.

Jackie Kay herself, in 'So You Think I'm a Mule?', produces a poem which suggests a dialogue between a woman of mixed race and the prying white questioner who wishes to categorise her – detrimentally – seeing her as 'half-caste', part of the 'mixed-race problem', when she is in no doubt of her own racial background, and her pride in it:

> and when they shout 'Nigger'
> ain't nobody debating my Blackness
> . . . I'm not mixed up about it
> There's a lot of us Blackwomen, struggling to define
> just who we are.[21]

Here the speaker and the language celebrate identity in a universalising statement which yet recognises difference. Others are speechless to define her, but she has her own voice now, content with her background and identity.

The 'schizophrenia' of retaining one's culture in another cultural environment is also noted by Black British women artists such as Sonia Boyce who said in 1983:

> I am British born of West Indian parents. I live a schizophrenic life, between an anglicised background and a West Indian foreground; to put it another way, between 'but look at my trials nah' and 'gaw blimey'. My work tries to reconcile both of these.[22]

Sonia Boyce focuses on the issue of language and expression here, as does Jackie Kay in her poem. Some might stutter, some might see radically different expressions: both Jackie Kay and Sonia Boyce create out of the fusion of these cultures and languages, through their own experiences, in their own form of expression. Others might be confused, but *they* are celebratory.

Jackie Roy's chapter in this volume (Chapter 3) is testimony to one woman's experience of being a Black woman in a predominantly white British literary/academic context. Jackie has been a post-

graduate student and is herself a creative writer. Her comments as
student, reader and writer reflect first-hand the confusions, contradictions and cross-currents affecting the writing, publishing, reading and studying of Black women's writing, with a particularly
British flavour.

Jackie Roy charts her personal feelings as a reader concentrating
on the received versions, for the student, of Black women's writing
set against the background of an overwhelmingly white (middle-
class male, too, of course) literary syllabus in higher education institutions. Many of the Black women students I work with on undergraduate and MA courses have reported similar feelings and experiences to those Jackie writes of here. They do not find themselves
represented on syllabuses, and the odd token black text studied does
not necessarily relate at all to their own culture or experience. Afro-
American and even African writing might be present on a syllabus,
discussed in class, albeit by white academics, but Black British writing
is rarely ever mentioned.

As readers and students they have discovered what Lauretta
Ngcobo also notes: that the theme, content, expression of Black
British women's writing is not easily assimilable in the context of a
white readership, for much of what is explored is a clear indictment
of the society from which that readership springs:

> We as Black writers at times displease our white readership.
> Our writing is seldom genteel since it springs from our experiences
> which in real life have none of the trimmings of gentility. If the
> truth be told, it cannot titillate the aesthetic palates of many white
> people, for deep down it is a criticism of their values and their
> treatment of us throughout history.[23]

It is a British context in which all the works written about in this
collection are read, by both Black and white readers, except in the
case of the Chapter by the South African academic and writer,
Dorothy Driver.

Black or white, inevitably we read out of a context riddled with
covert and overt racism and widespread ignorance. I am grateful to
the Black women students with whom I work – Jagdish Singh,
Adarsh Grewal, Joy Njenje, Rosina Abudulai and Sandra Young –
for the many points they have made to me about the overt and
covert racism in the syllabuses with which we work, in the assumptions about culture and lifestyle, and about the dearth of Black

writing on the degree syllabuses they encounter. One point several of these students have made is that while they do not in any way want to study *just* literature by Black writers, or *just* the history of the cultures from which they originate, they do wish to 'see themselves' as central rather than always marginal. Their interests are often tagged on to a lecture or are represented by one text in a seminar; they may be deemed to be thoroughly represented by the study of one example of an Afro-American text (usually *The Color Purple*!). While this might convey Black women's experience it doesn't have much to say about the students' versions of Black British women's experience.

This collection of essays confronts these issues directly without in any sense arrogantly asserting that they have been overcome, but out of a genuine need to discuss openly the tensions and contradictions inherent in the reading and studying process for largely white readers in a largely white literary and academic context. It is this intention that lies behind the focus on another form of autobiography; the reader's first-hand response to the texts, as recorded here.

Suzanne Scafe writes in *Teaching Black Literature*[24] of the difficulties Black children feel when studying texts by white writers in school. They find no model or representation of their own culture reflected there in the literary establishment, in what is 'accepted' as 'culture'. The other main problem, however, is their response to reading Black writing when it *is* taught in school. Here they respond out of the context of their previous reading and study practices. Since Black literature has not been much in evidence when 'the canon' of 'culture' has been mentioned, its introduction is greeted with suspicion. Perhaps this is an instance of fobbing them off with second-class writing?

> The schools transmit, for example, the notion, passed off as truth, that culture is white, male and middle class. This not only shapes Black students' expectations of the school, its purpose and function, but leads them to expect not to see aspects of their own culture and environment there.[25]

They might reject these experiences embodied in Black literature, or feel embarrassed to identify with them: they are too personal. Perhaps they feel any identification with the experiences and ideas represented in such texts will further equate them with the non-dominant group. Of Black culture represented in literature she writes:

Sometimes they see it as a powerful, enabling tool; at other times they express rejection of it, feeling that their identification with certain forms and practices disenfranchises them from British society and prevents their success in it.[26]

There is a problem, then, in reading Black writing if you are yourself a Black student. In her chapter, Jackie Roy looks at issues of studying and writing about Black women's writing in higher education today. She is wary of the interest of the white literary academy, since it seems like so much bandwagon-jumping at times. However, as she points out, once entry into the discourse of contemporary critical theory has been made (difficult for marginalised groups, among them many Black women students and returners) the essentially radical nature of this criticism will enable a variety of readings of texts, will underline the social and political message that social position and experience are the result of a particular mixture of effects at a particular moment. They are all open to change, and difference is recognised and valued. She points out the potential and the flaws of feminist theory which:

> presents a major challenge to patriarchal structures, though for black women it is limited by its failure to engage consistently and effectively with black issues, often subsuming these to encompass *all* women in a form of essentialism which denies the specificity of black women's experience.

Jackie argues for the inclusion of more books by Black writers on the syllabus, more Black lecturers to teach the courses, and for the widespread use of such Black literary criticism as has emerged, largely from America. This would go some way, she feels towards ensuring that the *only* voice on Black writing is not that of a white speaker or writer.

In putting together this collection we have attempted to include Black 'voices' in the debate, whether they be of Black students and readers and academics or of Black literary critics and the Black writers themselves. That there are still quite obviously too few Black voices represented here is yet further testimony to that absence Jackie notes and which we agitate against.

For many of us writing in this collection, however, the position of white feminist critic is the only one we can embrace. The white feminist critic's reading of Black women's writing is fraught with

problems. As Mae Henderson[27] comments on an essay by Houston
Baker,[28] one is not precluded from commenting on Black women's
writing by being non-Black, but one feels implicated, instead, and
this can actually silence, paralyse, force false responses: 'The incum-
bency for the non-Afro-American-woman critic is to finger the jag-
ged grain of a brutal experience in which – if he or she is white and/
or male – he or she is implicated.'[29]

One of the basic difficulties is in defining a limited object: Black
women's experience represented in Black women's writing. When,
for reading, personal or teaching reasons, one starts to define the
canon and define the characteristic of Black women's writing, one
runs up against the kind of essentialism which has dominated writing
about women since the dawn of literature and art and since the
dawn of (largely male-dominated) literary criticism. We must avoid
the rhetoric of a universality which elides and ignores difference
and, even for feminist critics, reconstitutes the Black woman and the
Black woman's text as an *object* of gaze, thus reproducing the *male
object of gaze* which has defined representations of women in a male
world. Representations of Black women as earthy, magical matriarchs
at the centre of society, rooted, are the most dangerous, for they
actually replicate the 'mother Africa' stereotypes and myths, the
white racist-based folklore which designates Black people, and
particularly Black women, as the source of a dark, fertile, wild power,
an alluring, dangerous Otherness, which can so easily slip into what
Bell Hooks points out lay at the roots of slave owners' misogyny:
'Since woman was designated as the originator of sexual sin,
blackwomen were naturally seen as the embodiments of female evil:
and sexual lust.'[30]

It is certainly a useful literary critical mechanism, however, excellent for teaching purposes, to attempt to define Black women's
writing. This results in comments on the use of magic of root-working,
of mixing the colloquial and dialect with 'standard' literary expression. It looks at the frequently Utopian endings, the celebratory note
found (and so often confusing to white readers) in so many Black
women's texts. Some general critical comments are perhaps necessary
to start off debate on the specific texts studied or read, but representations of Black women characters and of Black women's writing
should avoid the dangers of reification and essentialising, of a poetics
which locates Black women in a prelapsarian Edenic garden, or
as the archetypal embodiments of female lust. '[T]he danger is not
only that of essentialising but of reinforcing the most conventional

constructs of (black) femininity.'[31] Mae Henderson suggests that this essentialising is avoided by emphasising both the variety and difference of Black women as models and characters and the variety and difference of the literary texts in which they are described. We must also show critical, criticised models as well as celebrated ones and so, as Juliet F. MacCannell puts it: 'disrupt the male gaze by interrupting the pleasure of the visual'.[32]

Dialogue and difference are vital: 'We must deconstitute the notion of *the* black tradition. . . . as models *always* indicate boundaries . . . part of the commitment of the black feminist project however, is the privileging of difference.'[33] Henderson urges the recognition of models of Black women in literary works who are themselves not always described in a celebratory and positive manner, and cites the mother who burns her son, in Morrison's *Song of Solomon*, so that he is prevented from re-entering the womb; and the madness of Pecola, in *In a Bluest Eye*, when she is raped by men from the Black community; and the symbolic rabidity of Tea Cake, in *Their Eyes Were Watching God* by Zora Neale Hurston. Expression, discussion and criticism of Black women in texts should be a dialogue: there are many models. Difference should be recognised here, too, as in society.

Shabnam Grewal *et al.* also confront the problem, relating it to contemporary confusions over the existence or non-existence of a Black women's movement in Britain:

> Instead of at least the semblance of a Black women's movement the futile 'politics' of victim and guilt tripping runs rampant and is used to justify actions that any self respect would deem impossible. Or there is the collective adornment of moral and political superiority which is supposed to derive from the mere fact of being a Black woman.[34]

In their collection the editors include works reflecting both positive and negative aspects of the Black community to emphasise that there is no essential or universal Black woman. Still less is she a saint: difference is the foundation for self-identity and equality.

'Guilt tripping' is not the ideal impetus behind the white feminist critic's appreciation of Black women's writing either. In fact, as students in Gina Wisker's group testify, it confuses and silences. Arrogance, bandwagon-jumping and any attempts to pass off one example of Black writing, one image of Black woman, as universal and essential are equally critical traps to be avoided. What we have all attempted to do in this volume is to represent our varying experiences – and our students' experiences (where this is the relevant context of the essay) – to reading, studying and learning about and from a selection of Black women's very rich and very varied writing available today.

NOTES

1. A. Walker, *The Color Purple* (London: Virago, 1983).
2. C. Kaplan , 'Keeping the Colour in *The Color Purple*' in C. Kaplan, *Sea Changes* (London: Verso, 1986) p. 185.
3. A. Walker, in *Black Women Writers at Work*, ed. Claudia Tate (New York: Continuum, 1984) p. 183.
4. Maya Angelou, in *Black Women Writers*, ed. Mari Evans (London: Pluto Press, 1985) p. 3.
5. A. Walker, in *Black Women Writers at Work*, p. 185.
6. Audre Lorde, in ibid., p. 101.
7. Kaplan, 'Keeping the Colour', p. 177.
8. Zora Neale Hurston, *Dust Tracks on a Road* (London: Virago, 1986).
9. S. Grewal et al., *Charting the Journey: Writings by Black and Third World Women* (London: Sheba, 1988).
10. Ibid., p. 6.
11. A. Walker, *In Search of Our Mothers' Gardens* (London: The Women's Press, 1984).
12. L. Ngcobo (ed.), *Let It be Told: Black Women Writers in Britain* (London: Virago Press, 1988).
13. Ibid., p. 40.
14. B. Burford, 'The Landscapes Painted on the Inside of My Skin', *Spare Rib* (June 1987) p. 37.
15. Ibid., p. 37.
16. Ibid., p. 38.
17. Ibid., p. 39.
18. B. Burford *The Threshing Floor, and Other Stories* (London: Sheba Feminists, 1986).
19. Ngcobo, *Let It Be Told*.
20. Grewal et al., *Charting the Journey*.
21. J. Kay, 'So You Think I'm a Mule?', in *A Dangerous Knowing: Four Black Women Poets* (London: Sheba, 1987) p. 53.
22. Ngcobo, *Let It Be Told*, p. 4.
23. S. Boyce, 'Five Black Women': Exhibition at the Africa Centre (London, 1983).
24. S. Scafe, *Teaching Black Literature* (London: Virago 1989).
25. Ibid., p. 23.

26. Ibid.,
27. Mae Henderson, 'Response to "There is No More Beautiful Way: Theory and Poetics of Afro-American Women's Writing" by Houston A. Baker Jr', in *Afro-American Literary Study in the 1990s*, ed. Houston Baker and Patricia Redmond (London: University of Chicago Press, 1989) p. 159.
28. H. Baker, 'There is no More Beautiful Way', in ibid.
29. Henderson, 'Response : . . ' in ibid., p. 160.
30. Bell Hooks, *Ain't I a Woman?* (Boston, Mass.: South End Press, 1981) p. 33.
31. Henderson, 'Response . . . ', p. 159.
32. J. MacCannell, *Figuring Lacan: Criticism and the Cultural Unconscious* (Lincoln, Neb.: University of Nebraska Press, 1986) p. 135.
33. Henderson, 'Response . . . ', p. 164.
34. Grewal *et al.*, *Charting the Journey*, p. 3.

2

'Writing the Body': Reading Joan Riley, Grace Nichols and Ntozake Shange

GABRIELE GRIFFIN

Despite the fact that there exists by now a large, established body of writing by Black women writers such as Toni Morrison, Paule Marshall, Audre Lorde, Alice Walker, Maya Angelou and others, one becomes – when teaching their writing on a 'Women's Writing' course in a higher education institution in the home counties where one rarely sees more than one black face in any group of students – aware very quickly of otherness, the unknown, traversing foreign territory when reading Joan Riley's *The Unbelonging*, Grace Nichols's *I Is a Long Memoried Woman* (hereafter: *I Is*), and Ntozake Shange's *For Colored Girls who have Considered Suicide when the Rainbow is Enuf* (hereafter: *For Colored Girls*). From the questionnaire that I handed out to the third-year students on the 1988–9 'Women's Writing' course it transpired that more than half of them had never read any writing by Black people. Of those who had, most had encountered Black people's writing on the American Studies course at the same college. As one student, Ann Young, said about how the reading of these texts had affected her attitudes towards Black people: 'I have more respect for them now. Previously, my attitude was limited. I didn't think they could use language to express themselves, I didn't know how they felt.' Another student, Lisa Wares, wrote: 'Texts [by Black women] should be more widely available. I tried to buy *The Unbelonging* in a large bookshop in Birmingham and was told that I would have to order it. The area put aside for books by Blackwomen writers was minimal. I also feel that it would be helpful to publicise their work to a wider audience'. Between the unknown and the unavailable, the blank that was students' knowledge of Black women's writing is not surprising but worrying in the multiracial society we are supposed to live in.

The students' responses to the three texts we looked at, chosen in part to give them a cross-genre experience of Black women's work, revealed that no matter what their emotional response was to the content, it was its form which ultimately determined their liking for/dislike of a given text. Thus, many of the students were 'quite shattered' by *The Unbelonging*, as one of them, Judith Robinson, put it. They found it 'moving and distressing' (Lisa Wares); 'very negative' (Helen Jones); 'a depressing read' (Gillian Banks); and 'very disturbing' (Stephanie Margetts). Even 'irritation with the heroine' (Lyn Evans), however, did not prevent them from liking this novel better than any of the other texts by Black women we read. We visited a poetry reading at the Ritzy Cinema in Brixton where Jean Binta Breeze and Ntozake Shange performed their poetry in a context in which the almost exclusively white group of students experienced for the first time, 'what being a minority must feel like' (Ann Turnbull); what it means to be 'left out of a shared set of values' (Lyn Evans). This visit, despite a considerable and positive impact on the students, did not make *For Colored Girls* any easier for them: they liked it least of the texts we discussed.

In teaching Black women's writing within a limited temporal space one has thus to consider how to deal with white students' unfamiliarity with such writing *per se* as well as with their responses to the various forms and content of this work. It is in this context that focusing on the notion of 'writing the body' as foregrounded in the work of French feminist theoreticians like Hélène Cixous and Julia Kristeva can be useful for providing readings of texts such as *The Unbelonging*, *I Is* and *For Colored Girls*. In the remainder of this chapter I shall therefore indicate how one might analyse these texts in the light of concepts gleaned from French feminist theory, and end with some comments on the students' reactions detailed above.

When dealing with French feminist theory we have become used to the notion of a jump made from the body to the system of signification through which it finds expression, the analysis of language and form in terms of difference and heterogeneity which are supposed to be rooted in the female body, and which are meant to be celebratory as encountered in the text.

Kristeva's 'revolution in poetic language': does it refer to the presence of the cyclical, the non-linear in poetic discourse which supposedly echoes cycles such as the one of menstruation in women's physiological existence? Or does it refer to the presence of disruptive potential in poetic language, its defiance of grammatical and other structures? Whether as recurrence or as disturbance, what Kristeva offers us with her notions of *semiotic* and *symbolic* dispositions is celebration and cerebration of the female body. Both elevate – go to the head. They invite a formalist stance: animal existence and certain kind of physical reality are left behind in favour of metalinguistic explorations which deal in futures, possibilities of 'finding a woman's voice'.

Meanwhile, back in the here and now, another kind of reality asserts itself, an unfamiliar reality for the white readers of white women's writing, much of which is still so *nice*, so polite, so middle-class and educated, so anxious and out of touch with her body except in the most subliminal way. It is a reality they will not have encountered in the work of Virginia Woolf or Sylvia Plath where the rendition of the physical is always accompanied by a suitably distancing commentary, where being out of control physically is inevitably countered by being in control stylistically. The reality I am writing of is the reality relayed in *The Unbelonging*, where the body constitutes the site of oppression and becomes the source not of celebration but of permanent anxiety.

The body dominates this novel. Hyacinth Williams, the central character, experiences life in England through her body, through the absence of control she has over it and over her physical environment. Victimised from an early age, she is the object of perpetual abuse. The combination of psycho-terror and direct physical assault to which her father subjects her on a regular basis results in a sense of powerlessness expressed by Hyacinth through the body. She wets her bed. This loss of control over her bladder which happens at night while Hyacinth is in a state of unconsciousness is punished by the father through actions which refer her back to the body, now consciously experienced as being beyond her control.

> She knew he would keep her standing there until her nerve went; knew he would wait for the tears to slip out, the shaking to start. She could feel her eyes burning, misery and self-pity swamping her, and she fought back the tears determinedly. Her whole being was tensed, ears straining for what she dared not look at.   (p. 13)

Hyacinth's attempt to maintain control over her body avails her nothing. Spilling over provides her father with the excuse for containing her, subjecting her to 'stinging blows of the belt buckle', followed by 'the ice-cold bath, and the shaking, a mingling of cold and fear, as he . . . watched her sitting in the water' (p. 11).

Bodily fluids and all (in-)voluntary self-expression through the body become a source of anxiety to Hyacinth. This includes her menstruation, the onset of which is marked by a change in the nature of her father's attention towards her. It becomes more and more sexually marked until it finally erupts in an incestuous assault.

Hyacinth's history of being punished for spilling over alienates her from her body to the point where her attempt at sexual intercourse with a man classed by her as 'harmless' and trustworthy leaves her 'staring dry-eyed at the ceiling after the fumbling, the slipping and the pain had stopped' (p. 31). The discrepancy between these experiences and Cixous's jubilatory

> I, too, overflow; my desires have invented new desires, my body knows unheard-of songs. Time and again I, too, have felt so full of luminous torrents that I could burst – burst with forms much more beautiful than those which are put up in frames and sold for a stinking fortune. . . . I said to myself: You are mad! What's the meaning of these waves, these floods, these outbursts?[1]

is all too obvious. For Hyacinth, at the level of consciousness, the body is a source of unpleasure, fashioned as such by her father and his exploitative sexuality. His body, the focal point of which for her is the erection he has (described by her as 'the lump of his anger') when abusing her, becomes the memory which haunts all physical encounters in her later life. When Mackay, a young man who befriends her, feels she is playing games with him and gets annoyed, 'She had a compulsion to look down, to see the lump would be there, the anger she knew was waiting to burst out at her' (p. 105). One of the things that cause her to 'spill over', vomit, when she attempts sexual intercourse with Charles, another friend, is that 'he had turned that lump into a hateful, painful reality' and that there is 'that smell, so much like her father's pants' (p. 131).

Hyacinth's alienation from her body goes hand in hand with her experience of that body as the site of subjugation, upon which others demonstrate – through aggression – the power they have over her. Tutored by her father and her experiences outside the home she comes to feel that she cannot escape this fate as her body is the visual representation of the sexual and racial identity for which she is victimised. Unable to change either her sex or her colour she is the doubly marked scapegoat of her environment. At her school she is attacked by Margaret White, 'a mixed-race child adopted by white people' who seems 'to hate the black kids even more than the whites [do]' (p. 18). Maureen, Hyacinth's stepmother, sees 'nothing wrong with using Hyacinth to protect [her own kids]' (p. 36) from being beaten by the father. The staff of the children's home to which she is eventually moved ignore her suffering, 'the vicious pokes in her back, the slyly extended foot that tripped her' (p. 74).

The body always takes the blame for the physical encoding Hyacinth did not choose and cannot obliterate. The sheer physicality of her environment, the cold, the wet, the drabness of the places in which she lives, make her suffer. Her fate is in many respects not unlike that of Celie in *The Color Purple* but where Celie is redeemed through bonding with other women and the consequent rediscovery of her body, Hyacinth is condemned to permanent isolation. Maltreated by men and women, black and white alike, she trusts no one. The abuse by the father remains wedged between her physiological and her psychological growth.

> And always, behind it all, her father waited, crouching in the shadows, beating at her with all the horrors she had faced, laughing and mocking all her attempts at escape. And inside her, deep down, buried inside her woman's body, trapped and bleeding in the deepest recesses of her, a young girl screamed. As the scream echoed in her mind, the tears seeped out and Hyacinth knew she would never be free until that child had healed. (p. 143)

No solution as to how this might happen is indicated in the novel. Hyacinth's single sustaining escape route, her dream of her early childhood spent living with her aunt Joyce in Jamaica, is gradually blocked out in a careful narrative construction which juxtaposes this dream with the reality of her life in England.

At the outset of the novel Hyacinth's nightly dreams of Jamaica, in which she experiences sensual delight and contentment, are contrasted with the unpleasurable reality of her home life and her experiences in the outside world. The distance between these poles is gradually reduced when Hyacinth, in desparation, runs away from home and begins to make decisions about her life such as taking 'O' levels. As unpleasure is reduced in her 'real' life it surfaces in her dreams. It is as if the sheer need to have something to cling to for survival made her 'will' pleasurable dreams at a time when these dreams were literally all she might have some control over. But as she starts to gain control over her 'real' life she seems to 'lose her grip' over her 'dream' life; disturbing images of being persecuted in the playground by a menacing boy suffering from ringworm, of her friend Cynthia's father who, like her own father, 'lurked in the shadows . . . so big and aggressive' (p. 86), of Cynthia burning to death, and of her aunt not being so nice after all begin to haunt Hyacinth's dreams. The 'reality' of her former existence in Jamaica spills over from Hyacinth's subconscious into remembered dreams as the pressure in her day-to-day life subsides. Her dreams turn into nightmares, these nightmares eventually into lived reality when she returns to Jamaica, finally to be repulsed by the physical conditions under which her relatives and former friends suffer. Otherness and difference turn into sameness, the distinctions created in her mind between Jamaica and England prove to be non-existent. In the beginning lies the end: on the closing pages Hyacinth is back with her childhood friends in 'the little green cave' she dreamt she was in when the novel opened, helpless now as then. The return to her roots does not provide her with a new point of departure but with an affirmation of the position she has inhabited all her life: powerlessness. The movement was cyclical.

This cyclical movement makes for the unremitting negativity which informs the text, its remorseless rejection of all possibility of a happy ending. One of my students, Anna O'Neill, described this as 'Hyacinth's inability to help herself'; another, Lyn Evans, suggested that Hyacinth 'was doomed to disappointment'. Christine Bruley thought that 'when she was presented with chances to break out of it [her situation] she was too emotionally scarred to do anything about it'. Indeed, this issue of the 'hopelessness' (Samantha Maton) of Hyacinth's situation, which can cause readers irritation with the heroine, was raised in a discussion between Joan Riley, the author, and a group of white women who came to hear her giving a reading at the alternative bookshop in Leicester, Blackthorn's, shortly after the book was first published. In this discussion Riley said that she had deliberately avoided any possibility of a happy ending because she felt that a happy ending would allow readers to remain disengaged from the issues, that it would wrap up sexism and racism as something that could and would be overcome – as, in a sense, *The Color Purple* seems to suggest. In contrast, *The Unbelonging*'s insistence on the permanent isolation and alienation of the central character points to the persistence of sexism and racism and their effects on the individual in contemporary society, demanding a confrontation of these issues.

The other topic raised in the same discussion with Riley was her representation of incest in the novel, a problem that dominates other Black women's writing as well. As Anna O'Neill remarked, 'I can't think of a novel by a white woman which tries to cover domestic violence and incest in such an open way.' In the discussion Joan Riley said that incest was a problem in the West Indian community but that she was not prepared to talk about it in an all-white gathering as she felt it fuelled racial prejudice.

Incest is, of course, not a 'Black' problem, as anyone teaching in a special school will tell you and the Cleveland case on sexual abuse has highlighted. But it is true that incest as a topic is virtually non-existent in the white middle-class women's writing that tends to be on offer on 'Women's Writing' courses in higher education. Here the body is still very much taboo though *mental* breakdown, for example, has become more acceptable as a subject of enquiry. Here finding oneself means finding a voice, getting an education, deciding on the relationship between a career and one's private life. Finding the body, if not as a cerebral position, is a concern mainly in terms of discovering one's sexual orientation as in, for example, Jeannette Winterson's *Oranges Are Not the Only Fruit*. The body as a direct site of oppression, whether through the tyranny of sexual abuse or – to use another example – through the tyranny of the beauty industry, is dealt with predominantly in handbooks, 'factual' or 'documentary' accounts and reference material. The world of white middle-class women's fiction thus presents the fiction of a mind without a body or of a mind which dominates the body.

In *The Unbelonging* the body constitutes the point where self and other intersect and identity is forged. It is a battlefield rather than sacred soil. The internalisation of a power structure which is weighted against Hyacinth turns her body into a trap – being subject to the body equals being a victim. Nothing to celebrate, no joyful overflowing, no games with form. *The Unbelonging*, despite its refusal of a happy ending, has essentially a linear structure and belongs to the tradition of realism. It charts chronologically Hyacinth's development from childhood to adulthood, providing alternating currents of 'reality' and dream world, gradually completing and rectifying the images which make up Hyacinth's world. There is a truth to be discovered about her background, and we discover it. Boundaries visible and invisible remain intact. Dream is always identified as dream, and 'reality' as 'reality'. As J. P. Stern has put it:

realistic fictions are erected on firm ground which reveals no epistemological cracks, and . . . when such cracks appear, they are not explored but transformed into the psychology of characters: realism doesn't ask whether the world is real, but it occasionally asks what happens to persons who think it isn't.[2]

Hyacinth is a case in point. *The Unbelonging* is, in this respect, unlike either *I Is* or *For Colored Girls*.

I Is is a sequence of poems based on a dream Grace Nichols had: I dreamed of this young African girl who was swimming from Africa to the Caribbean – she had a garland of flowers around her. I took it to mean that she was trying to purge the ocean of all the pain and suffering she knew her ancestors had gone through.[3]

Here the revolutionary element which according to Julia Kristeva manifests itself in poetic language is very immediately present at the conception of the work through the invocation of what comes from the unconscious – the world of dreams – as inspiration; indeed, in 'Days that Fell', one of the poems in *I Is*, we read: 'all revolutions are rooted in dreams' (p. 11). The poems are aligned to an oral tradition which takes its rhythms and its inflections from the body. Breaks are created not by punctuation but by the need to draw breath, by how the body moves as it recites, raising questions such as 'What dance of mourning / can I make?' (p. 17). The body of the text is only very sparingly marked by the signs that come from a written tradition of language usage such as commas, questions marks, dots. In fact, nothing comes to an end with a full stop: there is no stopping the revolution. It is not over.

Nichols's Black woman goes through a series of stages. These, and the incidents which characterise them, are indicated as separate and specific through the titles given to the five sections into which the volume is divided, and the titles given to each poem. Together the five sections describe an unknown Black woman's history, from her capture in Africa ('But I was stolen by men / the colour of my own skin' – p. 19) to her life as a slave in the Caribbean, working in the sugar-cane fields, being made the white man's mistress, bearing his children. The Black woman mourns for her past and her home country, embodied by her ancestors, the gods she used to pray to, and her 'Mother'. Eventually, in the course of time and history, she acquires a new identity bound up closely with the body and her power of speech:

> I have crossed an ocean
> I have lost my tongue
> from the root of the old
> one
> a new one has sprung.
> ('Epilogue', p. 80)

The Black woman is both a specific person with an 'I'-dentity, and every-Black-woman who has been enslaved and shipped to a new land. Particularity and universality are also reflected in the easy move between past and present (tense). Timelessness

> It isn't privilege or pity
> that I seek
> . . .
>
>   but
> the power to be what I am/a woman
> charting my own futures . . .
> ('Holding My Beads', p. 79)

and immediacy

> It has come
> It has come
>
> Fireceremony
> and bloodrush
> an insane sunrise
> the black surge
> (' . . . and Toussaint', p. 77)

dominate.

As in *The Unbelonging*, the body takes the brunt, whether through slave labour or the bearing of the children of white men. And as in *The Unbelonging* the answer to

> the cutlass in her hand
> could not cut through
> the days that fell
> like bramble
>
> and the destruction that
> threatened to choke
> within
> ('Days that Fell', p. 11)

is 'We must hold fast to dreams'. There are two kinds of dreams in *I Is*: the dream that is a nightmare of the disintegration of self wedged between past and present as in ' . . . Like Clamouring Ghosts' (p. 41), and the dream that is 'piecing the life she would lead' ('One Continent / to Another', p. 8), the dream of a future different from the present. Even though the Black woman acknowledges:

> I must construct myself a dream
> one dream is all I need to keep
> me from these blades of hardness
>
> from this plague of sadness
>
> The Dream Must Not Be Tarnished
> ('One Dream', p. 39)

the dream she constructs does not have the regressive and distorting character of Hyacinth's dreams; rather, it is the dream of the revolution, of freedom from bondage.

Nichols's Black woman uses her body, her voice, her song to maintain her sense of selfhood, to support others and to subvert the structures that oppress her. Thus in 'Ala'. 'we the women sing and weep / as we work' for Ala, 'the rebel woman', horribly tortured to death for killing her newborn baby so that it might not have to live in bondage. In 'Waterpot' the Black woman at the end of a long day's labour in the cane fields

> tried very hard
> pulling herself erect
> . . .
> holding herself like
> royal cane.   (p. 14)

And although the overseer sneers at 'the pathetic display / of dignity', the image of the woman not bent under the burden remains as an undercurrent throughout *I Is*, an undercurrent bespeaking the refusal to adopt the position of victim. In 'Love Act' the Black woman brought into the white man's house as his mistress comes with the knowledge:

> time pass/es
> Her sorcery cut them
> like a whip

> She hide her triumph
> and slowly stir the hate
> of poison in.   (p. 49)

Nichols's Black woman refuses to be victimised either for being a woman or for being Black. In 'Web of Kin' she dissociates herself from a tradition of 'Black Oak women who bleed slowly at / the altars of their children' (p. 9), who offer 'gourds of sacrificial blood' at night:

> I will have nothing to do with it
> will pour it in the dust will set
> us free
> the whip will have no fire the sun
> no flame
> and my eyes everywhere reflecting.   (p. 10)

Such rejection of gestures of subordination and supplication does not signal a cutting-off from the African female community whence the Black woman has emerged. As she says in 'Web of Kin':

> even in my dreams I will submerge myself
> swimming like one possessed
> back and forth across that course.   (p. 10)

The connections she thus seeks to maintain stem from a recognition that she comes 'from a country of strong women' (p. 9) – it is the *strength* of the African female community which the Black woman conjures up in her mind for support, especially the strength of the mother (for example, in 'Sacred Flame', '. . . Your Blessing'. The Black woman's requests to the mother in this last poem

> With the power of your blessings
>
> Uplift me
> Instruct me
> Reclothe me   (p. 53)

uttered at a time of physiological change – she is pregnant, about to become a mother herself – chime perfectly with Cixous's:

There is hidden and always ready in woman the source; the locus for the other. The mother, too, is a metaphor. It is necessary and sufficient that the best of herself be given to woman by another woman for her to be able to love herself and return in love the body that was 'born' to her. Touch me, caress me, you the living no-name, give me myself as myself.[4]

In *I Is* female bonding operates on a diachronic and on a synchronic level: women from the past are invoked as well as the women among whom the Black woman lives in the Caribbean. The use of the first person plural, 'we', indicates this female community and a shared fate. In 'We the Women' a sense of collective strength is established through the non-completion of the main clause that begins each stanza. The labouring women ('We the women who toil / unadorn') who go unrecognised, are not broken by this experience. The final stanza's first word, denoting defiance, 'Yet we the women', is expressive of the resistance and resilience which informs the women's stance: despite the total lack of recognition which they experience. The last sentence of the last stanza – as is the case with the other three – remains incomplete and invites the reader/hearer to acknowledge the regenerative force in the women

> who deaths they sweep
> aside
> as easy as dead leaves.   (p. 13)

The Black woman's resistance to her victimisation is fed by the strength she gains from being part of this close-knit female community. Her resistance has direction. At the point where she has been sold into slavery she has lost control over her life:

> the truth is
> my life has slipped out
> of my possession.
> ('Sunshine', p. 21)

In this respect she resembles Hyacinth from *The Unbelonging*. But the persona of *I Is* never accepts this powerlessness as a permanent condition. She maintains that she

> must be forever gathering
> my life together like scattered beads.
> ('Sacred Flame', p. 20)

She sets about this by maintaining a sense of tradition, trying to carry on the rituals that were part of her life in Africa, by believing in change, in the future, in her own potential power, helped along by the magic she was taught by the women in Africa. Part Three of *I Is*, 'The Sorcery', begins to signal the change in the Black woman's condition through a series of poems that delineate the Black woman gathering her forces and feeling strong (see 'Nimbus', 'Night is her Robe', 'Old Magic'), or the Black woman's defiance of the white man (for example, 'I Coming Back', 'Hi de Buckras Hi!', 'Love Act', 'Skin-Teeth'). This gathering of forces reaches its climax in ' . . . and Toussaint', in which 'the black surge', like a wave breaking on the shore, finally overruns the country. As it recedes there is the Black woman

> Unforgiving as the course of justice
> Inerasable as my scars and fate
> I am here
> a woman . . . with all my lives
> strung out like beads.
> ('Holding my Beads', p. 79)

She has become a monument unto herself, enabled to sustain herself through the multiple connections she has with her past in Africa and the Caribbean, with tribal traditions, and with other women across and within time. These connections are emblematised through the recurrent symbol of the string of beads (reflected in how dots are used within *I Is*), scattered at first but gathered by the end of the sequence of poems which, at the level of content, form both a sequence (the move from Africa to the Caribbean) and a circle (from freedom to freedom) like a string of beads. What the persona finally desires is

> the power to be what I am/a woman
> charting my own futures/a woman
> holding my beads in my hands.   (ibid.)

The black woman's resistance and resilience in *I Is* is matched by an attitude Nichols expressed

I can't subscribe to the 'victim-mentality' . . . which seems so like wallowing in 'Look what they've done to us' . . . I reject the stereotype of the 'long-suffering black woman' . . . There is a danger of reducing the black woman's condition to that of 'sufferer'.[5]

This attitude, I would suggest, is crucial to Nichols's work. It is one she shares with Ntozake Shange and, as I shall indicate towards the end of this chapter, it is this which fuels the differences in the writing of these two women relative to Riley's.

Nichols's *I Is* has a fundamentally optimistic undercurrent. The poems appear to say, 'I am a Black woman. I have been used and exploited, as a labouring force and as a sex object, by Black and white men. But I come from a long line of strong women whose collective strength will support me in my move towards self-determination.' The poems bespeak this stance through their form as much as through their content. Again, Nichols writes:

> after reading a lot of English poetry . . . I want something different; something that sounds and looks different to the eye on the page and to the ear. Difference, diversity and unpredictability make me tick.[6]

This difference/diversity/heterogeneity is precisely what the French theoreticians like Kristeva, Cixous and Annie Leclerc celebrate as the expression of the female body in women's writing. In Nichols's poetry it is tied to what happens on the page and off the page. The layout of the poems express it; the presence of Creole, standard English and a mixture of the two indicates it; the way in which punctuation, that which comes from a written tradition of literature, is handled, marks it. Correspondingly, the students reading this poetry thought that it ought to be spoken, not read in silence, that not having it performed detracted from it. One student, Diane Tonkins, felt that the Brixton experience gave her a sense of the poetry being 'alive' and the audience getting 'involved' with it. Another student, Ann Turnbull, thought that 'the rapport between the audience and the performers was tremendous'; and Lyn Evans wrote that for her it was 'very important to see how poetry was regarded as co-operative.' The students came to realise that poetry created in the context of an oral tradition is an art form concerned with sharing, with communication. It expresses perfectly the tradition of a close-knit female community. More than that, as we saw in Brixton, movement and gesture become part of the performance of this poetry – voice and body are equally used in its presentation. Shange and Binta Breeze at Brixton embodied Cixous's description:

> Listen to a woman speak at a public gathering. . . . She doesn't 'speak', she throws her trembling body forward; she lets go of herself; all of her passes into her voice, and it's with her body that she vitally supports the 'logic' of her speech . . . she draws her story into history'. . . . In women's speech, as in their writing, that element which never stops resonating . . . . is the song: first music from the first voice of love which is alive in every woman.[7]

Cixous could be talking of *I Is*: Nichols's poetry is, in many respects, the perfect example of an *écriture féminine*, of the notion of writing the body.

This is one reason why the students found *I Is* difficult to read. It is poetry that needs to be performed, that requires the presence of the voice and the body – its appeal is not purely cerebral. Furthermore, it is written with the conscious aim of creating difference 'on the page', and 'in the ear'. In consequence, there are variations of lengths of lines and stanzas within and across poems, and the layout of the poems on the page varies considerably. Rhythmic incantations and repetitions such as occur in 'Drum-Spell', 'Hi de Buckras Hi!', or ' . . . Your Blessing' signal the *semiotic* disposition, 'the body in process' as Kristeva describes it,[8] the defiance of the authority of imposed, alien structures. This replicates the contents of the poems. There is thus a congruity between subject matter and form in *I Is*. But this very congruity proved a source of difficulty for the students: the revolutionary potential of writing such as Nichols's lies in the fact that difference means – for the students – unfamiliarity. Their main experience of literature is probably the realist novel. Being familiar with mainstream/conservative literary structures of the linear, progressive, logical variety they lack the experience of subversive 'feminine' texts. If they had sufficient experience of such texts they would, of course, come to constitute a norm, ultimately presumably losing their revolutionary potential.

As indicated above, Shange shares Nichols's defiant stance. This is highlighted in her very name:

> Shange changed her name from Paulette Williams as an act of protest against her Western roots. The Zulu names she embraced, *ntozake* ('she who comes with her own things') and *shange* ('she who

walks like a lion') emphasize both the independence and potential strength of the young black women for whom she speaks.[9]

Self-naming is one method of self-determination, expressing 'the power to be what I am'. There is a correlation between this stance and Shange's desire to enable young Black women to understand their own situation:

> The reason *For Colored Girls* is entitled *For Colored Girls* is that that's who it was for. I wanted them to have the information that I did not have. I wanted them to know what it is truthfully like to be a grown woman. All I had was a whole bunch of mythology – tales and outright lies. I want a twelve-year-old girl to reach out for and get some information that isn't just contraceptive information but emotional information.[10]

Much of the 'emotional information' relayed in *For Colored Girls* centres on 'interpersonal relations'[11] expressed in the choreopoem through representations of heterosexual relationships, from the post-finishing-high-school defloration in the back of a Buick, to the end of an affair that

> waz an experiment
> to see how selfish i cd be
> if i wd really carry on to snare a possible lover
> if i waz capable of debasin my self for the love of another.   (p. 14)

But, depressing though several of these poems are, especially 'a nite with beau wilie brown', *For Colored Girls* is not predominantly concerned with victimisation but with finding the young Black woman's voice and self. Shange writes as a woman for women trying to find a woman's voice – and 'writes the body' in the manner in which the French feminists talk of it. Her use of language de-struct(ure)s literary and theatrical conventions as a means of foregrounding 'the body', emotions and the workings of the unconscious.

As in the case of Nichols, Shange bases her writing on the oral/aural, and attempts to represent that on the page:

> The spellings result from the way I talk or the way the character talks, or the way I heard something said. Basically, the spellings reflect language as I hear it. I don't write because words come out of my brain. I write this way because I hear the words.[12]

Shange's spellings are not without system: the habitual dropping of
the final 'g' in the gerund and the contraction of auxiliary verbs
associated with the conditional – as in the line 'worn fron supportin
a wd be hornplayer' (p. 35) – are used throughout *For Colored Girls*.
Contractions (a word resonating strongly with women, as part of the
menstrual/reproductive/creative cycle) feature prominently – of
verbs and prepositions (such as 'usedta'), of two verbs (for example,
'cda' = could have), of verbs and pronouns (such as 'hadda' = had a).
These may be a function of the speed of verbal delivery; dropping
the 'h' in 'wit' is one of specific pronounciation. Both reflect the way
in which the body is used in speech: Shange's system of spelling as
detailed here is thus dictated by the body.

There are other elements of deviation from the written norm,
however, which cannot simply be ascribed to the body. The most
obvious of these is the constant use of small letters. In *Black Women
Writers at Work* Shange attributes this to the influence of writers like
LeRoi Jones and Ishmael Reed:

> It bothers me, on occasion, to look at poems where all the first
> letters are capitalized. It's very boring to me. That's why I use the
> lower-case alphabet.[13]

One might argue that the exclusive use of that alphabet is equally
boring. But if one looks for other explanations four things suggest
themselves:

(a) The lower case might reflect a particular sense of status, such as
     a sense of inferiority, on the part of the young Black woman who
     is the central 'everywoman' character of *For Colored Girls*. But
     while such a sentiment is expressed in *some* of the poems this is
     not the case for *all* of them: even at the end when the young
     Black woman self-affirmingly says:

>   i found god in myself
>   & i loved her/ i loved her fiercely   (p. 63)

     Shange uses the lower case. There is no movement from an 'i' to
     an 'I'.
(b) The lower case might be used to eliminate differences that be-
     speak a hierarchy/power structures. However, poems that ex-
     plore such structures, especially within heterosexual relation-
     ships, and poems in which the black woman asserts herself (as in

'i'm a poet who' or 'sorry') are not differentiated in terms of what case is used.

(c) The use of the lower case could be indicative of the democratising drive that underlies *For Colored Girls* which, in this respect, has much in common with *I Is*. In both texts the individual woman's experiences are representative of Black women as a whole. In consequence that 'I'/'i' has no name.

(d) As regards the first person pronoun, the form denoted by the upper case is rigid and immobile whereas the lower case 'i' – divided as it is into two, resembling a ball dancing on a single jet of water – suggests flexibility and possibilities of movement. Indeed, Shange has said:

I like the idea that letters dance, not just that the words dance; of course, the words also dance. I need some visual stimulation, so that reading becomes not just a passive act and more than an intellectual activity, but demands rigorous participation.[14]

Shange's desire for 'visual stimulation' mirrors Nichols's desire for 'difference on the page'. They also have much in common in terms of their refusal to use punctuation as prescribed by the norms of the written word: Nichols uses such marks sparingly, Shange virtually not at all (except in the didascalies). Both women introduce 'slashes' into their lines. But Shange moves further than Nichols in her refusal of the authority of the written word by substituting '&' for 'and', through the contraction of words, through a spelling that denotes spoken rhythms. Shange, in a more pronounced manner than Nichols, invites the reader's eyes to dance across the page by reserving the left-hand side for stage directions and keeping the right-hand space for the spoken/sung words. Activity is demanded at every level: of the text, of the performers, of the reader. Only activity promotes change.

As a *choreopoem*, *For Colored Girls* combines music, song, dance and poetry. What these four elements have in common is that their systems of signification foreground the characteristics of Kristeva's *semiotic* disposition, being rhythmic, repetitive, non-logical, non-linear and complex in their form as well as indeterminate in their meaning. As such they stand in direct relation to the semiotic *chora* which denotes 'an essentially mobile and extremely provisional articulation constituted by movements and their ephemeral stases'.[15] They signal the expression of 'discrete quantities of energy' which 'move through the body' in an as yet non-signifying manner. The body, through oral and anal drives, and the body relating to the body (child to mother) are 'the ordering principle of the semiotic *chora*'.[16] The semiotic disposition, as an utterance which expresses the self as body, is, in a sense, *pre*-social rather than *a*social, though its effects, especially in terms of its attack upon the unicity of meaning and the transcendental ego, might well be described as asocial. The semiotic is disruptive of all structures save those created by self. It threatens social and communicative processes by refusing their norms and setting up the self as a counter-authority. It is thus self-affirming rather than self-denying. It signals the body that will not be denied. In so doing it invites expulsion from the body that is society, the body which cannot tolerate otherness or non-integration. Even in small doses, assertion of self (is that what promotes fear of minorities?) can effect change: if the change is welcomed by the body social/politic it functions as an anti-allergen; if not, it is treated like a virus.

Shange, through the four-fold foregrounding of the semiotic by combining poetry, dance, song and music, 'writes the body' all-pervadingly. It is thus inevitable that at the end of *For Colored Girls* the young Black woman should 'find god in herself and love her fiercely'. This is what the choreopoem drives towards – literally and metaphorically. At the beginning 'she's half-notes scattered / without rhythm' (p. 5) – recalling Nichols's representation of her Black woman's lives as 'scattered beads' – but at least she *is* 'half-notes', music, not entirely divested of self, whereas the beads bear no relation to the semiotic, are wholly other, can be traded (see 'Taint'). Shange's Black woman's self gradually emerges as a separate, discrete entity, a formation signalling independence and love of self.

Naming belongs to the symbolic order, constitutes a social and socialising move. Not naming is therefore one way of refusing the symbolic order and thus the categorisations that dominate society. It is important in this context that 'choreo' refers not only to dance but also to the group, which in *For Colored Girls* is an anonymous group of seven 'ladies', differentiated by colour of dress rather than name. Without a name and therefore a specific identity they can move – literally, for the individual poems in *For Colored Girls* are separated from each other by the re-grouping of the performers – into and out of identities such as Sechita's, which they inhabit for the space of a particular poem. This ability to change roles indicates the possibility of change *per se* : the young Black woman is not fixed in a role in the same way that the performers are not. She can move on, change. Life, like the body, pulses – with each pulse providing the energy that brings change. It is for this reason that *For Colored Girls* offers movement, instability, the subject in process/on trial = the semiotic) as form and content.

The semiotic is rooted in the unconscious. Shange has said: 'I'm committed to the idea that one of the few things human beings have to offer is the richness of unconscious and conscious emotional responses to being alive'.[17] These responses, 'their special relationships to their dreams and their unconscious',[18] are, according to Shange, what differentiates one woman from the next. It is not the 'dream-come-true', however, which Shange seeks to represent but the relationship between dream and reality, the need to inhabit a particular kind of reality. Indeed, for her the difference between writing by women and writing by men is that 'In works by men there's usually an *idea* as opposed to a *reality*'.[19]

In *For Colored Girls* a number of characters live a dream, have an *idea* of how things might be, but, in the end, typically face reality. Such is the case with the young girl of 'Toussaint': for a while Toussaint L'Ouverture becomes her imaginary companion but in the end she settles for his name-sake, Toussaint Jones, a boy of her own age, living in her time. The woman in 'one' turns herself into a man's dream because she wants to be 'unforgettable' but at 4.30a.m. she reverts to being her 'ordinary' self, realising that the dream cannot last into the day. This is why the closing lines of *For Colored Girls* affirm the choreopoem's dedication:

> & this is for colored girls who have considered
> suicide / but are movin to the ends of their own
> rainbows

Their dreams may not be realisable but another kind of dream is: that of finding the self.

The three texts discussed, *The Unbelonging, I Is* and *For Colored Girls* all focus on the trials, tribulations and dreams of a young Black woman growing up in an environment where she has to deal with intra-racial and inter-racial hostility directed at her. Abused for labour and for sexual purposes, she tries to hang on to some sense of self, rooted in her own history and that of her background. The texts span three discrete genres: the novel, poetry, drama. The greater the formal requirements of each genre, the more experimental and divergent the representation. In this respect Riley's novel is the most conservative in form, and Shange's choreopoem the most radical, with Nichols's poetry situated somewhere in between. Correspondingly, Riley writes *about* the body, and the body dominates the mind, whereas Shange writes the body but the mind – or, rather, the emotions – is/are allowed to dominate the body.

Another interesting correlation is that the more radical the form of writing is, the greater is the self-affirmation and expressed optimism about the Black woman's condition in the text and by the author. One could argue from this that the representation of victimisation without the possibility of change goes hand in hand with a conservative style of writing whereas the affirmation of revolutionary potential is expressed through formal non-conformity. This equals a statement about the correlation between content and form: radical positions are expressed through radical forms, conservative positions through traditional forms. This does not mean that the latter cannot function as an incitement to change – Riley's comments, in the discussion at Blackthorn's bookshop referred to above, make clear that she had written precisely as she did in order to avoid people treating the problems presented as 'dealt with'.

I would suggest that the differences detailed here account for the students' responses to the texts in terms of which one they like best. Liking has to do with pleasure, and pleasure is closely aligned to passivity. Most people's notion of what constitutes a pleasurable experience is associated with non-activity: drinking; eating foods that do not require chewing (such as cakes, chocolate, cream); lying about in bed/in the bath/on the beach; seeing a favourite movie. Non-activity is related to the structure of the thing from which pleasure is derived, and to how familiar one is with it. Familiarity breeds content.

Predictably the students responded most easily to those aspects of the texts, both in terms of content and form, which they were familiar with from their own experiences. As regards content, what they identified with was 'the oppression of women'. Judith Robinson wrote:

> Sometimes the colour of the writer, and therefore the experiences they wrote about, acted as a barrier. The experiences they wrote about which were primarily concerned with being a woman I felt more at ease with – in the sense of being able to identify with them.

Difficulties arose where issues/experiences were raised that white
women are not familiar with. These include – and Christine Bruley's
list was typical here – 'colour prejudice, historical aspects of black
women's lives, tribal customs'; in other words, cross-cultural/racial
differences. These differences are handled differently by different
authors, depending, I suspect, on the author's political stance, projected audience and so on. To take the example of Black people's
history, an issue that comes up in many of the Black women's
writings: Alice Walker in *The Color Purple* treats Celie – and the
reader – both of whom are assumed equally ignorant on this matter,
to a potted history of Black people in Africa through the letters of
Nettie to Celie. The students liked this text (which we discussed on
the course) because the unfamiliar was explained. Shange takes a
completely different line. In *Black Women Writers at Work*, decrying
European ethnocentricity, she said:

> It annoys me when people think that my writing isn't intellectual.
> That to me is a denigration of Afro-American culture. I have an
> overwhelming amount of material I could footnote if I wanted to.
> . . . I'm not interested in an *annotated* Shange. I could let a Euro-
> pean do that, but I'm not going to. Either you know us or you
> don't. If you don't, then you should look it up. . . . We do not have
> to refer continually to European art as the standard. That's abso-
> lutely absurd and racist, and I won't participate in that utter lie.[20]

Here is the same refusal of a self-styled authority – that of European
history and art – as was encountered in Shange's style of writing in
relation to the written word. Ethnocentricity is thus made obvious;
most white people do have to look up who Toussaint L'Ouverture
was. Thus unfamiliarity demands activity.

Again, concerning the form of writing, students responded fa-
vourably to forms they 'recognised' – like *The Unbelonging*'s realist
novel form. Gillian Banks said of *I Is*: 'I had to read it several times
– found it a chore.' Christine Bruley talked of the 'difficulties experienced with the language' in connection with the same text. Howard
Jennings simply found it 'not as accessible as the novels'. Diane
Tonkins said of *For Colored Girls* that 'the form had not been encountered before'. Unfamiliar forms demand 'active participation'
(as Shange desires it of her audience), and this demand may correspondingly reduce the pleasure experienced in reading the text. As
any 'experienced' reader of unfamiliar forms, of, say, postmodern

texts, will know, the pleasure derived from reading such divergent texts is frequently associated with a process of 'recognition' – seeing the text fit into some pattern after all, being able to relate it to other texts one knows.

One can facilitate students' experience of reading unfamiliar texts in a number of different ways. One is, of course, simply to expose them to a large number of divergent writings. But on most courses such a move is not possible. Another one is to shift their 'familiarity focus' from the text to related areas of concern. Thus one can get them to investigate the mechanisms which govern their reading responses, to look at what constitutes pleasure, more specifically pleasure in reading for them. Once they recognise a pattern in their reading habit, become aware of the relationship between familiarity and liking in their reading, this can become the source of their pleasure. Or one can look at the texts in terms of theoretical positions such as that of the French feminists. Recognising traits of the *écriture féminine* can be another source of pleasure.

Familiarity breeds content. It also de-revolutionises – unless society changes to take account of the needs voiced in texts that challenge structure. The needs expressed in *The Unbelonging, I Is* and *For Colored Girls* are those of the young Black woman. As Shange demands:

> somebody / anybody
> sing a black girl's song
> bring her out
> to know herself
> to know you
> but sing her rhythms   (p. 4)

NOTES

1. Hélène Cixous, 'The Laugh of the Medusa', in *New French Feminisms*, ed. Elaine Marks and Isabelle de Courtivron (Brighton, Sussex: Harvester Press, 1981) p. 253.
2. J. P. Stern, *On Realism* (London: Routledge and Kegan Paul, 1973) p. 31.
3. Grace Nichols, in interview with Gillian Allnutt, *City Limits*, 17 June 1984, p. 24.
4. Cixous, 'Laugh of the Medusa', p. 452.
5. Lauretta Ngcobo (ed.), *Let It Be Told: Black Women Writers in Britain* (London: Virago Press, 1988) p. 98.

6. Ibid.
7. Cixous, 'Laugh of the Medusa', p. 251.
8. Julia Kristeva, *Revolution in Poetic Language*, trans. Margaret Waller (New York: Columbia University Press, 1984) p. 101.
9. Claudia Tate (ed.), *Black Women Writers at Work* (Harpenden, Herts: Oldcastle Books, 1985) p. 149.
10. Ibid., pp. 161–2.
11. Ibid., p. 159.
12. Ibid., p. 163.
13. Ibid.
14. Ibid.
15. Kristeva, *Revolution in Poetic Language*, p. 25.
16. Ibid., p. 27.
17. Tate, *Black Women Writers at Work*, p. 151.
18. Ibid., p. 153.
19. Ibid., p. 160.
20. Ibid., p. 164.

Main Texts

Grace Nichols, *I Is a Long Memoried Woman* (London: Karnak House, 1984).
Joan Riley, *The Unbelonging* (London: The Women's Press, 1985).
Ntozake Shange, *For Colored Girls who Have Considered Suicide when the Rainbow is Enuf* (London: Methuen, 1978).

3

Black Women Writing and Reading

JACKIE ROY

When I was asked to provide a commentary on Black women's writing, two main areas of concern came to mind. The first relates to my experiences as a mature student of English on a BA course at an inner-city polytechnic. The second concerns my own practice as a Black woman writer of fiction; my aims, interests and the way in which such writing is currently received. I wanted to use this double focus as a means of examining the difficulties which Black women invariably encounter when they enter either domain, both of which have previously been realms of exclusion and marginalisation.

Inevitably, perhaps, the task has proved more difficult than I anticipated. In reflecting on these two issues, I have come to recognise some of the uncertainties I have felt both as writer and student, and also the complexity of the position of Black women in either field. In Britain, Black women have only just started to be recognised as writers and consumers of texts. Consequently, provision for us and limited acceptance of us is only just beginning to occur. The ambivalence of the academic establishment towards us was indicated at a conference on Black women's writing at a university, where all the speakers were white men. In other words, there is considerable confusion about the role of Black women, where and who we are and what exactly our contribution is to be. It is no longer possible to ignore us entirely but it seems that our presence must be controlled by refraction through a largely white male perspective. There is also, I suspect, an element of opportunism in some of the recent interest that has been directed towards us. Academia is saturated with every possible discourse on the English literary canon; Black women's writing represents 'new' ground and for some, perhaps, a means of establishing a reputation in an area which may or may not turn out to be the next growth industry. Whilst I welcome the opportunity to speak about Black women's writing, I am wary; cynically, perhaps.

I sometimes suspect that current interest is a means of expiating white liberal unease regarding Black exclusion, and that as Black writing becomes more widely taught, guilt may begin to fade and present interest with it. This is not intended to suggest that all white responses to Black writing fit this particular mode. I have encountered white academics and editors (men as well as women) who demonstrated interest in Black writing long before it was even considered as a serious area of study and whose commitment to its promotion as a vital part of both Black and white inheritance is indisputable. However, it is important to recognise that tokenism and exploitation can and do occur. This was emphasised for me when I was asked to write for a BBC radio series on the Caribbean experience. The producer sought me out since Black writers were 'under-represented' but at the same time stated, 'We must be careful not to offend our white middle-aged female listeners.' It was made clear that our presence was required only as long as we did not cause unease or embarrassment.

I am stating my position here because complicity and/or passivity are often conditions of Black women being permitted to speak. Therefore, I must look at the way in which I present such writing now. What is required of me, and how far am I willing and able to meet it? These questions arise whenever I, as a Black woman, consider communicating my position. They are indicative of the fact that as yet there are relatively few Black women speakers. Until there are more of us, and we can be certain that it really is our voices that editors, producers and academics wish to hear, we will continue to be wary, uncertain and ambivalent about articulating our experiences in any capacity, including that of writer or reader.

The lack of Black women in all areas of literary study is perhaps my greatest concern at present. As a BA student at a polytechnic I was one of only four; by the end of the course there were only three of us. The reasons for this are many and complex, so I shall not be looking at them in depth here. However, several obvious factors are involved, particularly the under-achievement of Black school-children. Black pupils are not encouraged to perceive themselves in terms of academic success. Their attempts to learn are often viewed with indifference, and the courses they are taught mainly lack reference to their histories and experiences. Relatively few, therefore, obtain the 'A' level grades which give access to higher education.

In recognition of this, the polytechnic which I attended attempted to encourage the admission of mature and 'disadvantaged' students by offering courses that were relevant to their interests, such as New Literatures in English (comprising African, Indian, Canadian and Australian literature) and West Indian literature, which were options in the second and third year. The poly also had links with Access courses designed to prepare returning students, and often waived standard entry requirements for those who demonstrated the ability to work at degree level. However, these positive strategies were often undermined by low grants (now being made lower still by the introduction of loans) which tend to exclude students from disadvantaged backgrounds, since their financial situations are usually unstable even before such a course, making it a luxury they cannot afford. Additionally, crèche and nursery facilities were so inadequate that returning single parents in particular were effectively excluded, unless they were in a position to make alternative arrangements. Black women were, I suspect, particularly affected at times by this. These factors meant that students and staff were overwhelmingly white and middle class, which inevitably marginalised and/or intimidated those who fell outside either category. There were no Black women lecturers in the English Department whilst I was a student (nor were there any Black men). The importance of including Black women as members of the teaching staff cannot be overstated and I shall be addressing this issue more fully at a later point.

Courses at the polytechnic were taught mainly from current theoretical perspectives which students were required to adopt as part of their own critical practice. In introducing students to contemporary literary theory, the English course encouraged reading 'against the grain' and demonstrated those deconstructive techniques which enable the reader to detect the hidden ideologies and assumptions inscribed in a text that help to maintain relations of power. Clearly, this is an over-simplification of the functions of literary theory, but it indicated its importance with regard to oppressed groups such as Black men and women, since it shows that our position in the social order is not the consequence of a natural, unchanging hierarchy but a product of power structures, language and discourse and therefore open to change.

Of course, contemporary literary theory can be problematic for Black women, since it is complex and often employs terms which exclude those without access to higher education (usually the marginalised and oppressed) and in doing so reproduces some of the power relations it attempts to break down. Although I sympathise with this perspective, my own view is that when it is used with such objections in mind, literary theory challenges the existing order more often that it affirms it. This is particularly so with regard to feminist theory, which presents a major challenge to patriarchal structures, though for Black women it is limited by its failure to engage consistently and effectively with Black issues, often subsuming these to encompass *all* women in a form of essentialism which denies the specificity of Black women's experiences.

At this point, it would perhaps have been useful to have produced a feminist reading of a text by a Black woman writer based on my experience of seminars at the polytechnic. However, in thinking about ways of demonstrating the impact of feminism with reference to a specific text, I have come to recognise that little writing by Black women was included on any lists. They were dominated by white male writers on most courses and by Black male writers in New Literatures in English and West Indian literature. I can only recall being asked to read one poem by a Black woman in my time as an undergraduate, so rather than refer to texts which require lengthy summaries to make a reading comprehensible, I shall list the Black women's texts that we studied in the hope that interested readers will refer to these themselves and consider ways in which they might be examined. In West Indian literature, the following novels were read: Sylvia Wynter, *The Hills of Hebron* (London: Longman, 1962); Olive Senior, *Summer Lightning* (London: Heinemann, 1986); and Erna Brodber, *Jane and Louisa Will Soon Come Home* (London: New Beacon, 1980). And in New Literature in English: Bessie Head, *A Question of Power* (London: Heinemann, 1974).

The paucity of texts by Black women writers on these courses was repeated during my MA degree in Commonwealth literature at university. The Caribbean literature course included only one women writer – Michelle Cliff, *No Telephone to Heaven* (London: Methuen, 1988) despite repeated assurances from the (white male) tutor that feminist readings were desirable and welcome. When we queried this omission, one more text by a Black woman (Olive Senior, *Summer Lightning*) was added to the list.

Why then are academics so reluctant to examine texts by Black women writers? Even where there is a recognition of the importance of hearing Black women speak, their writing does not seem to be included; writing by Black men, or by white women such as Nadine

Gordimer, Jean Rhys and Phyllis Shand Allfrey, is examined instead. Obviously, this is largely attributable to the double marginalisation (that of race and gender) to which Black women are subjected. White male lecturers in particular, when teaching Black writing (consciously or otherwise) tend to evade those issues raised by Black women (whether as writers or readers). Often, such lecturers are aware that in teaching Black women's texts, they are inscribed as white patriarchs and therefore they find looking at such literature disquieting. Most are aware of their own limitations when Black feminist issues are raised and feel the instability of their position. This is also evident when white women are required to teach Black writing. Several have conveyed their unease in seminars and have indicated that their approach is uncertain as a result of their acknowledgement of the difficulties involved in white voices speaking about (and for) Black women. The lack of a clear and decisive theoretical framework through which to read Black women's writing also inhibits those who try to teach it. Most of the theorisation of black literature is coming out of America and is not widely available here. Often it is also specific to the Black American experience which differs primarily because the Black presence there has been established for several generations whereas here, as a major community, it is relatively new. This leaves tutors and students alike with insufficient support in their attempts to discuss Black feminist concepts. It is often safer to minimise engagement with this than to risk getting it wrong. Once again, this underlines the need for Black women lecturers and suggests that until more are employed, Black women's writing will continue to be inadequately addressed or largely ignored.

This need was specifically identified by a group of Black students at the polytechnic, who presented a paper to the English Department[1] which outlined the inadequacies of the English course with regard to Black writing. As it articulated several of the problems I am attempting to look at here, I shall be quoting it extensively. The paper focuses mainly on the core courses which all first-year students at this time were required to take, and lists these as Introduction to Poetry, Introduction to Drama, Poetics of Fiction and Discourse. The paper states:

> Within these four subject areas there were absolutely no positive images of black people portrayed. In the Poetics of Fiction, we were instead provided with racist stereotypical images of black people as savages as portrayed in Conrad's *Heart of Darkness*. We

understand that the presentation of this book was modified to include discussion of the racism reflected therein after complaints and a petition from BEd students, who were dissatisfied with the teaching of this material during the first semester. However, it is felt that this in itself was not adequate redress and it has been suggested that the inclusion of this work by Conrad could only be balanced by the inclusion of a black author in the curriculum. Zora Neale Hurston has been suggested as she fits into the period covered. It is with dismay that we note that the syllabus remains unchanged for first-year students this year.

The students' requirement that Black women writers be heard underlines the way in which such writing is neglected even in the more progressive academic institutions. By concentrating on texts from the literary canon, degree courses privilege and reinforce white male domination and inscribe (Black) women as other, confirming and repeating their marginalisation. I suspect that the emphasis on canon-based texts stems mainly from the belief sometimes expressed by (white) students and academics that a thorough knowledge of these is necessary to prove the validity of the degree and to indicate that the highest possible level of cultural attainment has been achieved. This raises all kinds of questions concerning notions of 'great' literature, aesthetic values and the status which an education in 'The Arts' confers, as well as the social structures which this inevitably affirms. These issues cannot be examined adequately in a study of this length, but they indicate that Black women writers have minimal value as cultural signifiers and affirmations of academic prowess, hence the relegation of such writing to the small dark corners of academia.

The paper was equally critical of the Introduction to Poetry course and raised the question of language:

> In the Introduction to Poetry dossier, there was a lack of anything written by black people once again and although individual seminar leaders introduced the work of black poets in seminar groups, it was felt that the tutors lacked adequate knowledge to explore the issues raised concerning black language. The result was that black language became denigrated through lack of understanding and discussion.

This comment highlights the need for Black teaching staff at all levels of higher education. The absence of Black staff members was frequently raised by Black (and white) students from all departments. By the end of last year the arts faculty had engaged a Black woman and a Black man as permanent members of staff. All British polytechnics and universities have a serious deficiency with regard to Black staff, particularly women. My own attempts to find a Black woman superviser at PhD level highlights the gap; the overwhelming majority of academic staff are white men, even where West Indian, Indian or African literatures are taught. If I want to pursue a research project (which at present is expected to focus on Black women's writing from a Black feminist perspective), I shall probably have to go to America.

The absence of Black staff was recognised by most lecturers at the polytechnic, who appeared to feel compromised by the anomaly involved in theorising about equal opportunities and anti-racist education while working within a structure which mainly excluded Black people, and this will perhaps lead to further Black appointments being made.

The lack of Black lecturers, particularly women, has serious repercussions for Black women students as the above quotation from the paper indicates. I would argue that when 'Black language' is interpreted and mediated by white readers, there is a sense that Black literature is alien and other, leading to a need to 'translate' it and to make it recognisable, which, when attempted by white lecturers is suggestive of appropriation and the kind of domination that Black writing constantly seeks to resist. It is important to stress here that I have no wish to exclude either white women or white men from considering issues of race and attempting to address them. To confine such explorations to the Black community is to ensure that racism remains a Black 'problem' and encourages the abdication of white responsibility. However, it is unacceptable for the white perspective to be the dominant perspective on Black issues and it is this position which I am attempting to challenge.

As long as Black women are excluded from higher education, the inference will be that Black women are incapable of achieving high academic standards, a notion which reinforces those stereotypical images which posit us as being inferior to white. In a learning situation, the absence of Black women lecturers places Black students at a disadvantage since we have neither role models nor access to readings of Black texts which adequately perceive Black women's histories and experiences or understand fully the significance of the oral tradition which is so evident and so important in much Black women's writing.

The lack of Black students, Black staff and a failure to incorporate Black writing on core courses is not only detrimental to the Black community; it narrows and restricts the experiences of white students and staff as the paper further suggests:

> If white students are not exposed to any black literature, dramatic art or poetry during introductory courses, then this is surely a reinforcement of racist ideas by effectively making black literature . . . invisible.

It is felt that introductory courses, by their very nature, should open up students to the diversity of English literature (which we understand to refer to literatures written in English) and it should not be left until second year options before black literature makes its appearance.

The paper also suggests that:

> By excluding material by black people, the course fails to capture the imagination of black students, leaving them with strong feelings of alienation.

This brings me to the second area of examination with regard to Black writing and Black receivers of texts. It concerns my own practice as a writer of fiction, since one of my aims in presenting Black characters is to combat some of the alienation I have felt when confronted by narratives which deny the existence of Black men and women or present us in terms of those stereotypical images which construct us as being lazy, animalistic, stupid and otherwise inferior to white.

My own novel for young adults, *Soul Daddy*[2] was an attempt to write against these assumptions by making the central characters young Black women who become aware both of the problems they face in attempting represent themselves in an inherently racist society and the way in which this need for self-definition can become a strength. I wanted to present intelligent young adults whose circumstances had provided them with very limited contact with other members of the Black community both in terms of their cultural background and in their day-to-day lives. They needed to learn how to place themselves in relation to their Black inheritance. Additionally, I wanted to examine the ways in which Black women, white women and Black men are often pressurised into adopting roles which fit social expectations and assumptions regarding gender and race and which are therefore inauthentic and constricting. There are problems involved in attempting to break down stereotypical images; there is always the danger that in the process they are reaffirmed or reproduced, and I was conscious of this throughout the writing of the book. The quotation selected by the publisher to describe and summarise some of the themes of the novel was, therefore, perhaps not the one I would have chosen, since it presents a largely sexual image of a Black man which is questioned and analysed throughout the novel as a white construction of Blackness, but quoted out of the context of the rest of the text it appears to uphold this particular image:

Hannah looked at the stocky man on the television screen. He wore tight, faded jeans and a jacket with broad, padded shoulders that made him look bigger than he really was. His Afro hair was plaited dreadlock style. His voice filled the room. 'Come to me, come to me, come to me sweet Isabèl.' Hannah wriggled in her seat . . . It was her mother in the garden he meant, the wife he'd walked out on before she was born . . . How much of him had she inherited? Were her eyes the same, her mouth? What did it mean to be Joe Delaney's daughter?   (p. 6)

This represents Hannah's first perceptions of Joe, which alter as the novel progresses. She realises, for example, that although her father left, her mother was not merely passive in the relationship and that the situation was far more complex than she had imagined, relating to the public image that her father is required to project. The TV representation of Joe is false, a publicity image that panders to public expectations of Black , male entertainers.

Social expectation of the Black community (and also of Black writers) was underlined for me in a recent reading from this book. A white male member of the audience asked why I had not represented young Black muggers on council estates. Implicit in this question was the assumption that this is the main pattern of behaviour for Black youth and that other presentations are both inauthentic and inappropriate.

Similar assumptions can also be made by editors and producers. I submitted a synopsis which concerned a fourteen-year-old girl with one white and one Black parent. This was queried on the grounds that such a perspective has already been explored in *Soul Daddy* and that I was therefore in danger of repeating myself. This clearly suggests that there is only one way of representing this form of Black experience and that it is therefore fixed and resistant to multiple approaches and definitions.

Similarly, a passage in a short story written for radio was queried on the basis that Black pupils were no longer subjected to subtle forms of racism in schools as I had implied and that this part should therefore be removed since it was likely to produce irate phone calls from teachers. The Black actress who was reading it supported my assertion that such attitudes were still prevalent and agreed with me that the passage should be retained. Without her help and the validation which her comments provided, an already watered-down script would have lacked engagement with any issue that might have been considered relevant to the Black community.

One thing I learnt from that particular experience was that Black writers are often rendered powerless to express their deepest concerns by those who handle the work at the various stages of its production. A Black producer would not have questioned the raising of such issues: her own experience of racism would have enabled her to see that such representations are still appropriate and necessary. Like the other Black writers involved in this project, I was commissioned to write the work hastily. I received no useful input. The resulting series was bland and poorly edited, fostering the (white) assumption that Black writers are second-rate and have little to offer. Once again, I can only conclude that until more Black people are employed at all levels of publishing, radio and television, the problems of Black representation (particularly as they relate to women) will remain, and will continue to reaffirm white prejudices with regard to Black input.

At the start of this investigation, I referred to the complexities involved in being both a Black woman writer and a Black woman student at present, and the uncertainties these tend to produce. It has been my intention to present some of these in the hope that changes can be made. I have frequently used the form 'us' and 'we' in referring to Black women here. It is a means of suggesting a political identification and the collective strength of Black women which I have felt the need to draw on in writing of my experiences. However, this does perhaps imply that I am somehow speaking for all Black women or that we have the same experiences; this suggests an essentialism which I am concerned to resist. In studying Black women's issues, and in writing about some of them, I have found that because there are so few Black women being heard at present, I am sometimes required, it would seem, to be representative of *the* Black feminist perspective. However, I am only one voice; I cannot purport to speak for all Black women and would not presume to do so. Our experiences are as varied and as diverse as those of white women. We are, of course, linked by the double marginalisation inscribed in Black womanhood, but there are many differences of perception which stem from differences of culture and class (an Afro-Caribbean woman's experience differs from that of an Afro-American, for example) and this needs to be recognised and acknowledged.

In writing about the polytechnic, I have mainly presented the shortcomings in its approach to Black women's issues. However, there were positive and constructive attempts to look at the positions of Black men and women. It is ironic, perhaps, that I am able to challenge the teaching at the polytechnic as I am doing here only as a result of the heightened perception afforded to me during my time there as a student. One of the poly's major achievements was to raise awareness so that racism, where it was clearly identifiable, was made unacceptable and was actively opposed by the majority of students and staff. This occurred more vigorously there than at any other institution I have yet encountered. Despite its limitations, the poly's approach to literary theory, courses such as New Literatures in English and West Indian literature and the examination of the concept of racial outsiders in the Shakespeare course in the third year, all challenged students' preconceptions regarding race and gender. By the end of these courses, students had a heightened sense of the implications of living in a racist and sexist society. Therefore, the importance of addressing such issues within institutions cannot be overemphasised. The way forward is clear, however; Black women must not merely be talked about, we must be in a position to speak for ourselves, and this can only be achieved when many more of us are admitted to those platforms which dictate the way in which representations are made, higher education and all areas of media communication must ensure that Black women hold positions that enable us to represent our own experiences and perceptions of ourselves. Until this happens, we will seldom be heard.

NOTES

1. Thanks to Elizabeth Turnbull and fellow students for permission to quote from their paper (for students' comments).
2. Jackie Roy, *Soul Daddy* (London: Collins, 1990).

4

'Long Memoried Women': Caribbean Women Poets

BRUCE WOODCOCK

HER STORY

Chilean novelist Isabel Allende argued in a Radio 3 interview that women writers from Central America have been 'strategically ignored'. This is not because women have not written – they have, from the time of the love songs and epics of the seventeenth-century nun Sor Juan Inés de la Cruz in colonial Mexico. But, as elsewhere, the literatures of Central America are male-orientated, and Isabel Allende pointed out the results: women writers don't get reviewed, are badly distributed, rarely published in Europe, and are not studied in universities (Radio 3 'Third Ear' interview, 2 April 1989).

The truth of her observations was reinforced by the concurrent publication of a book from The Women's Press of women's resistance poetry from Central America, *Lovers and Comrades*. Editor Amanda Hopkinson makes the point that despite the increased fashionableness of Latin American writing with the work of male writers like Márquez, Fuentes and Llosa, Latin American women's writing is generally under-represented, particularly the poetry. She prints 46 poets, of whom only half-a-dozen have had work previously translated into English. Among them are some astoundingly powerful and soberingly well-established poets like Claribel Alegría (b.1924, Nicaragua) and Alaíde Foppa (born in Spain of Guatemalan and Argentinian parentage; disappeared in Guatemala in 1980). Is it simply a confession of my white male Eurocentric ignorance that none of the works of these extraordinary poets was known to me?

If we look at the history of women poets in the English-speaking Caribbean – which will form the main focus of this essay – the situation is similarly one of marginalisation, though within a different context. Central American women have a long, if hidden, history of verse-writing albeit within a well-established male tradition. The women of the English-speaking Caribbean have only recently made inroads into what is itself a fairly new male literary domain. While there was always a rich tradition of oral culture often maintained through the experience of women as singers and storytellers, written Caribbean literatures emerged in their first full expressions as part of the nationalist movements after the First World War. The 1920s and 1930s saw a number of islands asserting growing demands for national identity and political independence, rediscovering roots in the suppressed history of African civilisations, the experience of slavery and the forces of resistance. Cultural expression formed an absolutely crucial part of this phenomenon, often with direct links to the political activity as in the case of Vic Reid in Jamaica, or the fruitful Trinidadian Beacon group with produced C. L. R. James and Ralph de Boissière among others. There is no doubt that women played vital roles within these movements. De Boissière has a marvellous scene in *Crown Jewel*, his novel based on the oil field strikes in Trinidad in the 1930s, in which the oppressed Cassie eventually asserts her importance as a woman in the political movement by telling her lover, the powerful male trade unionist Le Maître, 'We're lookin' to get rid of bosses, don't come bossin' me!' (p. 299). De Boissière has indicated in interviews that one of the projects of his novel was to reveal the overlooked contribution women made to the events he describes and witnessed first-hand. The transformation of Cassie through her involvement in political action is an eloquent and moving enactment of the personal-political premise so crucial to the European Women's Movement.

While de Boissière's case is undoubtedly correct, despite the limited documentaiton of it as yet, there is little information about the engagement of women in literary production during this period. As with any generalisation, there were significant exceptions. Paula Burnett's anthology of Caribbean verse records a number of women poets at work during the nationalist movements, notably Jean Rhys (1890–1979, Dominica), Phyllis Allfrey (b.1915, Dominica), Una Marson (1905–65, Jamaica) and Barbara Ferland (b.1915, Jamaica). None of these writers has left a significant mark on the generally acknowledged history of Caribbean poetry, though obviously Jean Rhys and Phyllis Allfrey have as novelists. Yet Una Marson, to take just one example, epitomised an active involvement by women in the nationalist and political movements from a literary as well as an ideological and organisational perspective. She was an ardent feminist, active in the 1930s in the Women's International League for Peace and Freedom and the International Alliance of Women, among other organisations. Her poems embodied this involvement: 'Gettin de Spirit' urges women to

> Shout sister – shout –
> Hallelujah – Amen
> Can't you feel de spirit
> Shout sister – shout.
> (Burnett, p. 160)

Her vibrant vernacular poems based on the Blues began to do for Jamaican English what Langston Hughes did for American English during the same period, a crucial area of development for later Caribbean poets.

It was not until the 1970s and 1980s, however, that Caribbean women began to find their voice publicly. It is arguable that, during this time, writing by women has been the most productive and most fruitful area of development in Caribbean writing generally, providing some of the freshest and most innovative material and offering an example of an emergent trend within an emergent literature. Quite simply, there has been a striking increase in the number of women writers being published and in the attention being paid to the cultural activities of women. This is evident in all areas. In the novel we have seen the emergence of Erna Brodber, Zee Edgell, Merle Hodge, Merle Collins, Joan Riley, Jamaica Kinkaid, Beryl Gilroy and Susan Cambridge, among others. There has been the remarkable example of the Sistren drama collective, formed by a group of working-class women in 1977 and developing a community-based theatre with accompanying discussions and workshops covering issues of particular relevance to rural and ghetto women, such as male violence, teenage pregnancy, the problems of female labour such as contract work in the sugar plantations, the problems of women organising for themselves, and so on. The Sistren group epitomises the attitudes of Carribean women to cultural activity: they cannot be contained within a pre-established category, 'drama'. What they do covers social work, consciousness-raising, assertion training, political organising, facilitating self-empowerment. Importantly, they also see themselves as documentors of the lives of women, as evidenced by their volume of oral history, *Lionheart Gal*.[1] It is their emphasis on collective creation which is striking.

In terms of poetry, the same rich pattern is evident. Of the women poets producing work now, Paula Burnett includes the following: Louise Bennett (b.1919, Jamaica), Claire Harris (b.1937, Trinidad), Judy Miles (b.1942, Trinidad), Pamela Mordecai (b.1942, Jamaica), Olive Senior (b.1943, Jamaica), Marlene Philip (b.1947, Tobago), Lorna Goodison (b.1947, Jamaica), Grace Nichols (b.1950, Guyana), Lillian Allen (b.1951, Jamaica), Dionne Brand, (b.1953, Trinidad), Valerie Bloom (b.1956, Jamaica). We can add to this list through reference to two significant publishing events which exemplify the emergence of women as poets. In 1977 Edward Kamau Brathwaite's magazine *Savacou* printed a special edition called 'Caribbean Woman', dedicated to the memory of Una Marson. It contains some significant essays by Hermione McKenzie and Merle Hodge among others, fiction by Christine Craig and poems by Jean Goulbourne (b.1948, Jamaica), Opal Palmer (Jamaica) and Lorna Goodison. *Savacou* went on to produce an anthology called *New Poets From Jamaica* which featured seven women out of a total of thirteen poets, including Pam Hickling (b.1945, Jamaica), Christine Craig (Jamaica), Beverley Brown (b.1945, Jamaica), as well as Pam Mordecai, Lorna Goodison, Jean Goulbourne and Opal Palmer.

The second publishing event was the appearance in 1980 of the Heinemann anthology *Jamaica Woman*, edited by Pamela Mordecai and Mervyn Morris, which for the first time gave new Caribbean women poets their own space within an international publishing imprint. It featured fifteen poets, and in addition to names already mentioned, including Jennifer Brown, Jean D'Costa, Dorothea Edmondson, Sally Henzell, Bridget Jones, Sally McIntosh, Alma Mock Yen, Velma Pollard, Heather Royes, Colleen Smith-Brown and Cyrene Tomlinson.

In addition, there are a number of women poets not included in these collections, but who can be found in other recent anthologies not devoted to Caribbean writing or in individual volumes.[2] They include: Jean Binta Breeze (Jamaica), Elean Thomas (Jamaica), Helen Joseph (Grenada), Christine David (Grenada), Merle Collins (Grenada), Amryl Johnson (Trinidad), Vivian Usherwood (1959–80, Jamaica), Gabriella Pearse (Columbia) and Barbara Burford. There are also examples of women poets of Caribbean descent but born in non-Caribbean countries. The best British examples are Jackie Kay (b.1961) and Maud Sulter.

Of the lists given, a number of poets are not working predominantly or entirely elsewhere than the Caribbean, most notably Grace

Nichols, Valerie Bloom, Jean Binta Breeze, Elean Thomas, Maud Sulter, Amryl Johnson, Merle Collins, Gabriella Pearse and Barbara Burford in Britain, and Dionne Brand and Lillian Allen in Canada.

HER VOICES

One of the most significant precedents for Caribbean women poets has been Louise Bennett, 'Miss Lou'. Born in Jamaica in 1919, Louise Bennett has achieved charismatic status for her work as a folklorist and performer. She has had a number of books published from the 1940s onwards, and her *Selected Poems* was published in 1982. But the best way to appreciate the extraordinary effervescence which she brings to her work is to hear her in performance, as in the 1983 live recording of her at the Lyric theatre, *Yes M'Dear*. Her work derives much of its inspiration and material from the oral tradition in Jamaican culture, both in terms of content (stories, proverbs, street chants, children's games) and language (voices, intonations, idioms). The two are inevitably indistinguishable: it is the oral quality of Jamaican language in its tones, gestures and expressiveness which embodies the experience, attitudes and outlooks of the voices Louise Bennett creates and records. Many of her poems are dramatic monologues addressed by a character, sometimes through letter form, and not surprisingly many of these voices are women's. Anecdotal, immediate, full of humour and ironies, Miss Lou's poems generally comment on matters in hand, social and domestic. Their pronouncements are often self-ironising by virtue of the strategy of adopting a dramatic persona as the vehicle of the poem. Many of them are celebratory, so it is not unexpected to find her producing a poem like 'Jamaica Oman':

> Neck an neck an foot an foot wid man
> She buckle hole her own;
> While man a call her 'so-so rib'
> Oman a tun backbone!
>
> An long before Oman Lib bruck out
> Over foreign lan
> Jamaica female wasa work
> Her liberated plan!
>
> (*Selected Poems*, p. 22)

Louise Bennett's legacy has been widespread. The performance poet Mikey Smith acknowledged her as 'the mother' of 'dub' poetry, the performance form related to reggae.[3] For women poets, her example has been vital. Later women performance poets have often added a more emphatic political dimension to their work, either covert or explicit, and this distinguishes them from Louise Bennett's more modulated satire. But they have carried on her pioneering use of 'nation language', Edward Kamau Brathwaite's coinage to replace the pejorative connotations of 'dialect' or 'creole'.[4] And as part of this 'people speech', they have followed her emphasis upon oral delivery as essential to the experience of their work, a collective sharing which is quite distinctive in their view of cultural activity.

The examples which spring most readily to mind are Merle Collins and Christine David from Grenada, and Elean Thomas, Valerie Bloom and Jean Binta Breeze from Jamaica. As we shall see, however, this in no way excludes other women as performance poets: one of the fundamental features of these women's work is that it often defies the orthodox categorisations into oral/performance or literary/written.

The two Grenadian poets were both galvanised by this involvement in the Grenadian revolution, and for Merle Collins that meant her work became 'all identification and eagerness, as a part of the people's process'. Chris Searle's book *Words Unchained*, from which Merle Collins's comment comes (p. 144), records the extent to which women and women's organisations were centrally involved politically and culturally in the period of the New Jewel movement, 1979–83. Christine Davis explained that her poem 'Ain't I Woman?' came out of the fact that women 'are more organised in our country, they're looking at themselves more clearly, they're more aware now . . . asking themselves all kinds of questions . . . doing things on their own, and things are coming *directly* from them' (Searle, p. 177). She sees her own poetry as not so much her voice as 'anybody's voice, the voice of the people, and in particular the voice of the people of Carriacou', her district. Her poems act like chants which encourage people to join in.

This emphasis upon relating to the experiences of particular communities and upon collective participatory cultural activity was a keynote for the women poets of Grenada and has remained a distinctive aspect of Caribbean women's poetry more generally. Equally there has been an emphasis upon transforming traditionally male cultural preserves. In Grenada, Valerie V. represented a significant

challenge by women to the chauvinistic traditions of calypso with
her song 'Women Be Free' (Searle, pp. 201–2), while Helena Joseph
articulated a central concern when she argued: 'Before, it was only
men really who were coming out and writing and saying poetry,
and if you look at West Indian literature it is mostly men who wrote
it. We never read poetry at school that was written by women, and
we know that women are not projected in most of the Caribbean
generally, particularly as writers' (p. 163).

Of the Grenadian poets, Merle Collins has received widespread
acclaim with her novel *Angel* and her volume of poems *Because the
Dawn Breaks*. She has worked closely with a group of African musicians called 'African Dawn', incorporating traditional oral, dramatic
and musical forms into the performance of her work. As with other
performance poets, her texts on the page are in one sense scores or
scripts to be brought to fullness through delivery and enactment.
She often takes local experiences as vehicles for what she wishes to
deal with. As she herself recognised in the work of other women in
her essay 'Women Writers from the Caribbean', 'it is the particular
dimension of the experiences as recounted and explored by the
women which gives it its special quality and presents a perspective
the exploration of which is important to the region's future'.[5] Her
poem 'Callaloo' uses the image of a popular Caribbean soup as a
metaphor of the 'mix-up' in the world, out of which will come some
positive transformatory synthesis:

> An' de promise o' de change
> Is sweet
> An' strong
> Like de soup
> When Grannie
> Cover it down dey
> And let it
> Consomme
> Like dat
> Hot
>   (Searle, pp. 137–8)

In 'The Lesson', Merle Collins's great-grandmother becomes em-
blematic of women living under the economic and psychological
weight of colonial oppression: she was familiar with British history
than with that of the Caribbean, and thought the name of resistance

leader Toussaint L'Ouverture was a curse. The poem envisages a transformation for women as they rewrite history and the future, but emphasises they will 'cherish / Grannie's memory' to include her in the new her-story (Searle, pp. 138–40).

Of the poets we have linked with Louise Bennett, Valerie Bloom from Jamaica is most directly in line. She has carried on Miss Lou's activities as a folklorist, lecturing and teaching in schools on folk traditions. She has one collection of poems, *Touch Mi, Tell Mi*. Much of her work uses similar forms to Louise Bennett's adopting the familiar four-line rhyming stanza and the dramatic persona addressing other characters through speech or letters about everyday experiences. And she has the same wry ironic manner of exposing inequities, oppressions and social foibles. Trench Town Shock' documents the death of Miss May's cousin, shot by police, but the telling of the incident as a validation for the police action is undercut by a wry chorus which questions the received version of the events:

> Dry yuk yeye, mah, mi know i'hat,
> But i happen ebery day,
> Knife-man always attack armed police
> At leas' a soh dem say.
>
> (Burnett, p. 94)

'Yuh Hear Bout?' uses a similar ironic underplaying of events and their implications:

> Yuh hear bout di people dem arres
> Fi bun dung di Asian people dem house?
> You hear bout di policeman dem lock up
> Fi Beat up di black bwoy widout a cause?
> You hear bout di M.P. dem sack because im refuse fi help
> im coloured constituents in a dem fights 'gainst deportation?
> Yuh noh hear bout dem?
> Me neida.
>
> (Berry, p. 105)

While not quite managing the ebullient vigour of Louise Bennett, Valerie Bloom does capture the authentic speaking voice of Jamaican people, the expressive gesture of idiom and intonation, as in the voluble banter of the customer insisting on a cheap deal in 'Longsight Market':

> What a mango dem fubba-fubba,
> Oonu wont sell tings force-ripe?
> Look ow di pitata dem twis up-twis up
> Lacka when jackass hab gripe.
>   (Allnult *et al.*, p. 16)

Also from Jamaica, Elean Thomas has had two collections published: *Word Rhythms From the Life of a Woman* and *Before They Can
Speak of Flowers*. Her work tends to be politically assertive in manner,
her orientation being evident from her membership of the Worker's
Party of Jamaica for which she is International Secretary. Central to
her concerns are the interrelationships between the tripartite oppressions of gender, race and class. She sees the need for 'People's
Liberation' rather than 'Women's Liberation' (*Word Rhythms*, p. 29),
and has argued in a recent interview that 'the woman question is not
only a woman question, it is a human question'.[6] Many of her poems
are combative, challenging men as oppressors and colonisers, ex-
horting women to develop self-dependency, and dealing with issues
such as child abuse and male violence against women. In his introduction to *Word Rhythms*, Dr Trevor Munroe, General Secretary of
the WPJ, describes Elean Thomas's presentation of

> the all too common abuses by the man – communist man, revolu-
> tionary man, reformist, and most of all reactionary man – all as
> man, however powerless under imperialism, set in a position of
> privilege in respect of women, and therefore in however small a
> way, beneficiary as well as victim of imperialism.
>   (*Word Rhythms*, p. xix)

There are poems about arrogant males like the speaker of 'What
More Could She Want', who indignantly justifies his own behaviour
against the demands of his wife:

> She is me women yes!
>   but she is old time thing
>   me no must have
> another little young thing
>   to rub up me jaw
> And make me feel young and sprucy
> What a wicked dreadful and unreasonable woman, eh.
>   (*Word Rhythms*, p. 64)

Such self-revealing poems are accompanied by others which are more directly critical such as 'Fact Is / April Fool' which deals with men who smugly assume women like Nina are merely petite and demure female stereotypes when she is actually manager of a 6000-acre tea farm:

> Fact Is
> He who tries to keep
> the Ninas behind
> Is who cannot see
>   these facts.
> (*Word Rhythms*, p. 88)

and has been left behind 'Like an April Fool'. Other poems present this critique of men through the voices of oppressed women, as in 'Concubine's Lament' in which a woman in the role of mistress realises her common bondage with the man's wife.

But Elean Thomas also signals the need for men to change in relation to the new sense of identity and political direction being achieved by woman, rather than be rendered ineffectual and resistant, as in 'Make Sure' (*Word Rhythms*, p. 109), while at the same time refusing to minimise the anger of women at the rejection by men of that process of change:

> I sang you love songs
> when you said
> I was no longer bright enough
> or good enough
> to attend the State dinners
> You were now being invited to
>
> I keep singing
>   you
>   love songs
> even as hate-songs
> threaten to smother
>   my very soul.
>   (*Before They Can Speak of Flowers*, p. 89)

The nature of Elean Thomas's poems means that they raise overtly some crucial issues for Caribbean women which relate to some of the debates in other forms. The poem 'To a Delinquent Father' invokes the issue of the absentee father and connects with arguments put by Hermione McKenzie in her essay 'Caribbean Women: Yesterday, Today, Tomorrow' when she states the problem of 'How to reconcile this search for fidelity and tenderness with harsh economic realities and the search for stable conditions for the family?' (*Savacou*, p. x). As Amanda Hopkinson points out, the questions around this issue signal one area of possible misunderstanding between Caribbean feminists and European feminists: in the face of the political invasions and repressions perpetrated by American imperialism and by corrupt regimes, Central American women seek to develop in their men a sense of responsibility and commitment to the obligations of the extended family structures which are part of the fabric of lived culture. Amanda Hopkinson points out that in the very different context of northern Europe, such an upholding of the family model might be questioned by European feminists accustomed to seeing the family in its Western nuclear form as the repository of hegemonic reactionary values. She concludes significantly:

> rather than develop a 'them and us' attitude in which Western women can criticise their Latin sisters for their expectations of men and we can be greeted with horror for the fragmentation of our family and social structures, the point is, surely, to be able to look at and understand, in this instance through women's writing, how women's individual and social lives shape both their politics and poetry. (Hopkinson, p. xxiii)

Within the context of such important arguments for women's movements the poems of Elean Thomas and the other women we are considering can be read as part of the process of making available different individual experiences within different cultures, the better to understand the tangible fabric of women's lives and circumstances within a variety of social contexts.

The other poet close to Louise Bennett who contributes powerfully to this process is Jean Binta Breeze. Born in Jamaica, Jean Breeze lives and works in Britain and has had wide recognition for her work through the British media, being included, for example, in Channel 4's series of programmes on new British poets ('Up and Coming', 1986). Jean Breeze has a quite clear political dimension to her work, too. She sees it as deriving from her multiple experience:

one as a woman, two as a black woman, three as a mother, then as
a single mother, as a member of an extended family, and then as
a citizen of a third world developing country and all that means in
present world economic and political terms.   (Channel 4, p. 20)

She deals with political issues in a manner which is more dramati-
cally enacted and less programmatically asserted than in the work of
Elean Thomas. Like Merle Collins, she sees music as integral to
poetry and her electrifying performances deliver her work with a
marvellous mix of drama, mime, song and personal dynamism. But
her texts on the page also capture the vibrancy of voice in language
and form, working with a controlled economy which can be almost
William Carlos Williams-like. Her poems have been collected together
for her first volume, *Riddym Ravings and Other Poems*. The title comes
from one of her most powerful and popular pieces, subtitled 'The
Mad Woman's Poem', which has also been printed as a poster poem.
Like many of Jean Breeze's pieces, it is a dramatic monologue, putting
it in the Louise Bennett tradition, but with a much fuller psychological presentation of character. It is spoken by a woman suffering from
mental instability in the Kingston ghetto. She is the victim of the
operations of the male 'dactar an de lanlord', akin to the persona of
Plath's 'Lady Lazarus', and Breeze's poem shares with Plath's a
savage comedy mixed with a distinctive pathos particularly evident
in the haunting manner in which Jean Breeze sings the chorus in
performance:

> Eh, Eh,
> no feel no way
> town is a place dat ah really kean stay
> dem kudda – ribbit mi han
> eh – ribbit mi toe
> mi waan go a country go look mango.
>   (Breeze, p. 58)

The imagery of riveting hand and toe is of a female crucifixion and
though Breeze's plaintive sing-song of this in her delivery emphasises the effect, it is tangibly built into the language on the page.
   Jean Breeze can equally turn a sharp eye on the pretensions of
male compatriots. In the vividly realised 'Hustler Skank' with its
vibrant sense of street talk, an ironic self-exposure of the arrogant
male speaker reveals the reality behind his delusions:

wait a minute
nuh you same one wuk dung a . . . a . . . a . . . yes
de firm weh hangle all dem big business
nuh yuh clean de floor
an all de shithouses
Well,
is de same man we wuk fah
you damn blasted fool
wen you haffi bow dung an sey
'Yes, sir, Mr. Austin'
who me – I jus say
'Comin, Mr. Cool'

'yes, boss'
'irie, boss'
'on my way, boss'.

(Breeze, p. 51)

Jean Breeze can also celebrate the contradictory triumphs and difficulties of loving men as in 'Lovin Wasn Easy', and she has some
wonderfully relaxed and tightly controlled poems of remembrance
and daily experience, 'de simple tings of life' (Breeze, p. 33).

HER WRITINGS

The poets we have considered so far we have seen as descendants of
Louise Bennett to some extent and as representatives of what Paula
Burnett distinguishes as the oral tradition. But as the discussion has
indicated, many of those poets see print and the written tradition as
important to their productions. No easy distinctions are available or
should be promoted, beyond the need for some 'packaging' for
discussion purposes. It is the very flexibility and mix of forms of
production, oral and written, that is partly what is distinctive about
the ways Caribbean women are choosing to develop their poetry.
They are pointing out that there should be no divisions between the
communal functions of their verse as delivered in a variety of audience contexts and its assimilation through print. There is an almost
inbuilt imperative that poetry is an activity of sharing.
    This argument is equally true of the other women poets we haven't
considered so far. It would be quite wrong to consider Grace Nichols,

Maud Sulter, Amryl Johnson, Jackie Kay as non-performance poets.
All of them have written pieces in the more open, emphatically
rhythmical performance modes, in so far as they can be distinguished. Even Lorna Goodison, Olive Senior and Christine Craig,
who might be seen as the most orthodoxly 'literary' of the poets,
share an interest in openly rhythmic forms, in the communality of
verse production and in 'nation language'.

The language issue, too, is one where there are no easy distinctions
to be made. Jean Breeze, for example, shares with a number of other
poets an interest in utilising both the resources of 'nation language'
and of 'standard English'. She joined James Berry and Fred D'Aguiar
in a radio discussion of this issue, agreeing that it is precisely that
mix of language possibilities which enriches the potential for Caribbean writers (Radio 3, 'Third Ear', 10 January 1988). For her, the
rhythmic voice of the poem itself determines the language choice,
and those in 'nation language' she sees as addressed to her local
village community in Jamaica. Merle Collins, on the other hand, has
indicated how recent the employment of 'nation language' as a
positive cultural force is: her Gran'aunt's reaction to the language of
her novel *Angel* was 'We don't talk as bad as that'; so that paradoxically the positive deployment of 'nation language' is possibly a
generational phenomenon.[7] It is also, of course, crucially a question
of power and the hegemonic force of 'standard English' and the
institutional promoters of it in the media and education, the recent
discussion papers on the primary national curriculum being merely
one contemporary example. The effect of this enforcement of a
'standard' English is not just the marginalisation of languages but of
cultures, and it is here that the colonial legacy for Caribbean cultures
links with that for the other cultures in Britain and Ireland – Irish,
Scots, Welsh, and even regions such as the North of England. All of
them have suffered from forms of imperialism, racial or class. What
the Caribbean women poets bring to this terrain is the consideration
of gender in relation to these other imperialisms, and in the cases of
Jackie Kay and Maud Sulter, their Scots origins allow them to make
overt links.

Jackie Kay appeared along with Grace Nichols, Barbara Burford
and Gabriella Pearse in the anthology *A Dangerous Knowing* (Burford
et al.). This was important anthology in making the work of some
Black British women writers more widely available, and in signalling
some of the issues. In their introduction, Pratibha Parmar and Sonia
Osman argue that Black women have been rendered invisible as

poets through the racism of the publishing industry. Jackie Kay's work has so far appeared only in anthologies, including *Dancing the Tightrope* (Burford *et al.*) and *The New British Poetry* (Allnutt *et al.*), She has a long sequence of poems in progress called 'The Adoption Papers', dealing with motherhood and adoption. She also considers lesbian experience, the poem 'Happy Ending' (Burford *et al.*(eds), p. 56) wryly rejecting the enforced tragedies of past writings on lesbianism, and this is an area also dealt with by Maud Sulter in her 'Scots Triptych' (Sulter, pp. 15–18). Like Maud Sulter, Jackie Kay's Glasgow origins have led her to write about the heterogeneity of Black experience in Britain. In 'We Are Not All Sisters Under the Same Moon', she addresses the need for white feminists to realise that Black women have their own specific experience, and that such differences are an essential starting point:

> Before this night is over and before
> this new dawn rises we have to see
> these particular changes speak to
> our guarded uncertain before singing
> Sisterhood is Powerful.
> (Burford *et al.*, p. 58)

This is a debate Grace Nichols has also addressed in her poem 'Of Course When They Ask for Poems about the "Realities" of Black Women' (ibid,. pp. 48–50). Grace Nichols's work is distinguished partly by her interest in the sequence poem, of which she has written two, *I is a Long Memoried Woman* for which she won the 1983 Commonwealth Prize, and *The Fat Black Woman's Poems*. Her latest volume is *Lazy Thoughts of a Lazy Woman*. *The Fat Black Woman's Poems* as a sequence focus around the title's persona. They are comic, satirical, celebratory, the Fat Black Woman 'Refusing to be a model / of her own afflication' and instead asserting her presence with vitality, humour and warmth. The function of the voices in many of Grace Nichols's poems is emblemised by 'Caribbean Woman Prayer':

> hear dis Mother-woman
> on behalf of her pressure-down people.
> (Allnutt *et al.*, p. 65)

Many of the voices in her poems speak with a solidity of language, idiom and experience which express the collective oppressions, traditions and futures of women. Her 'Twentieth Century Witch Chant' demands the resurrection of women victimised by men for their power as witches, prophetesses and priestesses, ending wryly:

> As for the boys playing with their power toys
> entoad them all.
>
> (Burford *et al.*, p. 47)

Paula Burnett chose an extract from *I Is a Long Memoried Woman* as the epigraph for her Penguin Book of Caribbean verse:

> I have crossed an ocean
> I have lost my tongue
> from the roots of the old one
> a new one has sprung
>
> (Nichols, *The Fat Black Woman's Poems*, p. 64)

The central argument of the sequence is that the Black diaspora was in effect a double dispossession for women. The colonial oppression of slavery and displacement from Africa was compounded by the more ancient subjugation of women by men. In the 'new world' Black women faced the multiple exploitation of being colonised by white Europeans, sexual colonialism being an essential factor within that economic parameter, as Jean Rhys's *Wide Sargasso Sea* makes clear, and continuing to be colonised by their own men. There are poems in the sequence directed at the white men to whom 'I bend / only the better / to rise and strike / again' (ibid., p. 55). But equally the section on sugar cane presents a critique of men more generally in the guise of the crop sugar cane with its legacy of violence:

> he isn't what
> he seem –
> indifferent hard
> and sheathed in blades
> his waving arms
> is a sign for help
> his skin thick
> only to protect
> the juice inside
> himself
>
> (Ibid., p. 56)

Similar testaments to history and the future are to found in Maud Sulter's work. She has one volume of poems, *As A Black Woman*. She too targets the imperialist male in poems like 'Urban Fox' (p. 47) and turns this critique on black men: '?Act of God' deals with violence against women, while 'Winter Solstice' asserts

> Sometimes as the months
> pass into years
> I think that
> looking for a responsible
> black man
> is an act of masochism

and ends asking 'Hey Brother / black man / Just who will father our future?' (Sulter, pp. 45–6). Maud Sulter can also be found addressing white sisters and white sympathisers for their unacknowledged racism and colonialism as 'they pilfer our culture' (p. 56).

While Maud Sulter addresses the legacy of colonialism from within Britain, Amryl Johnson has used her personal history of shifting from Trinidad to Britain at the age of eleven to reassess her origins. She has one book of poems, *Long Road to Nowhere*, in one of which she questions her place in the history of her islands as she returns on the new cargo ship of tourism, recalling the old cargo ships of slavery, and asking herself 'where was I in all this?' (Johnson, *Long Road to Nowhere*, p. 39). One notable strand in her book is a number of poems considering the Carnival, and experience she has also documented in her travel book *Sequins on a Ragged Hem*. She shares her use of this as a vehicle for investigating society and culture more widely with Trinidadian novelist Earl Lovelace in his novel *The Dragon Can't Dance* (1979). Amryl Johnson has a notable capacity to take local experiences and incidents and translate them into a means for comment. In 'Loaded Dice' she considers the fatalism which shackles oppression with hopelessness, the chance fall of circumstances as seemingly inescapable as thrown dice. But as the title suggests, the poem reveals that state of mind as part of a fixed situation, a 'con' which must itself be overthrown. Her poems also register a pervasive sense of social menace, as in 'Qu'est-ce Qu'elle Dit?', in which the song of the keskidee bird is translated into an image of interrogation in an oppressive society, or in the title poem of the volume with its obsessive vision of a crippled Black beggar swinging his legless torso back and forth across Kentish Town Road.

Amryl Johnson also has a wry eye for male pretensions. 'Peanut Vendor' ironises its arrogant speaker with his suggestive asides to passing women customers, leaving him perplexed when they don't buy as to 'wha' wrong wit' all yuh women' (Johnson, *Long Road To Nowhere*, p. 48). 'Conqueror of a Forbidden Landscape' exposes the sexual fantasies of a male adolescent, humorously playing them off against the comments of the women he idealises in an interestingly polyphonic form:

Slide into a curve

Boy, yuh ehn hah no shame?!!

slide to

Miss Millie!

slip further

Yes Miss Agnes!

deeper into

Is so you bringin' up yuh son?

the sweet

De boy eyein' up meh tut-tuts

gentle

Leroy!

waters

How he get to be so dam' fresh-up?

where no

boy is cut-arse fuh yuh

one could reach
him

(Allnutt *et al.*, p. 48)

More seriously, Amryl Johnson can link the experience of rape with the experience of colonialism in 'Tread Carefully in Paradise', and at the same time examine the phenomenon of dispossessed black youths raping white women in revenge for being 'spawned' from chattel houses with 'dubious foundations' (Johnson, *Long Road to Nowhere*, pp. 42–3).

In the work of Lorna Goodison, Olive Senior and Christine Craig a perhaps surprising general commitment to 'standard' English prevails despite the fact that these are the three poets who remain based in the Caribbean. All three were represented in the *Jamaica Woman* anthology (Mordecai and Morris) along with a number of other notable poets, none of whom has an individual volume available yet, although co-editor Pam Mordecai has a projected volume called *Shooting the Horses*.

Christine Craig has worked with the Jamaican Women's Bureau and has one volume published, *Quadrille for Tigers*. It contains some striking familial recollections like 'Prelude to Another Life', a five-page exploration of the past which echoes Derek Walcott's auto-biographical epic *Another Life* (1973) in its title. As with so many of the poets we are considering, this process focuses upon a matriarchal inheritance, Sarah the grandmother, who Christine Craig has to recreate for herself, 'Uprooted from my own past / I invented for her an inner past' (Craig, p. 20). The act of memory becomes an act of self-creation. She also has some wry views of the contained lives of women, as in 'Crow Poem' where she imagines herself like a ragged john crow.

Olive Senior has one volume available, *Talking of Trees* and, like Christine Craig, Pamela Mordecai and Lorna Goodison, is represented in Paula Burnett's Penguin anthology as well as Mordecai and Morris's *Jamaica Woman*. She has worked as a journalist and editor of *Jamaica Journal* as well as managing the Institute of Jamaica publishing company. A number of her poems deal with the splits between gender roles, as in 'Cockpit Country Dreams' where she recalls her father talking of bombs and her mother of babies, 'Portents of a Split Future' (Senior, p. 3), or in the muted hope for potential change in 'Birdshooting Season':

> We stand quietly on the
> doorstep shivering. Little boys
> longing to grow up birdhunters too
> Little girls whispering:
> Fly Birds Fly.
>
> (Senior, p. 2)

Olive Senior also has a number of notable 'nation language' poems, particularly a dialogue poem between mother and daughter dealing with incest and exploring the culpability of the mother's fatalistic resignation to the oppressed status of her daughter and son ('The Mother', Senior, pp. 68–9)

With two books of poems to her name, *Tamarind Season* and *I Am Becoming My Mother*, Lorna Goodison has already been the subject of an article by Caribbean poet and critic Eddie Baugh which indicates that she is working upon a long sequence poem called 'Heartease'.[8]

Her first book indicated some affiliations with the experimental jazz-orientated writing which characterised the work of one of the most interesting young male poets, Anthony McNeill's *Credences at the Altar of Cloud* (Institute of Jamaica, 1979): *Tamarind Season* contains one piece called 'Xcercise for Tony Mc' (p. 64), while both volumes have a number of poems about jazz musicians. Her second volume, though, has allowed Lorna Goodison to evolve more of her own voice and concerns, particularly in relation to the experience of being a woman. Here she has made an affiliation with the great Russian poet Anna Akhmatova as a model of that activity so many of the Caribbean women poets see as central: acting 'as a person who could speak for everybody, for people, for ordinary people, for people suffering' (Baugh, p. 15). Eddie Baugh sees this as an identification of the communal with the personal. Again, part of this process involves a reclamation of history. Like Jean Breeze in her 'Soun de abeng fi Nanny' (Breeze, p. 45), Lorna Goodison has a poem celebrating Maroon resistance leader Nanny, heroine of Jamaican national culture. She is, as Eddie Baugh points out, one of a lineage of powerful female figures, public and private, in Goodison's work, including Rosa Parks of the Alabama bus boycott, Winnie Mandela and Goodison's own mother, as in the powerful 'For My Mother (May I Inherit Half Her Strength)'. Nanny's poems ends prophetically:

I was sent, tell that to history.

When your sorrow obscures the skies
other women like me will rise.
(Goodison, *I Am Becoming My Mother*, p. 45)

The historical continuity of this female experience is central to Goodison's stated commitment to 'write about women more than anything else, the condition of women' (Baugh, p. 17), and she does so with a continual insinuation of hope and promise. 'We Are the Women' ends with a familiar image from Afro-Caribbean ancestry, the buried navel string of the new-born child, the guarantor of future safety:

We've buried our hope
too long
as the anchor to our
navel strings

> we are rooting at
> the burying spot
> we are uncovering
> our hope.
> (Goodison, *I Am Becoming My Mother*, p. 13)

'Bedspread' presents an imaginary monologue by Winnie Mandela addressed to her imprisoned husband from the bright Azanian colours of the quilt woven in the past by 'woman with slender / capable hands / accustomed to binding wounds' and ingrained with 'ancient blessings / older than any white man's coming'. It is a process of weaving the future which continues, the poem argues, despite the long confinement of Mandela and offers the certainty of change (ibid., pp. 42–3).

Lorna Goodison also has a number of poems about children and child-care, a crucial area of concern for Caribbean women. The *Savacou* article by Hermione McKenzie puts the complexities of the case when arguing for the need to create a consciousness of the possibilities of choice for women, rather than allowing women to be subordinated. McKenzie qualifies this by saying that it is not child-bearing itself which makes women subordinate, since it is a socially valued and personally rewarding experience:

> the problem seems to arise when complex cultural factors induce young girls to see early child-bearing as their essential route to womanhood, and induce women throughout their lives to see multiple child-bearing as their only role and future. (*Savacou*, p. xi)

Lorna Goodison has a sharp awareness of the emotional complexities of such issues. She manages to present the ambiguities of hope during the present time while keeping faith with the progressive potential of the future and particularly the role of women in that transformatory process. It is this commitment that allows the woman speaker of her title poem to see herself as giving birth to herself, and becoming her mother in a double sense.[9] In this awareness, Lorna Goodison is representative of much of the freshness and vigour to be found in Caribbean women's poetry. Given the recent emergence of these writers and the fact that most of them are at the very beginnings of their poetic developments, they promise a very bright future and new directions for Caribbean literature itself.

NOTES

1. See unpublished dissertation on Sistren collective by Kate Valentine for BA Drama, Hull, 1988. 'The Use of Popular Theatre in Non-Formal Adult Education in the Third World with Reference to Africa and Jamaica'. Also report by Anne Bolsover for BBC Radio 4 'Woman's Hour', 7 April 1986.
2. The other anthologies used for this essay are *News for Babylon*, ed. James Berry, and *The New British Poetry*, ed. Gillian Allnutt *et al*. In addition there are a number of sources and poets I have not had space to deal with. They are: a new anthology *Black and Priceless* which includes work by young British women of Caribbean descent; Jamaican poet Michelle Cliff's volume *The Land of Look Behind*; Guyanan poet Meiling Jin's volume *Gifts from my Grandmother*; Dionyse McTair's *Notes Towards an Escape from Death*; and the work of Mahada Das, Lioness Chant and poets included in *Blackwomen Talk Poetry*, ed. Da Choung.
3. Quoted in Mervyn Morris, 'People Speech: Some Dub Poets'.
4. See Edward Kamau Brathwaite, *History of the Voice*.
5. Merle Collins, 'Women Writers from the Caribbean', p. 21.
6. 'We Are the World', interview with Elean Thomas by Rachel Silber and Caroline Brandenburger, *Guardian*, 15 April 1989, p. 21.
7. Merle Collins information from interview with Robin Eyre for Radio 4 'Midweek', 1 June 1988.
8. Eddie Baugh, 'Goodison on the Road to Heartease', *Journal of West Indian Literature*, vol. 1, no. 1 (October 1986) pp. 13–22.
9. Lorna Goodison gives this view of her poem in an interview for Radio 4, 'Some Caribbean Writers', 1987.

BIBLIOGRAPHY

Allnutt Gillian, Fred D'Aguiar, Ken Edwards and Eric Mottram (eds), *The New British Poetry* (London: Paladin, 1988).

Baugh, Edward, 'Goodison on the Road to Heartease' *Journal of West Indian Literature*, vol. 1, no. 1 (October 1986), pp. 13–22 (University of the West Indies).

Bennett, Louise, *Selected Poems*, ed. Mervyn Morris (Kingston, Jamaica: Sangsters, 1983).

—, *Yes M'Dear* (Island Records, ILPS 9740, 1983).

Berry, James (ed.), *News for Babylon: The Chatto Book of West Indian–British Poetry* (London: Chatto and Windus, 1984).

Black and Priceless, anthology ed. Cindy Crocus (London: Common Word, 1988).

Bloom, Valerie, *Touch Mi Tell Mi* (London: Bogle L'Ouverture, 1983).

Brathwaite, Edward Kamal, *History of the Voice: The Development of National Language in Anglophone Caribbean Poetry* (London: New Beacon, 1984).

— (ed.), *New Poets from Jamaica* (Kingston, Jamaica: Savacou, 1979).

Breeze, Jean Binta, *Riddym Ravings and Other Poems*, ed. Mervyn Morris (London: Race Today, 1988).

Burford, Barbara, Gabriela Pearse, Grace Nichols and Jackie Kay, *A Dangerous Knowing* (London: Sheba, 1983).

Barbara Burford *et al.* (eds), *Dancing the Tightrope* (London: The Women's Press, 1987).

Burnett, Paula, *The Penguin Book of Caribbean Verse in English* (Harmondsworth, Middx: Penguin, 1986).

Channel 4, *Up and Coming* (London: Channel 4 television, 1986).

Choung, Da (ed.) *Blackwomen Talk Poetry* (London: Blackwomantalk, 1987).

Cliff, Michelle, *The Land of Look Behind* (London: Firebrand, 1985).

Collins, Merle, *Angel* (London: The Women's Press, 1987).

—, *Because the Dawn Breaks* (London: Karia, 1985).

—, 'Women Writers from the Caribbean', *Spare Rib* (September 1988) pp. 18–22.

Craig, Christine, *Quadrille for Tigers* (San Francisco, Cal.: Mina Press, 1984).

de Boissière, Ralph, *Crown Jewels* (London: Picador, 1981).

Goodison, Lorna, *Tamarind Season* (Kingston, Jamaica: Institute of Jamaica, 1980).

—, *I Am Becoming My Mother* (London: New Beacon, 1986).

Hopkinson, Amanda (ed.), *Lovers and Comrades: Women's Resistance Poetry from Central America* (London: The Women's Press, 1989).

Jin, Meiling, *Gifts from my Grandmother* (London: Sheba, 1985).

Johnson, Amryl, *Long Road to Nowhere* (London: Virago, 1985).

—, *Sequins on a Ragged Hem* (London: Virago, 1988).

McTair, Dionyse, *Notes Towards an Escape from Death* (London: New Beacon, 1988).

Mordecai, Pamela and Mervyn Morris (eds), *Jamaica Woman* (Kingston, Jamaica: Heinemann, 1980).

Morris, Mervyn, 'People Speech: Some Dub Poets', *Race Today Review*, vol. 14, no. 5 (1983) pp. 150–7.

—, *New Poets from Jamaica*, ed. Edward Kamal Braithwaite (Kingston, Jamaica: Savacou, 1979).

—, *I Is A Long-Memoried Woman* (London: Karnak House, 1983).

Nichols, Grace, *The Fat Black Woman's Poems* (London: Virago, 1984).

—, *Lazy Thoughts of a Lazy Woman* (London: Virago, 1989).

—, *Savacou: Caribbean Woman* (Kingston, Jamaica: Savacou, 1977).

Searle, Chris, *Words Unchained: Language and Revolution in Grenada* (London: Zed Books, 1984).

Senior, Olive, *Talking of Trees* (Kingston, Jamaica: Caliban 1985).

Silver, Rachel, and Caroline Brandenburger, 'We Are the World – Interview with Elean Thomas', *Guardian*, 15 April 1989, p. 21.

Sistren Theatre Collective, *Lionheart Gal* (London: The Women's Press, 1986).

Sulter, Maud, *As a Black Woman* (London: Akira Press, 1985).

Thomas, Elean, *Before They Can Speak of Flowers* (London: Karia Press, 1988).

—, *Word Rhythms from the Life of a Woman* (London: Karia Press, 1986).

5

'Disremembered and Unaccounted For':
Reading Toni Morrison's *Beloved* and
Alice Walker's *The Temple of My Familiar*

GINA WISKER

Toni Morrison's *Beloved* [1] articulates and embodies a history and experience which has been ostensibly, literally and 'safely' recuperated but is actually still raw. The final page claims 'it was not a story to pass on' (p. 275), using an established literary trick: creating a readership *ensures* it will be passed on.

Beloved directly confronts racism in a novel which combines lyrical beauty with an assault on the reader's emotions and conscience. It traces, embodies and focuses on the legacy of slavery, using forms derived from a traditional Black folk aesthetic. Both content and form are controversial for the reader or teacher/student and I should like consequently to focus here on these issues and the nature of the controversy, arguing that *Beloved* provides a paradigm for critical issues related to our reading of Black women's writing.

For those of us teaching Black women's writing in the academy, *Beloved* will take its place in our lecture and seminar booklists alongside *The Color Purple* [2] as a novel which is both highly crafted *and* confrontational in its dealings with racism and sexism.

The second novel I wish to deal with here, though in less detail than *Beloved*, is Alice Walker's *The Temple of My Familiar* [3]. As I have not yet had the opportunity to teach the text I shall confine myself to my own comments, rather than setting these alongside those of my students.

The Temple of My Familiar has had very mixed reviews, largely due, it seems to me, to the deliberately mixed nature of the work itself. It is a fitting companion to *Beloved* here because it raises similar issues: the confrontation of racism and of sexism, and is written in a style which contains polemic integrated with the literary, the spiritual reference with the historical reference.

Beloved engages with racism. Its exposure of the pathology and the legacy of slavery directly confronts the reader and, as a white reader in the academy, I feel I have a (necessarily problematic) responsibility to try to deal with the treatment of these issues, in context. Secondly, *Beloved* is a mixed mode, and for me, as for others I have discussed it with (BAAS conference workshop, York, 1988) this raises particular difficulties of reader response, but yields particular richness also. The combination is disturbing: social and historical realism; overt political impetus in its confrontation of both racism and sexism; the supernatural; a dead baby ghost who returns as a young woman – Beloved – disrupting relationships and nearly destroying the mother whose mother-love caused her to be sacrificed in the face of re-enslavement. These two central issues of how to read and appreciate the novel cause us to consider reading, reception and response in relation to that rich variety of Black women's writing now available to us.

Toni Morrison has an established literary reputation. The novel has also received much acclaim in England, with a whole 'South Bank Show' in early 1988 devoted to discussion with Toni Morrison on its publication. It is this kind of acclaim which highlights the changing climate of opinion over the reading and studying of Black women's writing. From the critically well-documented silences and total lack of publication, through a recognition of individual ability and technique of quality, to being 'the flavour of the month', perhaps. It is no longer anything other than embarrassing to read such critical comments as that of Sara Blackburn in 1973, reviewing *Sula*:

> Toni Morrison is far too talented to remain only a marvelous recorder of the black side of provincial life. . . . she might easily transcend that early and unintentionally limiting classification 'blackwoman writer' and take her place among the most serious, important and talented American novelists.[4]

An example of white female racism which ignores and undervalues the basis of Morrison's polemic. And it is the creative writing of such as Morrison which has given a voice to Black women:

> Afro-American woman remained an all-pervading absence until she was rescued by the literary activity of her black sisters in the latter part of the C20th.[5]

The stated aim of Morrison and other Black women writers is to provide such a historically contextualised, political voice for themselves and their black sisters:

> In our work and in our living we must recognise that difference is a reason for celebration and growth, rather than a reason for destruction.[6]

Alice Walker states:

> I think my whole program as a writer is to deal with history just so I know where I am.[7]

and Toni Morrison identifies her main aim in writing:

> To bear witness to a history that is unrecorded, untaught, in mainstream education, and to enlighten our people.[8]

This needs to be set against what can too easily be forgotten, due to the complacency which high sales-figures induce, that 'all-pervading' absence and silence due, as Lorraine Bethel puts it, to an essential devaluation:

> The codification of Blackness and femaleness by whites and males is seen in terms 'thinking like a woman' and 'acting like a nigger' which are based on the premise that there are typically black and female ways of acting and thinking. Therefore, the most pejorative concept in the white/male world view would be that of thinking and acting like a 'nigger woman'.[9]

We are also reminded of Zora Neale Hurston's famous lines, in *Their Eyes were Watching God*, when Janey is told:

> Honey, de white man is de ruler of everything as fur as ah been able to find out. Maybe its some place off in de ocean where de black man is in power, but we don't know nothing but what we see. So de white man thrown down de load and tell de nigger man tuh pick it up. He pick it up because he have to, but he don't tote it. He hand it to his womenfolks. De nigger woman is de mule uh de world so fur as ah can see.[10]

This triple burden which so long silenced and disempowered Black women has been challenged by those women whose novels and poems are now widely available to us through the well-packaged and marketed women's and radical presses: they are successful marketing commodities. If we read these works and if we teach them and encourage our students to read them, it is our duty to ensure that they are read in context, with full recognition of their polemical purpose. It is vital that we avoid jumping on the bandwagon of a transient popularity, and that we ensure that the literary merit of these works and their vital contribution to literature and popular literature is never ignored again.

Barbara Burford points to the short-livedness of earlier recognition,the Negritude movement in France, the Harlem Renaissance:

> This time we must not allow ourselves to be turned on and off, and we must not disappear quietly, when it is decided that we as an 'issue' have suffered from over exposure.[11]

We have a problem as critics and readers, then, faced with the cultural imperialism of appropriation and alternative canonisation of writing by Black women, which colonises them for the literary academy. Faced with the fear that we might be jumping on the bandwagon, we need to ensure that we recognise their works for *all* their merits: as literature, as popular literature and as polemical works by women whose colour makes them particularly well placed to write about the triple burden of race, sex and class.

I have worked with *Beloved* now with two groups of students studying the novel on a contemporary women's writing seminar during their third year of an English degree course (CNAA). Some of the students involved in the seminars have experience of writing by Black writers, male and female, others have no such experience of which they are aware, although occasionally they discover a writer they have been reading is Black, which says a great deal about contextual reading! In our reading we were aware of the problem of dealing with *Beloved* as if it were typical of all texts by Black writers and we discussed tokenism, the impropriety of assuming that we had 'done' Black writing by reading the one text. In order to provide a context I produced extracts from critical works by Susan Willis, Barbara Burford and others, quotations from which appear here, and we also looked at some of Toni Morrison's critical comments from interviews.

Responses to the book were an interesting mixture of the personal and the critical, something which many of us are aware of when teaching women's writing to a predominantly female group, and something I encourage as a grounding for the integration of analysis and experience. Several students felt silenced by the shock of the novel's indictment of racism in which they felt implicated merely by being white, and over which they felt unable to act usefully, directly. As one, Julie Palmer, put it:

> the central issue for the late, and possibly complacent twentieth-century white reader must surely be that of post-colonial account-ability. . . . It hurt, as a white reader, to be the target of what felt like an undercurrent of 4th and 5th generation black resentment, especially when you considered yourself reasonably principled and unprejudiced.

But it was difficult to know how to act, in the face of such deep resentment and guilt. The polemic within the novel was what was perceived immediately, and it was the least tractable to being dealt with, using standard literary critical strategies. Enjoyment of the text was itself felt to be something of a guilty activity because of the 'close to unbearable' content; and responses which brought in all sorts of other oppressions and tried to equate them, deal with them all together, led to a sense of drowning and losing direction. Another student, Lyn Morgan, noted:

> I do not think I can be the only reader who is shocked to discover how little I understood the extent of the brutality of slavery. Before reading *Beloved* my impressions of slavery had largely been based on old 'forties films.

Like other seminar members, Julie felt a sense of oppression in the indictment against her inherited and assumed racism, but she went on to reason that this can lead to growth, clarity and change:

> 'Colour' which was never a problem to me became an issue as I confronted the other side of the coin – I too was stamped, labelled and racially resented (very mildly by comparison) and I didn't like it. . . . I had not experienced racism directly, now I was made to feel my 'otherness' through reading black literature. . . . I learned something: it doesn't take much to make me feel oppressed.

However:

> Toni Morrison's book went some way towards helping me to understand black anger. OK, so it hurt, but I value highly the brave, vital spirit of survival that forced me to think through these

issues. . . . It is not enough to be passively 'unprejudiced', we must find ways of acting individually to undo our inherited collective wrongs.

While a seminar with a group of relative strangers is not a very fruitful situation for such brave developments, it can be a crucible in which the beginnings of such changes are made. One of the very obvious changes is in the images of Black people, and it is impossible after *Beloved* to swallow the genial stereotypes of Uncle Tom and the Black mammy which provided such a usefully sugarised, consumerised version of the fatal pill of white oppression of Black people throughout history and particularly under slavery.

Lyn commented:

> Toni Morrison deconstructs the myth of the genial slave who is content and happy with his or her lot. Images we have been fed in the past have been of the 'Uncle Tom' type figure taking the little white boy fishing or of the laughing mammy character with her hair done up in a red and white polka dot scarf whose main delight in life is seeing her little white charge bedecked in expensive frills.

This is an image undercut by the figure of Sofia in *The Color Purple* also, she suffers her servant role caring for the Mayor's children while her own grow up far away from her.

Cora Kaplan outlines the teaching and reading problem clearly:

> Our more than usually fragmented and partial knowledge of the history, politics and culture in which they were produced and originally read frequently leads us into teaching and thinking about these texts through an unintentionally imperialist lens conflating their progressive politics with our own agendas, interpreting their visions of humanism through the historical evolution of our own.[12]

These texts by Black women writers interrogate a continuum of attitudes towards racial difference which make us feel uncomfortable because they upset our unconsciously held beliefs: they confront us with our own racism, and our own guilt.

This is nowhere more true than in Toni Morrison's *Beloved*, for the novel's dramatic exposure of the horrors of slavery and its legacy forces white middle-class readers to be uncomfortably aware of their national and historical complicity. One warning of the care we must take in reading and studying this text not to misappropriate it for our own ends emerges from our consideration of its indictment of the slave owner, Schoolteacher, the intellectual whose dehumanising cruelty to his slaves dresses up the denial of human rights in the cloak of academic authority. Schoolteacher's pupils are told to study Sethe and the other slaves, drawing up lists with their animal characteristics on one hand, their human on the other. This misuse of knowledge gives Schoolteacher and the white man power over those designated as only fit for scientific categorisation rather than human relationships and respect. Study in itself is not devalued. Later, herself not an object for formal study, Denver's own studying provides her with an opportunity to develop insight and articulacy.

Beloved focuses on the all-pervading dehumanisation of slavery and, in a dramatic and concrete form, its legacy which is made manifest in the figure of Beloved herself.

As readers, teachers and students of this novel, we need to discover the context of the history of slavery, the torture, murder and economic sources and descriptions of the institution, the treatment of slave women used by slave owners, denied family lives yet forced to be breeders of future slaves, and the historical changes which the period of the novel focuses on, when the free states gave homes to freed slaves, but were unprotected from slave-catchers crossing to recapture their escaped slaves.

The story of*Beloved* is based on a real historical incident involving Margaret Garner, a *cause célèbre* in 1855. At that time slave owners could cross into free states to recapture escaped slaves. Margaret, who had escaped with her family, saw the slave-catchers coming and tried to kill her four children. The baby girl died, the boys lived. She was convicted of escaping (a property issue) rather than murder.

The novel dramatises the incident, which starts, apocalyptically, 'When the four horsemen came'. The fugitive slaves are described as if they are children playing guilty games. Dehumanised, they are also described as wild animals:

Caught red-handed, so to speak, they would seem to recognize the futility of outsmarting a whiteman and the hopelessness of outrunning a rifle. Smile even, like a child caught dead with his hand in the jelly jar, and when you reached for the rope to tie him, well, even then you couldn't tell. The very nigger with his head hanging and a little jelly-jar smile on his face could all of a sudden roar, like a bull or some such, and commence to do disbelievable things . . . . (p. 148)

They are considered valuable only as property, and of less use than an animal when dead:

Unlike a snake or a bear, a dead nigger could not be skinned for profit and was not worth his own dead weight in coin. (p. 148)

In the face of such 'humanity', the 'crazy' mother, Sethe, murders her child to save her. It is a stark description:

Inside, two boys bled in the sawdust and dirt at the feet of a niggerwoman holding a blood-soaked child to her chest and an infant by the heels in the other. She did not look at them; she simply swung the baby toward the wall planks, missed and tried to connect a second time. (p. 149)

The 'pickaninnies' are now considered worthless, and Sethe's anguished act a mere product of the nephew's 'mishandling' of her, as one might mishandle a dog: 'Suppose you beat the hounds past that point thataway. Never again could you trust them in the woods or anywhere else' (p. 149).

Beloved is essentially a novel about the vitality and intrusiveness of memory, the memory of racial oppression under slavery. Memory or 'rememory' is acknowledged as present, solid, vital: 'If a house burns down, it's gone, but the place – the picture of it – stays; and just in my rememory, but out there in the world . . . it's when you bump into the rememory of someone else' (p. 36). This suggests that history is a tangible, visible existent that a community can experience, bump into. In this novel, the insanity and absurdity upon which a capitalist society which is dependent on slavery is founded, translates itself into the lived madness the haunting of the past within no. 124, the house where first Baby Suggs, the grandmother, then Sethe, the mother, and Denver, her daughter, live.

It is over the issue of this tangible history that readers face a problem. *Beloved* is an historically situated, politically focused novel, but it is equally a novel essentially based on an acceptance of the supernatural and magic. We suspend our disbelief when we are told that the baby whose throat Sethe cut to save her from the slave-catchers haunts the house on Bluestone, no. 124, whose red aura provides a lifeforce, however occasionally malevolent and spiteful, and whose presence effectively isolates Baby Suggs from the community. Previously the centre of community root-working, herbal medicine and mystical powers, as a lay preacher Baby Suggs represented the socially acceptable face of the supernatural's place in shared society. Like the community around her, however, we have problems as readers, when Beloved actually appears, right at the moment of a new family harmony and sexual unity for Denver, Sethe and Paul D., one the last of the Sweet Home men who has come to stay in Sethe's life. Footsore and weary from a long journey, confused in her memories about who gave her her clothes, taught her her ways, Beloved intrudes on family harmony, upsets Sethe's sexual relationship with Paul D. by sleeping with him and forcing him to recognise her. She demands: 'call me by my name' and 'touch me on the inside'. Sexuality, here as elsewhere in Toni Morrison's works, is used, as Susan Willis points out, as a register for the experience of change: 'sexuality converges with history and functions as a register for the experience of change, ie historical transition'.[13] Through her new sexual relationship with Paul D., Sethe began to be able to reopen and cope with the memories of the slave past, as did Paul D. Beloved challenged her sexually, and won, her past literally refusing to be so easily laid.

At the novel's close Sethe and Paul are reunited, with a return of the honesty which recognises that much must be left unsaid, cannot be fully faced if sanity is to be possible.

Beloved is a succubus. She drains the house of love and vitality, both spiritual and physical, then forms a strong bond of dependency with Denver, finally turning to Sethe when her mother recognises her as the daughter she sacrificed. She grows fast as Sethe shrinks and shrivels, and she causes the whole house to be united in a crazy bond. Too much recognition drives Paul D. away, drains Sethe of life as she both serves and battles with the ghost-made-flesh whom she in particular cannot hope to lay.

Beloved is manifest history, the guilt and pain of slavery as it enters personal lives and causes brutal, dehumanised actions in self-defence from those who have been denied human rights. For the community this is too much to face, as their own culpability is involved. Sethe and Baby Suggs were richly celebrating the family's freedom the day before the slave-catchers came, and the community, while joining in, became jealous of too much happiness and expense which dulled their reactions so that they failed to warn Sethe in time.

Here as elsewhere in Toni Morrison's work there is a focus on the relationship of the individual to the community:

> The novels may focus on individuals, like Milkman and Jadine, but the salvation of individuals is not the point. Rather, these individuals, struggling to reclaim or redefine themselves, are portrayed as epiphenomenal to community and culture; and it is the strength and continuity of the black cultural heritage as a whole which is at stake and being tested.[14]

The role of the community response is crucial, as the events at no. 124 are a metaphor for the sufferings, memory and guilt of the whole community. As this central metaphor of slavery's history and guilt-made-manifest, the visitation of Beloved is perfectly acceptable to the reader, but its presentation as 'fact' destabilises the novel's documentary realism.

It is this integration of the metaphoric and the metonymic which also causes problems with our reading of The Color Purple. The Utopian ending, with the return of the presumed drowned Nettie and her 'family' of husband and Celie's lost children was recognised as the stuff of mass-audience dreams by Spielberg in the movie. There, fecundity and new hopes were represented by the run over the cornfields and the sun setting on the united family group on the porch, which even managed to incorporate Mister, the brutal and brutalised sexist husband, who was 'satisfactorily' (for Celie) tamed and incredibly (for reader/viewer) rendered kindly and caring. (In the movie he is the link in the chain which reunites Celie and her sister and family.) If the focus on Black male sexism rather than white racism upsets some readers, The Color Purple's insistence on a Utopian ending upsets just as many. But perhaps we are reading both this ending in the one novel and the factually documented supernatural events and presences in the other with the same kind of contextual ignorance so detrimental to our full appreciation of the text when it is considered as a social, historical and political document.

The Color Purple, Beloved and The Temple of My Familiar are all written against the dominant white male structural and formal norms for literary production. They are products essentially of Black, female folk-culture and it is against this background, in this context that we need to read them.

Lorraine Bethel points out the political motive of the maintenance of traditional forms for Black women writers:

Women in this country have defied the dominant sexist society by developing a type of folk culture and oral literature based on the use of gender solidarity and female bonding as self affirming rituals. Black women have a long tradition of bonding together in a community which has been the source of survival, information, and psychic and emotional support. We have a distinct Black women identified folk culture based on our experiences in this society: symbols, language and modes of expression that specifically reflect the realities of our lives as Black females in a dominant white/male culture. Because Black women rarely gained access to literary expression, this Black women identified bonding and folk culture have often gone unrecorded except through our individual lives and memories.[15]

The structure, forms and expression of Black women's writing come out of their position in the community: 'Toni Morrison and Alice Walker incorporate the traditional Black female activities of rootworking, herbal medicine, conjure, and midwifery, into the fabric of their stories.'[16] And Toni Morrison also acknowledges the central importance for her as a Black woman writer of writing in a mixed mode, incorporating the supernatural and the historically credible, when she talks of her intentions in *Song of Solomon* (1977). What she sought is:

the tone in which I could blend the acceptance of the supernatural and a profound rootedness in the real world at the same time with neither taking precedence over the other. It is indicative of the cosmology, the way in which Black people look at the world. We are a very practical people, very down to earth, even shrewd, people. But within that practicality we also accepted what I suppose could be called superstition and magic, which is another way of knowing things. But to blend these two works together at the same time was enhancing, not limiting. And some of these things were 'discredited knowledge' that Black people had; discredited only because Black people were discredited therefore what they knew was 'discredited'.[17]

There is always the danger of appropriating and misreading Black women's texts, which we must guard against. But in the case of writing in a mixed mode, as Toni Morrison clearly does in *Beloved*, it seems legitimate to look not only at the sources of such writing in the work of politicised Black women writers, but also in the literary precedents set by such familiar, canonised white male or female writers as Dickens, Hardy, Emily, Brontë, and more recently, Pynchon, to name but a few, if any argument is necessary about the literary acceptability of such forms of writing.

Brontë mixes the supernatural passion beyond death of Heathcliff and Cathy with historical and social detail, thus securing the uptake of the more 'poetic' imaginative, mystical and magical elements of *Wuthering Heights*. In the grotesque figure of Miss Havisham in *Great Expectations* Dickens gives us concrete metaphors of sterility, soured monuments to a falsely directed, entombed love redolent of the misdirection and culpable dependence on illusion and appearances of Victorian society. Criticisms of Hardy's confusions in his writing, mixing the supernatural, melodramatic, balladic and the socially and historically pertinent are legion. The mixed mode has its own specific power: the problem lies not with the author but with the reader. The mixture of metaphor/the imaginative and even the magical, with metonymy/the historically, socially and politically documented, realistically presented and credible is widespread among our 'greatest' writers of the literary canon. As readers and critics we are not so dated and hamstrung that we accept the earliest dictats of Marxist criticism and insist that the only really engaged works are those which are fully and only grounded in (the appearance of) historical reality (see, for example, critical reception of modernist works in Rosemary Jackson[18]). The specific version of such deliberate, not naïve, mixed modes produced by Morrison and Walker, for example, should therefore pose no problems of critical reception.

Darwin Turner pays tribute to the storyteller's skill of Toni Morrison through this use of the supernatural, the encouragement of the reader to suspend disbelief:

> she continues to demonstrate her artistic skill in memorable, sometimes startling, but always illuminating metaphors, vivid and credible dialogue, and graceful syntax. . . . Above all she commands the storyteller's skill to persuade a reader to suspend disbelief by discovering credibility in the magic of the tale.[19]

Writing in a mixed mode is typical of Toni Morrison. In her earlier work *Sula*, Sula cuts off the tip of her finger to warn threatening white boys that she can match violence with worse, and a township believe in the establishment of a day when individuals can choose to kill themselves, a 'suicide day'. These incidents are narrated with realistic detail, but they are also metaphors for the cruelty and madness of social sickness, and suffering, which produce extreme behaviour in response.

Like *Beloved*, Alice Walker's *The Temple of My Familiar* confronts both racism and sexism, investigating the legacy of racism before, during and since slavery, and charting back, as does *Beloved*, through the history of racial oppression. It goes much further, however, in the range of this investigation as it looks at Black oppression of Black, at the origins of violence among the pygmies and the Indians, and at the origins of sexism. This it does through using memory. Unlike *Beloved*, Alice Walker's novel does not concentrate on a single, embodied memory; instead it explores the memories of various characters, notably Miss Lissie, partner of Uncle Rafe, uncle of one of the protagonists, Sowelo.

Miss Lissie can be many women, and a photographer captured this variety, a variety which is not just the social role-play of women, but the different lives Miss Lissie lived over hundreds of years, each reincarnated in her pose in individual pictures. I read the novel shortly after watching a TV programme about two children recalling past lives, one in Yorkshire, one in India. Nor is this kind of claim particularly rare; it just is not usually treated as historical *fact* testified to by both personally claimed testimony and the 'unequivocal' proof of photography. When such events are treated in a realistic style in a novel, less-flexible readers may well baulk – and they have done, as reviews testify. The baby ghost in *Beloved* can be explained as easily, as a metaphor representing the unspeakable, the inheritance of a race memory of endless oppression. Those of us who are not always surprised by the existence of the mystic in the everyday need not stop at reading *Beloved* and Miss Lissie's tales as merely metaphoric, however.

Black and white society have sold out, repressed and denied the spiritual and denied equality also, in the face of difference. This is a major statement in Alice Walker's novel and it is embodied and dramatised in a central scene reminiscent of the mystical writing of Doris Lessing. A dream image offers explanation for the cause of racism, sexism, oppression, division, the end to the speech of animal and the beginning of the destruction of other people and of nature. Miss Lissie tells of an earlier self, the woman priest who ignored the source of her magic, her feathered familiar, trying to contain it in a variety of restraining forms and under covers while she was responding to the enticements of a formal record, of verification, as demanded and offered by the white male explorer who reached her temple. He could not understand the religious and spiritual source of her powers unless he categorised and labelled it. The familiar fled; the magic disappeared from the temple and from the world. It is a woman who betrays the lively, beautiful, fish-like, feathered bird to the man, and this incident also represents the disenchantment of relationships between the sexes.

The central activity and metaphor of the interweaving of bright bird feathers suggests the interweaving of ostensibly unrelated stories, the intertwining of other textual references and other Alice Walker characters within the novel. As Zedé and Carlotta make and sell cloaks of fine plumage for priests, then the rich rock starts with magical music, so Eleandra Peacock's tales of native Africans reweaves, redesigns and redraws the memories of the peoples she loved.

Tales of Zedé and Carlotta, Sowelo, Fanny, Miss Lissie and Hal are interwoven and interlinked as the story progresses, and all are rewritings of warped or silenced versions of racism and sexism, of oppression through the years and across different continents. The image of weaving recalls that of quilting in Alice Walker's *In Search of Our Mothers' Gardens*, as she sought images of her mother's and grandmother's creativity. It also recalls the harmony and co-operation of the essentially female art of quilting practised in *The Color Purple* between Shug, Sofia and Celie.

Ironically, we are told, the production of beautiful feathered robes and cloaks which once represented the priestly powers of female priests in a matriarchy, became the image of their subservience under an encroaching patriarchy when men, jealous of female creativity, stole the priestly role and turned the women into mere producers of cloaks for male glorification. By the time Zedé grows up, feathered headdresses and cloaks can only be sold in *gringa* boutiques, as the American capitalist has outlawed village traditions and religion, and the new god is the dollar.

Throughout there is a link drawn between art, creativity and the possibility of valuing difference, co-operation, growth. So the feathered garments suggest self-expression and glory, Arveyda's music is seen as therapeutic and spellbinding, and Hal's painting was a brilliant self-exploration until denied by his father, who crushed his spirit when he refused its value.

This book, attempts to recall as does *Beloved*, that which lies behind all the rewriting, the horrors and inhumanity of oppression, slavery and its legacy. It also celebrates the glory of female creativity, and racial and sexual harmony in past cultures, in a semi-magical past. Alice Walker has her characters speak of the unspeakable using magic, but she also balances the unspeakable with hope, since what was positive and creative in the past could come again, with the kind of insight that characters such as Sowelo learn within the novel, through listening to their ancestors, their relatives, their friends, nature, themselves.

The mixed mode of writing in *The Temple of My Familiar* was complex for the reviewers, and that of *Beloved* for those students in the seminars I taught. Responses to personal elements within *Beloved* were also very mixed. Student groups contained both women with and women without children. *Beloved* challenges the paradigms of the 'good mother' and responses were personal and strong. Lyn comments:

> The desire to protect one's own children validates almost unimaginable actions thus a new anarchic value system has to be constructed, this . . . is about coming to terms with a personal morality and junking the established norms which belong to a different world.

From discussions which closely touched personal feelings and experiences, we moved on to close critical analysis of parts of the novels, particularly the arrival of Schoolteacher to collect his property. Students noticed here in particular the point of view we are forced to take, which is initially that of the slave-catcher. This distances us from the real drama which goes on at the margins. We discussed how we could deal with such a passage, and realised that its effect would not have been so deep had it occurred earlier in the novel or if it had been seen directly through Sethe's eyes at this stage, when it would have been more sensational and we would have felt less implicated, less really stunned into a response. As it is, our position is that of the slave-catcher, a totally untenable position. We are thus able to view Sethe's act as inevitable, and then as right, within the horrific inhuman value system in which she is placed. With her mother-love totally invalidated by the society and the system in which she lived, Sethe could only express her love for her children through the cruel irony of taking them out of that life-denying situation and trying to kill them.

It is not only the haunting and reappearance of Beloved that exemplify Toni Morrison's use of the mixed mode. The depiction of Sethe's murder of her baby is an assault on the reader's senses, an embodiment of the logical and necessary results of dehumanisation under slavery. This racist society drives its victims to respond defensively: murder is considered more humane than recapture. Essentially, as does *The Temple of My Familiar* with its use of race memory, letters, diaries, testimony, *Beloved* gives voice to the unvoiceable, rescues from silence that which perhaps must be acknowledged but cannot be faced fully, daily, if life is to continue, because it is too great a denial of life. Silence and breaking silence are central issues in the novel's plot, also, as vehicles for this argument.

The bit which Paul D. is forced to wear dehumanises him, reducing him in his own eyes below the level of Mister, the liberated rooster:

> Mister was allowed to be and stay what he was. But I wasn't allowed to be and stay what I was. Even if you cooked him you'd be cooking a rooster named Mister. But wasn't no way I'd ever be Paul D. again, living or dead. Schoolteacher changed me. I was something else and that something was less than a chicken sitting in the sun on a tub.   (p. 72)

The bit literally enforces silence, but Paul D. maintains his own silence, his sense of self worth and identity diminished, as expressed by his describing his heart as being replaced by a tobacco tin. Under his previous master he had been boasted of as sexually potent, a 'nigger man' whose own potency was seen as a reflection of the power of his master's control over him and the other Sweet Home men. The uses of language, as of learning, are warped, additional control mechanisms in white hands. So reading is rejected by the Sweet Home men as 'the naming done by a white man who was supposed to know' (p. 125). In his relationship with Sethe he and she gradually unwind enough to start to talk of their stories, 'He wants to put his story next to hers' (p. 273) but the pain is too great for Paul D. to acknowledge how far he has lost his identity and pride, and when he discovers Sethe's 'crime' he cannot accept her any longer. After all 'humankind cannot bear very much reality'.

Learning the message about her own mother who valued her as the only child born of love, Sethe was 'picking meaning out of a code she no longer understood' (p. 62). She is finding a language, a form, an image to help her understand her past here, as do Sowelo, Mary

Anne and principally Miss Lissie in *The Temple of My Familiar*. If she has been isolated and ostracised by the community, Sethe is also rescued by them when they too recognise their own involvement, their own culpability, their own need to face up to a shared guilt and suffering. The women came to no. 124, returning to a pre-linguistic, powerful noise which denies the symbolic structures of the white man's oppression, and its legacy in Sethe's and their own guilt, the haunting of Beloved:

> They stopped praying and took a step back to the beginning. In the beginning there were no words. In the beginning was the sound, and they all knew what that sounded like.   (p. 259)

The noise unlocks Sethe's mind, reunites her with the community:

> For Sethe it was as though the Clearing had come to her with all its heat and summer leaves, where the voices of women searched for the right combination, the key, the code, the sound that broke the back of words – . . . it broke over Sethe and she trembled like the baptised in its wash.   (p. 259)

The religious imagery is obvious: this is an exorcism, a re-baptism, a cleansing and renewal. The women's exorcism takes place at the instant of the white man's riding up to take Denver to her new job: and the parallels with the earlier incident are too great for Sethe. Beloved disappears, quite literally into thin air, though some fear she could return.

In *The Temple of My Familiar* the writing of Miss Lissie and of Eleandra both disappear, but are recorded in the novel and so passed on. Paradoxically, the powerful novel *Beloved* seems initially to end denying its own force, its own articulacy: 'This is not a story to pass on'. But finally it recognises this power, for 'It was not a story to pass on' has been passed on, in the shape of the novel itself. For Sethe, articulating her story and her feelings was almost too much to bear, but her story ends, with Paul D. in a recognition of the vital, human importance of self-worth despite dehumanisation of the past. She learns, as Paul points out, 'You your own best thing, Sethe.'

NOTES

1. Toni Morrison, *Beloved* (London: Chatto and Windus, 1988).
2. Alice Walker, *The Color Purple* (London: The Women's Press, 1983).
3. Alice Walker, *The Temple of My Familiar* (New York: Harcourt, Brace, Jovanovich, 1989).
4. Sara Blackburn, in Barbara Smith, Gloria Hull and Patricia Bell Scott (eds), *But Some of Us Are Brave: Black Women's Studies* (London: The Feminist Press, 1982).
5. Marie Evans, *Black Women Writers* (London: Pluto Press, 1984).
6. Audre Lorde, in Claudia Tate (ed.), *Black Women Writers at Work* (New York: Continuum, 1984) p. 101.
7. Alice Walker, in ibid., p. 185.
8. Toni Morrison, in *Race Today Review*, 1985.
9. Lorraine Bethel, in Smith *et al.*, *But Some of Us Are Brave*, p. 178.
10. Zora Neale Hurston, *Their Eyes Were Watching God* (Champaign, University of Illinois Press, 1978) p. 29.
11. Barbara Burford, 'The Landscapes Painted on the Inside of My Skin', *Spare Rib*, no. 179 (July 1987).
12. Cora Kaplan, 'Keeping the Color in *The Color Purple*', in Cora Kaplan, *Sea Changes* (London: Verso, 1986)
13. Susan Willis, 'Eruptions of Funk: Historicising Toni Morrison', in *Black Literature and Literary Theory*, ed. Henry Louis Gates Jnr (London: Methuen, 1984).
14. Ibid., p. 270.
15. Bethel, in Smith *et al.*, *But Some of Us Are Brave*, p. 179.
16. Ibid., p. 164.
17. Toni Morrison, in Evans, *Black Women Writers*, p. 341.
18. Rosemary Jackson, *Fantasy* (London: Methuen, 1981).
19. Darwin T. Turner, in Evans, *Black Women Writers*.

6

Art, Action and the Ancestors: Alice Walker's *Meridian* in its Context

CHRISTINE HALL

In an essay called 'Coming in from the Cold',[1] Alice Walker writes about the word 'mammy'. She considers the racist stereotype associated with the word and explains her own decision to use it in *The Color Purple*.[2] She concludes her discussion thus:

> And yet, we can learn from what has happened to 'mammy' too. That it is not by suppressing our own language that we counter other people's racist stereotype of us, but by having the conviction that if we present the words in the context that is or was natural to them, we do not perpetuate these stereotypes, but, rather, expose them. And, more important, we help the ancestors in ourselves and others continue to exist. If we kill off the sound of our ancestors, the major portion of us, all that is past, that is history, that is human being is lost, and we become historically and spiritually thin, a mere shadow of who we were on earth.   (p. 62)

The issues Walker raises here – the suppression of language, the need to recontextualise, the need for a sense of the self in history as a prerequisite of spiritual and psychological health – seems to me to be central to her work. In this essay I want to propose that it is in *Meridian*[3] that Walker problematises and works through these issues, charting through her protagonist the psychological and physical struggle necessary for Meridian to arrive at conclusions similar to those Walker herself espouses in 'Coming in from the Cold'. I hope then to contextualise the work within the body of Walker's novels and, in doing so, to raise some questions about the political and ideological implications of the ideas under discussion.

The fragmented nature of *Meridian*'s structure immediately suggests a broken narrative in which the silences and gaps feature prominently. The title of the book reflects the idea of circularity which is so important to the structure of the novel and, metaphorically, to its central issues of revolution and change. Only in 'Ending' (the final section) is there any movement beyond Chickohema, the small town in which Meridian and Truman meet in 'The Last Return' (the first chapter of the book). Even then, Meridian departs only to be replaced by Truman Held, and later, perhaps, Anne-Marion:

> Truman turned, tears burning his face. . . . It was his house now, after all. His cell. . . . He had a vision of Anne-Marion herself arriving, lost, someday, at the door, which would remain open, and wondered if Meridian knew that the sentence of bearing the conflict in her soul which she had imposed on herself – and lived through – must now be borne in terror by all the rest of them.   (p. 228)

The circles intersect and overlap. The movement of time in the novel is cyclical rather than chronological; the fragmented form, with its rapid movement from past to present, and its start and finish in the house of Chickohema offers a structural representation of issues and attitudes which entrap Meridian. At the end of the novel, Meridian herself, 'cleansed of sickness', breaks from the circle, leaving Truman, Lynne and Anne Marion still trapped and needing to seek their own means of release.

Questions about how to read and the whole hermeneutic enterprise are thrust to the forefront from the initial page, which offers a variety of definitions of the word 'meridian'.[4] The novel is divided into three broad chapters, within which are over 30 short sections containing stories which, because of their fragmentary nature and textual context, often have about them the quality of folk-tale, parable or fairy story. The possibility of alternative perspectives and a variety of readings is seen as a fruitful one; no one reading is particularly sanctioned within the text. The isolation of the stories encourages the notion of the reader as the active maker of meanings, a role which is paralleled within the novel by Meridian's own search for an interpretation which will make sense in and of her life. The gaps and spaces surrounding the stories make a structural link with the gaps and silences that are given thematic consideration within the plot (Mrs Hill, Camara, those who have not registered to vote . . .). Alan Nadel, in an interesting article on *Meridian*, has pointed out the contrasts between the first chapter, 'Meridian', and the second chapter, 'Truman Held', which has a stronger linear narrative. Central to the 'Meridian' chapter is the image of unearthing nuggets of (fools'?) gold, an enterprise encouraged by the chapter's structure and movement back and forth in time. Nadel's point is that, in contrasting the two chapters, 'Walker forces us to read not only one history against another but also one kind of writing – one way of attributing significance – against its alternatives.'[5] He sees this as exemplified in the final tale Meridian tells of the husband who favoured his dog over his wife. Meridian's reading places primary significance on the patterning of events, whilst Truman demands the resolution of the linear narrative. (' "And did he kill the dog?" Meridian shrugged. "I suspect that is not the point," she said' – p. 225).

The first chapter, 'Meridian', begins with three key narratives, none of which is fully resolved in the present of the novel. Each of these stories illustrates the suppression of women's voices; there are urgent reasons why each needs to be recontextualised, to be located within a context other than that of the dominant white culture. These three stories – of 'Marilene O'Shay', 'The Wild Child' and 'The Sojourner Tree' – are concerned with, respectively, the wife's role, the child's role and the mother's role, though in each case the situation is distorted and the possibilities for interpretation are left open.

Marilene O'Shay, the 'mummy', was murdered by her husband for dereliction of wifely duties. The leaflet written by her husband explains:

> Marilene had been an ideal woman; a 'goddess' who had been given 'everything she *thought* she wanted'. She had owned a washing machine, furs, her own car and a full-time housekeeper-cook. All she had to do, wrote Henry, was 'lay back and be pleasured'. But she was 'corrupted by the honeyed tongues of evildoers that dwell in high places far away', had gone outside the home to seek her 'pleasuring', while still expecting him to foot the bills. (p. 6)

The narrative is condensed, in melodramatic form, reminiscent of Flannery O'Connor, into four dramatic stages:

> a red and gold circus wagon . . . glittered in the sun. In tall, ornate gold letters over the side were the words, outlined in silver, 'Marilene O'Shay. One of the Twelve Human Wonders of the World: Dead for Twenty-five Years, Preserved in Life-Like Condi-

tion'. Below this, a smaller legend was scrawled in red paint on four large stars: 'Obedient daughter', read one, 'Devoted Wife', said another, the third was 'Adoring Mother', and the fourth was 'Gone Wrong'. Over the fourth a vertical line of progressively flickering light-bulks moved continually downward like a cascading tear.   (p. 5)

The crudity of the tale, and the patent charlatanry of the context in which it is presented, help to isolate the four starred stages of the woman's life, encouraging the formation of ironic or sceptical readings. But the schematic outline offers a recurring pattern for the main women characters in the book. Meridian herself explores the categories of obedient daughter, devoted wife and adoring mother, before 'going wrong' – or perhaps 'going wrong' in each. Mrs Hill's and Lynne's stories also follow similar patterns. The narrative structure of the Marilene O'Shay tale is, therefore, worked out in different contexts within the novel. But in order to re-contextualise and interpret the tale, one needs critical access to it. So Meridian's stand is for the black children's right of access to the story, and thus their chance to interpret and demythologise it – which they use ('she was a fake. They discovered that. There was no salt, they said, left in the crevices of her eyesockets or in her hair. . . . They said she was made of plastic' – pp. 12–13).

The fate of the wild wife is paralleled by that of The Wild Child. No one's daughter, she cannot be accommodated within the community, because of her cursing, her dirt and her manners. Similarly, Louvinie's distorted 'maternal' contacts with the Saxon children result in a child's death and her own mutilation. The stories are symbolically tied together in the episode of the authorities' refusal to accept the public importance of The Wild Child's story (by conceding the right to the ceremonies of death) and the Black students' failure to respect the symbolic importance of Louvinie's story as represented by The Sojourner Tree. These are private tales of silenced females, tales made public in different ways which make them both part of 'public' history and of Meridian's private, personal history. The difficulties of contextualising these stories and of arriving at interpretations which are coherent in both a personal and a more broadly political way, are perhaps best illustrated by the story of The Sojourner Tree.

Louvinie, a slave whose African heritage has been 'the weaving of intricate tales with which to entrap people who hoped to get away with murder' (p. 31), had been enslaved before she could be taught the art of interpretation, by means of which one could 'identify the guilty party'. The only son of the Saxon household dies of a heart attack whilst Louvinie is relating a particularly blood-curdling story, requested by the children and recorded only by a white child. Louvinie's tongue is cut out and ground underfoot by the master. Retrieved and smoked by Louvinie, her tongue is planted under a magnolia tree which subsequently flourishes and is believed to possess magical qualities. The tree, later in the grounds of a college for Black women, comes to symbolise many aspects of creativity, self-expression, security and comfort for the students. It offers a tangible link with Black history, and is the site of the commemoration of Fast Mary's suicide, a ceremony which unites all the students. Withstanding threats from a liberal benefactor who offers to build on the site, the tree nevertheless falls foul of women students themselves, who, in their fury at the authorities' refusal to accept The Wild Child for burial, riot and very nearly destroy the tree.

Meridian and Anne-Marion are both involved with the final stages of this narrative, though they adopt different positions. Anne-Marion participates in the destruction of the tree, perhaps seeing it as rooted in white brutality against Black women, and the violent act as severing the oppression and suffering of the past from the present. Meridian, on the other hand, 'begged them to dismantle the president's house instead' (p. 38), presumably valuing the non-verbal forms of creativity – music, dance, love-making – which have flourished from the tree's roots, and distraught that the act of destruction should be turned against the students' own symbolic sanctuary and link with the past.

At the end of the novel Truman, looking around Meridian's room, notices 'an addition to the line of letters. A blank sheet of paper and, next to it, forming the end of the line, a photograph of an enormous bull's-eye' (p. 223). On closer inspection he discovers what the 'bull's-eye' is: a photograph of The Sojourner sprouting a new branch. The paper is not blank either, though 'the handwriting was grotesquely small'. 'It contained one line: "Who would be happier than you that The Sojourner did not die?" She had written, also in a minute script, "perhaps me", but then had half erased it' (p. 224).

The half-erased writing is Anne-Marion's. The tentative, both literally and figuratively self-effacing nature of the communication indicates the changes this previously decisive, dogmatic woman has gone through. Early in the novel she is described as brash and eager to argue over the smallest issues. Her temper was easily lost. When she was attempting to be non-violent and a policeman shoved her, she dug her nails into her arms to restrain herself, but could never resist sticking out, to its full extent, her energetic and expressive pink tongue. (p. 27)

The history of The Sojourner Tree might be interpreted as demonstrating that the energetic and expressive tongue will be stilled; the rebirth of the tree might then symbolise hope for non-verbal forms of representation, rather than oral or written ones. Significantly, the photograph comes at the end of a line of letters; immediately preceding it is Anne-Marion's half-erased text. Truman, reading this sequence, sees the paper as blank and the image of the sprouting tree as something to be shot at, a bull's eye.

Within the text, then, a variety of interpretative possibilities are hinted at. Margaret Homans, commenting on *Meridian* in an essay entitled 'Her Very Own Howl',[6] compares this final photographic image of the tree with the howl which is the final expression of Nel's feelings at the end of Toni Morrison's *Sula*,[7] a novel which graphically illustrates the difficulties of communication for and between women. Relating these novels to the different feminist schools of thought on language acquisition and use, Homans contends that

> both Walker and Morrison conclude their representations of language in ways that radically call into question the very possibility of that representation. Necessarily standing outside the question in order to represent it within discourse that can be printed and read, these novelists paradoxically undermine the ground they stand on.[8]

It is undoubtedly true that *Meridian*, like *The Third Life of Grange Copeland*[9] before it, offers potent illustrations of the problems of verbal communication, especially for women. These are examples of women's voices being discounted, suppressed and repressed. Early in her life Meridian is taught that, publicly, conformity is required – from her mother, her high school audience and her revolutionary college friends. Only by mouthing the correct sentiments, divorced though they might be from her beliefs, can Meridian win approval from any of them:

> Meridian was reciting a speech that extolled the virtues of the constitution and praised the superiority of The American Way of Life.

The audience cared little for what she was saying, and of course they didn't believe any of it, but they were rapt listening to her speak so passionately and with such sad valor in her eyes.

Then, in the middle of her speech, Meridian had seemed to forget. She stumbled and then was silent on the stage. The audience urged her on but she could not continue . . . . Meridian was trying to explain to her mother that for the first time she really listened to what she was saying; knew she didn't believe it, and was so distracted by his revelation that she could not make the rest of her speech.   (p. 119)

Her explanation is lost on her mother, who, in her bitterness and repressed fury with her role in life, her 'war against those to whom she could not express her anger or shout 'it's not fair!' (p. 41), refuses any real communication with her daughter, just as Meridian is later unable to communicate with or care for her own child. The children in the novel, as in *The Third Life of Grange Copeland*, are portrayed as vulnerable, isolated, voiceless individuals. The Wild Child's story epitomises many of the themes concerning children's neglect, sexual exploitation and ultimate lack of voice – 'cursing is the only language [The Wild Child] knew' (p. 24).

Meridian's difficulty in communicating with Truman, even at the time of her most intense love for him, is symbolised by Truman's insistence on speaking in French, a language 'she understood . . . better than she spoke'. 'When he talked to her she had to translate every syllable into English before answering. Their conversation moved slowly' (p. 96).

Thematically, then, there is an exploration of issues about the silencing of women which is important to characters like Lynne and Mrs Hill, as well as to Meridian. The theme is developed both in The Sojourner story itself and in the varying interpretations of it which are suggested in the text. To some extent, therefore, Margaret Homans's point is clearly a good one: to the extent that she examines the handicaps, problems and obstacles to women's self-expression, Walker may be seen to be undermining the ground of verbal discourse upon which her own work rests. She radically questions the possibility of representation, yet it seems to me that the final image of the sprouting stump of The Sojourner Tree is not necessarily as inconclusive or paradoxical as Homans suggests.

Presented in a non-verbal form – a photograph – the image of the sprouting tree can obviously be seen as symbolising the resurgence of non-verbal forms of expression and growth. Yet the roots are clearly in verbal forms, story telling and oral history. Meridian's concern for the tree might be interpreted as, in part, a concern for rights of access to the means of self-expression, in whatever form, that The Sojourner symbolises. (A concern which has been prefigured in the novel by Meridian's stand over the Black children's admission to the Marilene O'Shay side-show.) The image of rebirth is an optimistic, positive one, and it is linked in its positioning at the end of the narrative, and in its symbolic qualities, with Meridian's own healing which enables her to break from the circle that has bound her.

Meridian's own 'rebirth' is a result of the culmination of her struggle to define her personal role within broad political and artistic contexts. Early in the novel Meridian announces to Truman that 'what you see before you is a woman in the process of changing her mind' (p. 12). This change of mind eventually occurs in church, when Meridian eventually finds herself able, theoretically at least, to come to terms with the idea of righteous murder.

The section 'Camara' begins with an image of Meridian with a sense of herself as 'an outsider, as a single eye behind a camera that was aimed from a corner of her youth, attached now only because she watched' (p. 197). In many ways, her sense of herself as alienated, committed yet in some way uninvolved, an outsider whose perspective might well be askew, is the most typical of her life – with her mother, with Eddie, with Truman, at college and with her revolutionary friends. This sense of alienation has been incorporated into the direct political action she is able to take, such as her stand against the tank at the beginning of the novel.

As she enters the church, the sense of art and artifice is pervasive: she mounts the step 'as if into an ageless photograph'; she is aware that 'If she were not there watching, the scene would be exactly the same, the "picture" itself never noticing that the camera was missing' (p. 197). Finally entering the church, she hears a familiar story, about a father's loss of a son, sacrificed for a greater good. As a version of the Christ story the narrative is in keeping with the context in which it is presented; the history of a murdered civil rights worker, it is also self-consciously disjunctive with it. The ceremony in the church is a carefully constructed performance, highly self-conscious with an emphasis upon form and performance. Audience tension and expectation are aroused; before the backdrop of the young man's photograph, the father utters a ritualised three word speech – 'My son

died' – the essence of a longer, 'laboriously learned' oration. He
pauses and is led away. Music accompanies the collection of money.

The sermon itself has been an even more self-conscious performance – a direct and deliberate imitation of Martin Luther King:
'all his congregation *knew* he was consciously keeping that voice
alive. It was like a *play*' (p. 200).

For Meridian and for the congregation, these are not just traditional
distant forms being emptily reworked; they are vibrant and relevant,
a means of keeping the image of their own dead before the living.
The music remains the same, but the words have changed; the Christ
story has new characters; Martin Luther King's sermons are celebrated
for their form and delivery which are so much a part of their message.
The image on the stained glass window is of a Black man holding his
guitar and singing, but brandishing a bloody sword with his free
hand. Experiencing this leads Meridian to the important conclusion
that it is by means of art, whether it is story-telling, performance, the
visual arts or music, that history can be transformed to be truly
meaningful to the present, and to engender action. The process is a
slow one of collectively working through the events and becoming
familiar with them; fundamental change will occur, she concludes,
only by working within the culture, extending the shared forms to
the limit of their usefulness.

> If you will let us weave your story and your son's life and death
> into what we already know – into the songs, the sermons, the
> 'brother and sister' – we will soon be so angry that we cannot help
> but move. 'Understand this', they are saying, 'the church' (and
> Meridian knew they did not mean simply 'church', as in Baptist,
> Methodist or whatnot, but rather communal spirit, togetherness,
> righteous convergence), 'the music, the form of worship that has
> always sustained us, the kind of ritual you share with us, these are
> the ways to transformation that we know. We want to take this
> with us as far as we can.'   (p. 204)

Meridian's liberation – a physical as well as philosophical one
('There was in Meridian's chest a breaking as if a tight string binding
her lungs had given way, allowing her to breathe freely' – (p. 204) –
lies in her understanding that her role is not to be a revolutionary
leader, a heroine, but a recorder of the past, not in the detached
impersonal manner of the eye behind the camera, but as an engaged
performer, a repository of songs and stories.

It was this . . . that has caused me to suffer: I am not to belong to the future. I am to be left, listening to the old music, besides the highway. . . When they stop to wash off the blood I will come forward and sing from memory songs they will need once more to hear. For it is the song of the people, transformed by the experience of each generation, that holds them together, and if any part of it is lost the people suffer and are without soul. If I can only do that, my role will not have been a useless one after all.   (pp. 205–6)

Margaret Homans's essay suggests that, in offering the photograph of the sprouting stump as one of the final images of *Meridian*, Alice Walker aligns herself with feminist theoreticians who make out a case for the ultimate impossibility of women adequately being able to represent themselves in language. Whilst there is obviously much in the novel to suggest the obstacles to women's representation in language, such an interpretation seems to me at odds with the whole thrust of the novel. Both structurally and thematically, Walker has underlined the importance of narrative and performance, of weaving together story and history, art and politics. The major distinction drawn, it seems to me, is not between the verbal and the non-verbal, but between the rooted and the rootless. Truman, with his spoken French, his African prince performance and his Che Guevara outfit, represents an example of cultural expressions which are not rooted in the community. Meridian's way forward, out of the cyclical pattern that has bound her, is from the base of the black community's cultural heritage and practices, verbal and non-verbal. It is from this starting point that Meridian concludes that personal and political change can be built.

she understood, finally, that the respect she owed her life was to continue, against whatever obstacles, to live it, and not to give up any particle of it without a fight to the death, preferably *not* her own. And that this existence extended beyond herself to those around her, because, in fact, the years in America had created them One Life.   (p. 204)

Analysing this passage in an article on race, gender and nation in Walker's work,[10] Lauren Berlant writes:

The movement in these phrases from the solipsism of everyday life to the symbolic unity of 'One Life' takes place under the symbolic and political force of 'years in America'. Despite its crucially oppressive role in the historical formation of racial consciousness, America in this novel remains the sign and utopian paradigm of national identity. Meridian's new selflessness, born of an American-inspired melding of individual self interest with populist social concerns, serves as a model for the future nation Afro-Americans can construct.[11]

Berlant's view is that in *Meridian* 'personal' relationships are seen as symptoms of the political situation, but that

> Meridian subordinates the struggle within gender to the 'larger' questions raised by the imminent exhaustion or depletion of the (Civil Rights) movement itself. Meridian's theory of 'One Life' dissolves the barriers of class and education between herself and the black community at large and effectively depoliticizes the struggle with the movements patriarchal values and practices by locating the 'personal' problems of sexism within the nationalist project.   (p. 835)

My own reading of this would be quite different. Like Berlant, I would wish to focus on the political and symbolic force of 'years in America' in the position Meridian defines for herself. it seems to me, however, that it is because of (rather than despite) the crucially oppressive nature of these years that Meridian's emphasis is upon the process of Black history and the cultural forms that have been evolved over the years, rather than on a model of American national identity. In the context of the novel it seems to me that the word 'years' is weighted as heavily as 'America'. Meridian's new position acknowledges the importance of knowledge (and access to knowledge) abut these years. Progress will come, not from a cynical conjunction of 'individual self interest with populist social concerns' but from understanding, accepting and valuing Black history, locating oneself within Black culture and society and working from there. The notion of 'One Life', it seems to me, is based on a depth of understanding of shared oppression and resistance, and a refusal to deny or diminish what has gone before – in Walker's terms, a refusal to 'kill off the sound of our ancestors'. Meridian does not find a 'new selflessness' – and selflessness has been an important and not always productive aspect of her personality before this point. Nor, I think, does she find a way of depoliticising gender issues by placing them within a 'broader' nationalist politics. What she finds, it seems to me, is a political approach which allows her to value herself and her personal history rather than collude with the kinds of divisions between the 'personal' and the 'political' which have tormented her physically, emotionally and intellectually throughout her association with the Civil Rights movement.

The association between Meridian's body and the body politic is central to the novel. The resolution of the problematic relation between the two is suggested by the final restoration of Meridian's body to health. Her health arises from a more confident sense of self, rooted in her own community, from which she can view her own decisions and relationships. The splits between Meridian's moral, intellectual and emotional selves within the political arena are symbolically represented throughout the novel by her grappling with the problem of revolutionary murder. The understanding she arrives at acknowledges the need for coercive political action but also acknowledges that she is unlikely to be amongst 'the real revolutionaries – those who know they must spill blood in order to help the poor and the black and therefore go right ahead.' (p. 205). But as artist, recorder and creator of histories, working within and on behalf of her community, she can find a sense of wholeness and a clarity of purpose:

> even the contemplation of murder required incredible delicacy as it required incredible spiritual work, and the historical background and present setting must be right. Only in a church surrounded by the righteous guardians of the people's memories could she even approach the concept of retaliatory murder. (p. 205)

There is, I think, a development of thoughts and ideas from *The Third Life of Grange Copeland* through *Meridian* which achieves a certain resolution, however tentative, in *The Color Purple*. All three novels explore the suppression of women's voices and the damage done, both to the women themselves and the broader social group, by the denial of the right of self-expression. In *The Third Life of Grange Copeland*, Margaret and Mem are brutally silenced; Ruth, given greater opportunities, is nevertheless set very definite limits by Grange. Grange encourages self-expression, creativity and independent thought, but within very carefully controlled boundaries which reflect the limits of his own position; he does not want her to be empowered to the extent that she feels that she can attempt to

change things or act in a genuinely radical way. Meridian's struggle
– to express herself in forms and contexts which have personal and
political coherence and are genuinely (rootedly) radical – is in many
ways a legacy of Ruth's. Meridian's conclusions, about the importance
of context and the valuing of black cultural forms, point the way to
the setting, the narrative structure and many of the issues explored
in *The Color Purple*.

  The Color Purple's most radical quality, for me, is its giving of
voice to a silenced woman. Celie's letters are an affirmation of the
quality of the imaginative life of a woman forced by her physical and
social circumstances to live almost entirely in her imagination. With
the use of first-person narration, the Margarets, Mems, Josies and
Mrs Hills of earlier novels are given a centrality previously denied to
them. The creation of Celie's voice seems to me the single most
successful element of the novel; powerful and highly individual, it
challenges any construction of the character as simply a victim.

  Reading *The Color Purple* as a radical challenging novel is, of course,
dependent upon the contexts in which one chooses to place the
work. In the context of fairy stories and American rural family sagas,
The Color Purple has seemed uncontentious and sentimental to many
critics. Trudier Harris, for example, writes in an article called 'On
The Color Purple, Stereotypes and Silence':

> It affirms, first of all, patience and long suffering. . . . In true fairy-
> tale fashion, it affirms passivity; heroines in these tales do little to
> help themselves. It affirms silence in the face of it, if not allegiance
> to, cruelty. It affirms secrecy concerning violence and violation. It
> affirms, saddest of all, the myth of the American Dream become a
> reality for black Americans, even those who are 'dirt poor'.[12]

  Cora Kaplan, in 'Keeping the Color in *The Color Purple*',[13] argues
that, set in its racially, culturally and historically specific context, *The
Color Purple* can be kept from being 'bleached into a pallid progressive
homily'. She suggests considering *The Color Purple* in the context of
Black men's works which have preceded it, particularly those of
Wright, Ellison and Baldwin:

> The utopianism of *The Color Purple* and its seemingly apolitical
> model of change as a familial dialectic looks rather less simple
> when read as a polemic against the deeply negative imaginative
> interpretation of southern Black life in much male Black fiction
> and autobiography.[14]

Similarly, Kaplan would want to see the novel as part of a continuing dialogue taking place in sociological and historical writing, as well as in fiction, about Black family life. Part of its context would then be works like the Moynihan Report or Alex Haley's *Roots*. In this context 'the reconstruction of "family life" in Walker's novel which includes resistance to both heterosexuality and the nuclear family must be seen as a feminist response to a specifically racial set of discourses about the family and femininity'.[15]

In the context of Walker's own work to date, I see the enterprise of giving voice to Celie as an artistic resolution of the ideas and concerns she has dramatised and documented in earlier novels. In *The Temple of My Familiar*[16] Walker pushes her project on to the next stage: exploring, primarily through the character of Lissie, the idea of tuning in to the voices and contexts of the 'ancestors', of empowering them through art. A consideration of the sequential development of the works can offer important insights. Within this context *Meridian* must take the central, pivotal position that its title implies, for it is here that Walker theorises a position (which we might take to be analogous to her own) that insists that suppression of one's own language is unhealthy, that contexts must be clarified and that knowledge of the past must inform the present and the future.

NOTES

1. Alice Walker, 'Coming in from the Cold: Welcoming the Old, Funny-Talking Ancient Ones into the Warm Room of Present Consciousness, or Natty Dread Rides Again!', in Alice Walker, *Living by the Word* (London: The Women's Press, 1988).
2. Alice Walker, *The Color Purple* (London: The Women's Press, 1983).
3. Alice Walker, *Meridian* (London: The Women's Press, 1982).
4. Alan Nadel in his article 'Reading the Body: Alice Walker's *Meridian* and the Archaeology of Self', *Modern Fiction Studies*, vol. 34, no. 1 (Spring 1988) considers the fact that 'meridian' can be defined as a noun 'that is, as something defined in and of itself; and as an adjective, that is, as something that modifies another subject. The merging of the modifier and the noun in Meridian's name thus signifies the reconstituting of a self both personal and political'.
5. Ibid., p. 67.
6. Margaret Homans, 'Her Very Own Howl', *Signs* (Winter 1983).
7. Toni Morrison, *Sula* (London: Triad/Granada, 1982).

8. Homans, 'Her Very Own Howl'.
9. Alice Walker, *The Third Life of Grange Copeland* (London: The Women's Press, 1985).
10. Lauren Berlant, 'Race, Gender and Nation in *The Color Purple*', *Critical Inquiry*, vol. 14, no. 4 (1988).
11. Ibid., p. 835.
12. Trudier Harris, 'On *The Color Purple*, Stereotypes and Silence', *Black American Literature Forum*, vol. 18, no. 4 (1984).
13. Cora Kaplan, *Sea Changes: Culture and Feminism* (London: Verso, 1986).
14. Ibid., p. 185.
15. Ibid., p. 187.
16. Alice Walker, *The Temple of My Familiar* (London: The Women's Press, 1989).

7

'Not My People': Toni Morrison and Identity

ELAINE JORDAN*

'I write what I think is of interest to black people.' Black women's experiences and, in particular, the meanings they attach to motherhood, are central themes in *Beloved*. For Morrison, these issues cannot be divorced from a different, deeper contradiction: the tension between the racial self and the racial community. . . . The story is based on the case of Margaret Garner, a young woman who killed her children rather than let the slave-catchers take them back to bondage. . . . 'the questions about community and individuality were certainly inherent in that incident as I imagined it. When you are the community, when you are your children, when that is your individuality, there is no division. Margaret Garner didn't do what Medea did and kill her children because of some guy. It was for me this classic example for a person determined to be responsible.'[1]

Toni Morrison's conversation with Paul Gilroy in *City Limits* indicates the scope of *Beloved*. This essay explores what it meant for me as a white woman, the same but different, to look at Morrison's writing. She herself is exploring a woman who is different from herself, a woman of the past; can *she* inhabit that person she imagines? In the history of the US Black people have not been represented, or have figured in the narratives of others. The question of Morrison's novel is, how can Black people reinhabit that history, cease to forget, without being overwhelmed? The astounding figure she finds for this problem of being too much there and not there at all is 'Beloved'. My interest is in the figure of Beloved, who does not exist, is a logical contradiction (both x and not-x), and yet can hold things together and move strong emotion. Toni Morrison suggests how different identities, psychological and political, are split apart and stitched together within an individual or between individuals and groups;

within and between Afro-Americans, within and between women. Such divisions may be generally felt to be a bad thing, whether in political or in psychological terms, unless one is ready to think that living is always in process, that the identities from which active commitments arise are also, always, divided and mobile, and that this has hopeful as well as treacherous potential.

I take one epigraph to *Beloved* as my starting point: 'I will call them my people, / which were not my people; / and her beloved, / which was not beloved.' This comes from St. Paul's Epistle to the Romans, 9:25, in which he seeks to persuade Jewish Christians to tolerate the different practices, within the same faith, of Gentile Christians. One tactic of persuasion is to refer back, in the words quoted, to a theme of reconciliation in the Old Testament Book of Hosea. From a modern point of view this is a difficult and obscure text, though it has many moving rhetorical resonances for a reader of *Beloved*: of that which was rejected being finally welcomed home; of a daughter, for example, who is deliberately given a name, Lo-ruha-mah, which means not 'She is my beloved' but 'it is not pitied'.[2] The prophet Hosea's purpose is quite unlike Paul's, at least according to modern biblical scholarship: he seeks to separate off the One God's Chosen People from Canaanites, who may have worshipped female divinities. But his persuasive metaphors are drawn from sexual relationships, a rhetoric which is not Judaic but typical of the fertility religion he wants to exclude.

Both Sherley Anne Williams in *Dessa Rose*, published a year earlier, and Toni Morrison in *Beloved* engage with the significance that the past can have for the present moment.[3] They look back at the significance of slavery in the United States, and forward with anxiety and hope for new generations: '*Oh, we have paid for our children's place in the world again, and again*' – the last words of *Dessa Rose*. The escaped slave Dessa's determination to record her story recalls the reminiscences of slaves, such as those quoted in Barbara Omolade's essay 'Hearts of Darkness', in which painful memories are set within an account of history which becomes deliberately, lyrically, affirmative:

> But others sold down the river survived and remembered their mothers and fathers. . . . They, in their turn, gave their daughters and sons the gifts of determination and freedom, the will to love and the strength to have faith.[4]

History here has the deliberate force of myth, with a will to remind and empower younger generations. Morrison's third novel, *Song of Solomon* (1977),[5] puts the story of Black Americans in place within the history of the United States and lays claim to a historical right to citizenship, along with native Americans, through research into an individual family history and through the naming of America's places and folk heroes (pp. 302–4, 328–9). In one of her articles for the *New York Times*, 'Rediscovering Black History' (1974),[6] she indicates that Black Americans in general have a longer native-born inheritance of America than the twentieth-century immigrants who claim citizenship, given that 'heritage' is an issue. It was important at that time to say to all, from within the Black community in the States, 'we belong here, it's our place, and our names and histories are inscribed on the road signs, on the culture, in memory'. But what are the implications for immigrants to the United Kingdom, and their children: do they somehow have less right to the place because their history here is shorter? This problem only arises if we universalise what Morrison writes, rather than reading it as an intervention in a particular time and place. But to say that is to identify it with tactical 'truth effects', not truth.

In another article, 'A Slow Walk of Trees . . . ' (1976),[7] Morrison writes that the modern Blacks she celebrates have not always been popular with the Black community they served (James Baldwin is an instance; it was the posthumous recognition of his value by Black writers and critics that inspired their living tribute to Toni Morrison in 1988). She has been attacked herself, since her commitment to exploring Black experience without worrying what whites might think enables her to address myths within Black cultural politics critically. She is certainly not over-anxious to sound nice to white women. My way into talking and writing about her work can't be easy. In the fourth novel, *Tar Baby* (1981),[8] Gideon, or Yardman as his white employers call him, warns the wanderer, Son, about the mulatto woman Jade, or Jadine, that 'yallas' like her 'don't come to being black natural-like. They have to choose it and most don't choose it. Be careful of the stuff they put down' (p. 156). Later Jade strays into a swamp that coats her in black stuff. In this novel the natural environment, a Caribbean island near Dominique, is 'animised' in contrast to the human characters, who are all rootless; and the swamp is identified with Black women, who are arrogant – mindful as they were of their value, their exceptional femaleness; knowing as they did that the first world of the world had been built with their sacred properties; that they alone could hold together the stones of pyramids and the rushes of Moses's crib; knowing their steady consistency, their pace of glaciers, their permanent embrace.   (p. 184)

Such language recalls the novel *Of One Blood* (1902–3) by Pauline Hopkins,[9] which claims that all world culture has one origin in Ethiopia. It also recalls 'A Slow Walk of Trees' (trees don't walk, but over time tree lines may advance, as glaciers may), which represents Morrison's grandmother's cautious optimism about the progress of Blacks in the States. At first glance the swamp-women in *Tar Baby* thought the struggling Jade was a runaway child restored to them, but then they see that she is 'fighting to get away from them . . . to be something other than they were'. What is being allegorised is the difficulty that the 'yalla' has in identifying with the Black side of her inheritance, but also, very strongly, suspicion and hostile judgement from Blacks. On the level of the story after all, Jade is here struggling literally to survive.

She is highly educated, has been a model and acted in films in Europe: an ideal of assimilation. In the allegory of the swamp-women, both femaleness and Blackness are identified with a long mythical history and with nature. This is not presented as the way Jade sees it, though later she does have a dream of Black women passing judgement on her and inhibiting her. Like the deliberate animistic atmosphere of the whole novel, the image exists beyond any individual consciousness. Its positive claims for Black femaleness are made at a cost, and it is the educated, Europeanised woman who (nearly) goes down. To Gideon, natural Blackness appeared far better than coming to Blackness by choice; so that Jade's chances of being acknowledged, trusted, respected, are narrow. Again, positive representations of Blackness (and of femaleness) have a history: they intervene to counter negative representations and exclusion. But who goes down to set them up? Young Blacks now are saying that they are not to be identified with something in the past, or in Ethiopia, but that they are here, now.

At this point Toni Morrison might say, like many a woman, 'Damned if I do and damned if I don't.' All writers in the United States who achieve any status are called on not just to 'represent' mimetically, but also to be representatives responsible to their cultural, ethnic or gender group. In Sondra O'Neale's 'Inhibiting Midwives/Usurping Creators',[10] Morrison is a major target of attack. Black writers, O'Neale complains, have not given the Black woman reader 'representative and enhancing self-images' of normal Black women, but have shown them as deformed or mutilated – suffering from the idealisation of white beauty or as the 'tragic mulatto' with no secure identity as white or Black, or as escaping such problems through psychosis or mysticism or lesbianism. O'Neale's poetics, her understanding of metaphor and of identification are terribly restrictive; moreover she ignores the extent to which Morrison *has* written from a position of identification with 'normal' Black women. In 'What the Black Woman Thinks about Women's Lib' (1971),[11] Morrison begins with an ironic acceptance of segregated signs for toilets, 'White Ladies/Colored Women' – 'ladies' are those who are willing to let others do the work, but 'colored women' were already identified, before 'women's lib', as 'tough, capable, independent and immodest'. In this light white feminists are said to have stolen Black women's roles – 'shacking up' rather than marrying, taking on single parenthood, and so on – while also (some of them) depending for their 'liberation' on Black women as cleaners and childminders. Morrison here defends the positive potential within some stereotypes which activists had tended to reject out of hand. It was with the same positive purpose of identifying with and speaking up for Black women generally, that her 1974 article took the opposite tack of querying the slogan 'Black is Beautiful' – 'black women are already O.K.' even if their necks are shorter than Nefertiti's.

In that tactic she united defence of the 'average' Black woman with the feminism she otherwise seemed to mock: why should any woman be made to feel at a disadvantage in comparison to some ideal model? Right from the start she had queried one term of her title: ' "The Black Woman" is a dangerous misconception, for it encourages lump thinking.' While all of her writing represents Black women in their differences from each other and from stereotypes, the other term of her opposition, the white lady, remains in the lump. This article is disturbing for a white woman to read precisely because of its whole-hearted commitment to Black women whoever they may be, which Sondra O'Neale would deny Morrison. The end of the article transfigures it by mentioning the potentially positive achievements of a coming conference involving both white and Black women, for whom the feminist aims of the conference would have to be seen from the perspective of the interests of the Black community.

As a journalist and as a novelist Toni Morrison is a canny, a tactical writer, not from bad faith but from responsibility and commitment. In this article she lets Black women know that she knows from the heart why they might be leery of feminism and white women, and she certainly lets white women know why there is no easy sisterhood. Yet in the last instance, from which the whole can be reread, she recognises the possibility of Black and white feminisms working together.

Interviewed by Paul Gilroy in *City Limits*, Morrison spoke of Afro-American music as the parallel to the strategies of her art, the mirror 'that gives me the necessary clarity': 'Music makes you hungry for more of it. It never really gives you the whole number. It slaps and it embraces, it slaps and it embraces.'[12] That is the best account I've seen of why her art is such a compelling emotional and intellectual experience. It helps explain the effect in reading *Beloved* when Sethe and her two daughters, the living one and the dead one, skate together, laughing and falling in delight together though 'Nobody saw them falling' (pp. 174–5). It is an ecstatic moment, all the more so for the threatening possibilities of the word 'fall' and the fact that the reunion is at the same moving moment a dangerous fantasy, skating on thin ice. The episode gives us our heart's desire – we have been made to want so much what Sethe wants, and now has, her recognition of the daughter she has killed, restored to her. All sufferings are redeemed, all antagonisms are resolved, and there is no outside observer to cast doubt on this. Except for the very language that defines the ecstasy: 'Nobody saw them falling.' Why think of that, then? Ecstasy in classical Greek means literally 'standing outside' – that which goes beyond reason, and a reminder of an objective point of view.

Beloved stands outside realism; its poetics (the principles of its making) are more analytic and complex. It satisfies desire at this point, but the wish fulfilment is also a turning point from which the object of desire comes to seem increasingly a horror – the beloved becomes something pitiless, which should not be desired. That does not cancel the validity of the desire for reunion or its imaginative gratification. In retrospect, the scene is both the one thing and the other, both positive and negative, depending on which way you look at it – a logical contradiction, like the living dead, Beloved and Not-Beloved.

When I write of what 'we' feel, this is a fictional identification, hoping that it may evoke something of what other readers have felt.

Whether it does so or not, what else do I have to call on except the surprises, mistakes, pleasures, that the text worked on me at a first reading? Any 'reading' of an imaginative narrative is gutted, that does not rest at some point on the dynamics of a first reading, how it seemed before 'we' knew it all, how it felt when we (historically, politically, generically determined) were finding out.

The restoration of her daughter to Sethe is a fantasy, embodied. If we move beyond Sethe's own remorse and desire, it is obvious that the uncannily revived daughter whose throat the mother cut to save her from slavery will have at least as much antagonism to, as desire for, her mother. Most movingly, it is only late in the text that we have access to the full consciousness of the living daughter, Denver, who has also desired this impossible restoration to life of her sister. That equal desire puts her in a different position from her mother in relation to the beloved. It is late in the text that we learn that, although Sethe's maternal love is equally towards her living daughter, that daughter is mortally afraid of her mother, since she has drunk in her sister's blood with her mother's milk. She has always been afraid that her mother could kill her too. 'First cut is the deepest', into the imagination as into the flesh. This is a text that does not disregard the imagination, or the flesh, or history.

So the lovely skating party of Sethe, Denver and the one they love, which includes a reader in its exhilarating satisfaction of desire, is threatened not only by the observer which it attempts to exclude ('Nobody saw them fall'), but also from within, by the differences of their desires, especially those of Denver. It is also threatened by what Stamp Paid, a male observer, can hear. We may at first feel that as a man he's simply got it wrong, but he is able to 'hear' the surrounding voices of the 'angry dead', and it is true that Beloved belongs to the dead as much as to the living (pp. 169, 172). The skating party as a kind of icon, an emblem of ecstasy between sisters and mothers and daughters, is simultaneously fractured from without and from within.

Whatever else she is, Beloved stands for all those who suffered under slavery and did not survive. In the long psychic and historical regression of this novel, the story of Margaret Garner and her daughter, recorded in *The American Baptist* in 1856,[13] is no more than the last recoverable individual story. For all her obsessive desire for her mother, an absolute and mutually destructive desire such as is appropriate for a revenant who *really* lived only as a child of no more than two years, Beloved also desires her father. Denver's desire for her sister is in reality her desire for the return of her father also. *Beloved* tells more than one story, patiently and lovingly releasing possibilities for recovering memories which can be pieced together to make some sort of a history: Paul D. Garner's story as well as Sethe's, together with the difficulties they have in telling even each other. It is not simply a matter of remembering, but a painful labour of research and recovery and communication. *Beloved* acknowledges stories which are beyond recovery: 'Sixty million' (another epigraph) 'and more', exceeding calculation and imagination – unnarratable and undramatised pain. The story of Halle Garner, the father and the man Sethe loved, is always promised within *Beloved*, but it is the story which can never be told, the story of those women and men who did not escape or survive, who suffered the worst beyond what can be recalled. The literary form of tragedy offers a significant, a human, death; the appalling deaths, beyond tragedy, are those which are rendered insignificant: no closing speech of defiance and affirmation.

'It was not a story to pass on / This is not a story to pass on' – that statement rings three times through the epilogue or coda to *Beloved* (pp. 274–5). It is ambiguous: it could mean something you should not *pass* on, as in a game of chance. The main meaning, however, I take to be 'something that should not be preserved by communicating it', and I want to develop some implications of that. The strong and enduring Sethe becomes a hysteric, the woman overcome by what she remembers but can't face. Her obsession is powerful enough to colour the atmosphere and impose itself on others. In this light, Beloved is her symptom – a physical manifestation of her desire that the infanticide should not have happened or can be redeemed. In the language of the women of this Black neighbourhood on the edge of Cincinnati, her 'devil-child'. This fantasy remains as if unconscious, an uncanny haunting, until Paul D. comes by, one of the brotherhood of slaves on the plantation, Sweet Home, Kentucky – symbolically a return of the father, the nearest to Halle that the novel gets. Until this point Sethe has been stoical, not helpless in the grip of her emotions. One of the reasons why white women have responded so enthusiastically to writing by Black women is because it so often offers such uncompromising identifications with women who are tough and enduring, often humorous. As an hysteric Sethe massively subverts the identification she had seemed to offer. In her desire to be forgiven by her dead daughter, she shrinks.

The final achievement of a loving and supportive relation between Sethe and Paul D. releases Denver to education and employment in the cities with which her name identifies her (one
comparison might be with the child Anna in D. H. Lawrence's *The
Rainbow*, who is freed from supporting one or the other parent by the
achievement of sexual equilibrium between her mother and stepfa-
ther). In contrast to Son's attitude to Jade/Jadine in *Tar Baby*, Paul D.
holds his peace about Denver's opportunities, albeit uneasily. *Beloved*
is the first of Morrison's novels to end with a heterosexual relationship
promising a better future – offering the man an alternative identity
to that of the wanderer who leaves women to bear the burden of
children and therefore of cultural transmission. On this reading, to
always hark back to the story of suffering is something that has to be
abandoned if individual and historical life is to continue, to progress.
Nevertheless, the last word of the text is still that yearning and
recalcitrant 'Beloved'.

'It was not a story to pass on.' At the end of *Beloved* the shed where
Sethe cut Beloved's throat is locked: 'Where the memory of the smile
under her chin might have been and was not, a latch latched and
lichen attached its apple-green bloom to the metal. What made her
think her fingernails could open locks the rain rained on?' (p. 275).
This is not the baby's smile in the photograph album which mother
and daughter delight in looking back on together: Beloved's 'smile'
was under her chin, where her throat was cut. The scar signifies her
mother's will to free her, which she never ceases to resent. I want to
appeal here to Toni Morrison's 1974 account of her response to the
story of Margaret Garner, which she found during her editorial
work for Random House on *The Black Book*, a collection of memo-
rabilia from the seventeenth to the nineteenth centuries: this and
other such records produced a despair too deep for passion or tears,
she writes.[14] A trauma, or wound, on which she was, nevertheless, to
work for more than a decade. In the 1856 account, 'A Visit to the
Slave Mother Who Killed Her Child',[15] emphasis is laid on the ra-
tionality of the mother: asked if she had been 'excited almost to
madness when she committed the act', she replied 'I was as cool as
I now am', but preferred to end the sufferings of her children rather
than 'have them taken back to slavery, and be murdered by piece-
meal'. The story is told as propaganda, to make a point; possibly it
may have been no more than propaganda (the scandal then would
be that the land of liberty needed such propaganda against slavery).

It is not until late in the novel that we come to a point when 'how it must have been' can be imagined, and it is not until Stamp Paid has tried and failed to tell it to Paul D. as something more than a newspaper sensation, that Sethe can retell the story herself:

> So Stamp Paid did not tell him how she flew, snatching up her children like a hawk on the wing; how her face beaked, how her hands worked like claws, how she collected them every which way: one on her shoulder, one under her arm, one by the hand, the other shouted forward into the woodshed filled with just sunlight and shavings now . . . . (p. 157)

> Sethe knew that the circle she was making around the room, him, the subject, would remain one. That she would never close in, pin it down for anybody who had to ask. If they didn't get it right off – she could never explain. Because the truth was simple, not a long-drawn-out record. . . . Simple: she was squatting in the garden and when she saw them coming and recognized school-teacher's hat, she heard wings. And if she thought anything it was No. No. Nono. Nonono. Simple. She just flew. Collected every bit of life she had made, all the parts of her that were precious and fine and beautiful, and carried, pushed, dragged them through the veil, out, away, over there where no one could hurt them. Over there. Outside this place, where they would be safe. And the hummingbird wings beat on. (p. 163)

When Sethe tells her story Paul D. leaves her, sharing the local community's rejection of this mother who is not a mother, not nurturing, because the system in which she existed had imposed a more terrible kind of responsibility on her, though not one Toni Morrison can imagine her performing in cold blood. Isolated with her daughters, mad, Sethe is locked in an impossible attempt to atone, locked in repetition which reaches its crisis when the white man again invades her place, comes into her yard – although this time she directs her attack on him not her child – even though *this* white man is one who 'never turned us down' (p. 265).

It's one of the text's bitter months, when white abolitionists are said to just hate slavery more than they hated black people (p. 137) – a judgement on liberal 'principle' as opposed to the total love of Baby Sugg's sermon, which calls on a love of self totally identified with other Blacks, produced by white hatred (p. 88). At that final, cathartic re-enactment of Sethe's original violence, the women of the community have already gathered to the aid of those *they* have outcast, to rescue Sethe and Denver from enclosure within a private emotional world. Perhaps their mass action has somehow magically summoned up the re-enacting which puts an end to the repetition of the story: certainly they redeem themselves as well as Sethe, by acting in the spirit of the holy woman, Sethe's mother-in-law Baby Suggs, whom they had envied as too proud and lucky. They live up to her wonderful sermon, to love themselves and their own. Their role here needs to be contrasted to the climax of *Dessa Rose*, where it is a white woman who rescues the black heroine.

'It was not a story to pass *on* / This is not a story to *pass* on.' The 'South Bank Show' on BBC TV in 1988 when Toni Morrison was interviewed about *Beloved* seemed to me a fine vindication of how popular media can address literature. Toni Morrison spoke for the value of poetic language, operating between the general investigations of historical research and popular culture. Her point was to 'place' her work on *Beloved*. On the one hand, she said, she could find historical accounts of the slave trade and slavery which gave her not only numbers but information about objects – instruments of punishment and torture, that somebody designed, like the iron bit placed under the tongue. On the other hand, there was Black oral culture, its stories and songs – of mourning, defiance and delight – but these did not tell of the appalling things recorded in the history books. Her novel attempts to inhabit that silence. Between the extremes of 'the objective' (the historical or sociological) and communal subjectivity, she made her massive and imperative claim for *Beloved* as one instance of the work of the imagination, the only discourse that could operate between those other discourses, to make those who are outside go through what it was like to live with those things, or at least the memory, the record, of them.

Morrison's novel and Williams's *Dessa Rose* are elements in a rethinking of Afro-American history, which derives from the celebration in the late 1970s and early 1980s of the Bill of Rights and the American Constitution, reviving discussion of just who was and may now be considered free and equal. Hazel Carby in *Reconstructing Womanhood* is right to question approaches which focus too much on ideal retrospection, celebrating 'the black people' as the folk of the rural south, while ignoring the problem for Black intellectuals of how they can be said to represent the urban working class in the north.[16] Toni Morrison was born a northerner in the 1940s, in Lorain,

Ohio, like Claudia, the narrator of her first novel, *The Bluest Eye (1970)*;[17] but when her narratives travel south into myth and history, and retrace the emigration north and west of Blacks in search of work, there are political reasons for wanting to do so, in terms of this contemporary discussion of the place of Afro-Americans in America's history and future. These political investments in accounts of history, and the demand on writers to 'represent' their people, produce totalisations: *the* Black experience, *the* Black community – identities from which claims can be made; but which also cover over differences and make for coercive judgements like Sondra O'Neale's.[18] A term such as 'the Black community' becomes purely discursive, transcending any particular person or neighbourhood, and as a concept it is available to discipline individuals. This is the problem which Morrison counters when she refuses to represent 'the Black community' as an object under observation, an entity defined by its outside – which as such an object might feel impelled to conceal its internal differences, between women and men, between different localities, between different generations.

Tar Baby is a significant precursor of *Beloved* for the degree to which it opens up divisions which *Beloved* seeks to heal. My early quotations made *Tar Baby* sound less questioning than it really is: the judgements I quoted earlier, On those not 'wholly and naturally' Black, are themselves judged in relation to other possibilities. Though I thought at first it was too close for comfort to the vertigo of Morrison's New York journalism (the vertigo which she says racist social relations induce in her) it is formally brilliant in its crossings over of positions. Its argument takes the form of the rhetorical figure *chiasmus*), or what Morrison called 'slap and embrace'. Interestingly it is the older generation who become more self-assertive, while the younger pair come together but end essentially where they were. Although the end leaves the 'culture-bearing black woman' Jadine and Son the 'mama-spoiled black man' divided, the effect is to call their division in question. Feminist critics have idealised the three-woman households which occur in all Morrison's novels except *Tar Baby*; but they are increasingly subject to a criticism: that social relations which exclude men are unbalanced, which *Beloved* brings to a head. Commitment to all Black people, women and men, transcends feminism.

Morrison's first two novels were woman-centred, but also concerned with 'who the black community respected, and what they considered an outlaw'.[19] Sula, in the second novel, is rejected partly because she will not care for her grandmother but puts her in a home. In contrast, the grandmother who had once saved her son's life takes back that life when she sees him destroying himself with drugs; trying to crawl back into her womb, she calls it. She sets fire to him – a murder which prefigures the extreme paradox of infanticide as ethical responsibility in *Beloved*. I would explain this immense challenge as the most radical break Morrison makes in feminist thinking. Motherhood is more usually represented in terms of nurturing the infant and child; and from the point of view of the child, its most immediate needs and demands and defiances, which the mother must serve and survive. Morrison, like Kristeva, thinks beyond infancy; motherhood is a model of 'her-ethical' responsibility, because it ultimately (and indeed from the moment of birth) involves letting go, as well as a nurturing embrace and containment. Of course it does; but this is very rarely represented except in terms of the mother who can't let go.

Eva Peace, Sula's grandmother, commits an exemplary crime which, like Sethe's, is offered symbolically as a challenge to thought, not as something easily to be judged. They kill because they care for the fully human, responsible freedom of the young. Sula is culpable because she is incapable of caring. In *The Bluest Eye*, the self-hating Breedlove family had been the outcasts, especially the abused child-victim Pecola. Sula is the outcast as rebel – whose refusal to be the carer could be read positively, from a feminist point of view, since too many women's lives are crippled, across the world, by lack of community provision for care. Such outlaws and outcasts, rebels and victims, define 'community' precisely because they mark the boundaries of what is 'inside' or 'outside'. Morrison celebrates communities; she also celebrates accepting love of the different one, the one on the edge, who lets 'us' know who we are, whether this marginal and limiting case is victim or rebel, or a writer who breaks ranks through a more difficult sense of responsibility. Sula and her girlhood friend Nel are opposed types: the reckless and the respectable woman (akin to Milkman Dead and Guitar in *Song of Solomon*). It is the triumph of these novels that Nel and Sula, Milkman and Guitar, are ultimately together – in spite of and because of their differences.

'Woman' is the only one of the identities that Morrison is stitching together (and unpicking) in her writing. From a white feminist's point of view, this has been a major specific role of Black women writers. They have stood in the way of totalising a female identity – precisely because it would have been scandalous for them not to be

at least as much concerned with their identity as Blacks. It is true
that, with some exceptions, the women's suffrage movement in the
States was racist – hence Black suspicion of feminism (just as in
England there was class bias in the argument: why should working
men have the vote when *we* do not?). Obviously there are many
different identities for women. An identity as white can be something
'we' don't need to consider, and at another moment, something we
might like to disavow: the kind of disavowal I experienced when
reading 'What the Black Woman thinks about Women's Lib'. 'I'm
not that' – a political moment of self-definition, by negation; having
to take up a position on what almost everything lets me take for
granted. Affirmation of an identity depends on what it is not; a
difference is taken for an identity. By the same token, identities are
not single and immutable. Though Black, white, female, male are the
identities most likely to seem beyond choice, the full acceptance of
such identities, and what that can mean, what other identifications
can be combined, is a matter for decision.

   'Love your hands: they do not love them' (*Beloved*, p. 88): in Baby
Suggs's sermon communal self-love is produced by antagonism; the
community is defined by what it is not. It is significant that in both
Beloved and *Dessa Rose* rebellion is triggered by awareness of being
made 'other than human', an object for investigation by whites.
Sherley Anne Williams's novel combines two historical records, one
of a woman who helped lead an uprising with one of a white woman
who gave sanctuary to slaves, so that the white woman has a far
larger part in the story than in Morrison's novel. The resolution of
Dessa Rose is concerned not with reconciliation within a Black community or between a Black woman and man, but with the possible
friendship of Black and white women. A friendship, however, born
and continuing in antagonism, like that of siblings. There *is* a white
girl who helps Sethe in *Beloved* – a poor white, and feckless as Ruth
Elizabeth is in *Dessa Rose*. She plays a much smaller role; however,
Denver is named after her. The point I want to make is about naming.
Naming, and calling someone out of their name, is important as a
mark of recognition or insult (travestying identity, refusing participation in humanity) in both these books: Dessa insults Ruth Elizabeth by calling her Miz Ruint – later she stiffly calls her Miz Lady;
Ruth Elizabeth ultimately lays claim to being called 'friend', furious
with her Black co-conspirators for a wary politeness which excludes
friendship, fobbing her off with phrases like 'it's not my place'. But
the name she has been called by her Black nurse, the 'Mammy' she

disputes with Dessa, is the name by which she is identified in the narrative, and that is Rufel (rueful!). The first name of the white girl in *Beloved* is Amy – that is, Beloved: Aimée, in another language.

The title of *Beloved* signifies an absence in the wording on the headstone of the dead child's grave. It should be 'Dearly Beloved' – the mother could not afford to pay for the whole. 'Dearly Beloved' however is not an intimate endearment but a timeworn address to a Christian community, and therefore to many different communities (Sethe has heard the words at the funeral service). Moreover, the novel shows the beloved to be 'dear' to her mother and her sister in a bitterly ironic sense. It is concerned with antagonism *within* the most intensely loving relationships – and with a double imperative: that personal lives should not exclude responsibility to a community and that communities should think twice and again about whom they exclude. In discussing *Beloved* I find myself making gestures of embrace, to explain how I respond to its form and arguments: nursing and cradling and containing movements, but also openings out from that circle, births, letting go; and letting in, recollection, an embrace that understands the need to go out yet again.

Morrison's art, the complex and sensitive multiplicity of her language, shows that many changing self-definitions and commitments are possible and do not necessarily entail treachery, fragmentation, impotent confusion, but can produce harmony and happiness actively. A crime such as infanticide is a crime entailing terrible remorse, but Morrison uses it to symbolise the difficulties of asserting humanity; personal love together with responsibility to a community. Understanding takes time and imaginative intelligence, as reading *Beloved* shows wonderfully. Her writing represents many possible positions for Black people and for women, divided within and without by different calls on their allegiance. She resists being swallowed up by those with whom she nevertheless identifies, and shows that this is the opposite of irresponsible. We could just as well fill in the absence in the title, 'Dearly Beloved', from the epigraph: 'Not Beloved'. With its promise of affirmation recoiling from negativity: 'I will call them my people, which were not my people; and her beloved, which was not beloved'.

NOTES

* I should like to acknowledge my indebtedness in revising this paper to discussions with Sally Keenan, Jim Philip, Richard Gray and Paul Gilroy. The way I have thought about identity and difference in Morrison's writing was formed by a seminar paper by Slavoj Zizek, now incorporated in *The Sublime Object of Ideology* (London: Verso, 1989).

1. Paul Gilroy, 'Living Memory', an interview with Toni Morrison, *City Limits* (London), 31 March–7 April 1988.
2. Book of Hosea, chs 1 and 2; see also the remarks on Romans and Hosea in Peake's *Commentary on the Bible*; and on Hosea in G. W. Anderson, *A Critical Introduction to the Old Testament* (London: Duckworth, 1979).
3. Toni Morrison, *Beloved* (US: 1987; London: Picador 1988); Sherley Anne Williams, *Dessa Rose* (US: 1986: London: Macmillan, 1987).
4. B. Omolade, 'Hearts of Darkness', in A. Snitow, C. Stansell and S. Thompson (eds), *Desire: The Politics of Sexuality* (US: 1983; London: Virago, 1984) p. 375.
5. Toni Morrison, *Song of Solomon* (New York: 1979; London: Triad Grafton, 1980).
6. Toni Morrison, 'Rediscovering Black History', *New York Times Magazine*, 11 August 1974.
7. Toni Morrison, 'A Slow Walk of Trees . . .', *New York Times Magazine*, 4 July 1976.
8. Toni Morrison, *Tar Baby* (London: Triad Grafton, 1981).
9. Pauline Hopkins, *Of One Blood* (1902–3; quoted in H. Carby, *Reconstructing Womanhood: The Emergence of the Afro-American Woman Novelist* (Oxford: Oxford University Press, 1987).
10. S. O'Neale, 'Inhibiting Midwives/Usurping Creators: the Struggling Emergence of Black Women in American Fiction', in T. de Lauretis (ed.), *Feminist Studies/Critical Studies* (US: 1986; London: Macmillan, 1988).
11. Toni Morrison, 'What the Black Woman Thinks about Women's Lib', *New York Times Magazine*, 22 August 1971.
12. Morrison, 'Living Memory'.
13. Quoted in Morrison, 'Rediscovering Black History'.
14. Ibid.
15. 'A Visit to a Slave Mother who Killed her Child', quoted ibid.
16. Carby, *Reconstructing Womanhood*. An excellent study, which should be consulted along with Susan Willis, 'Eruptions of Funk: Historicising Toni Morrison', in H. Carby (ed.), *Specifying: Black Women Writing the American Experience* (Madison, Wis.: University of Wisconsin Press, 1987) ch. 4; originally in *Black American Literature Forum*, vol. 16 (Spring 1982); reprinted in H. L. Gates Jr (ed.), *Black Literature and Literary Theory* (London: Methuen, 1984).
17. Toni Morrison, *The Bluest Eye* (US: 1970; London: Panther, 1981).
18. O'Neale, 'Inhibiting Midwives/Usurping Creators'.
19. Diana Cooper-Clark, *Interviews with Contemporary Novelists* (London: Macmillan, 1986). See also Toni Morrison, 'Rootedness: the Ancestor as Foundation', in M. Evans (ed.), *Black Women Writers* (London: Pluto Press, 1985).

8

Autobiography: The Art of Self-Definition

EVA LENNOX BIRCH

This essay arises out of my teaching on a course on Women's Writing offered as an optional special study to third-year undergraduates at Manchester Polytechnic. The initial focus of the course is on autobiography, in the belief that this genre facilitates discussion of some issues we think are seminal to our appraisal of women's writing. The autobiographies chosen were by twentieth-century women writers, whose historical placing and cultural setting separated them. Texts included Zora Neale Hurston's *Dust Tracks on a Road*[1] and Buchi Emecheta's *Head Above Water*.[2] The issues raised, and which will be addressed in this essay, were: (a) Do women's autobiographies have pre-occupations that are particular to all women? (b) How does racial awareness shape self-definition? (c) How does this relate to the writer's concept of class? (d) What conclusions could be drawn about gender socialisation? (e) How did we relate to the issues raised? (f) How did we evaluate the texts as literature?

It might be assumed that as women in a privileged academic situation we had little in common with a Black American who emerged from the Harlem Renaissance of the 1920s, and a Nigerian woman whose position in British society was implicitly that of an outsider. Furthermore, the seminar group included women whose ages ranged from 20 to 60. Yet we learned much of value from our study. Despite the differences between our own and the autobiographers' social and cultural backgrounds, we found ourselves nodding in agreement and recognition at the articulation of experience we shared as women, irrespective of colour. A published life-writing by a woman who is writing in her own right, rather than as a female relative of a famous man, is doubly welcomed as successful invasion of a hitherto male preserve. To provide a theoretical base for our reading of these texts, we consulted Stephen Butterfield's work,

Black Autobiography in America,[3] and the essays edited by Estelle Jelinek on women's autobiography,[4] against whose theories we read our selected texts. Within the tradition of Black American literature, Butterfield stresses the importance of the autobiographical statement which originated in the slave narratives. These accounts collectively stand as testimonials of the inhumanity of the slave system and are distinguished by a social rather than a personal impulse, on the assumption that what was true of one slave was true of all. Hence Butterfield said that the Black autobiographer is not an individual with a private career, but a soldier in a long historic march towards Canaan. The self is conceived as a member of an oppressed social group, with ties and responsibilities to the other members'.[5] He identifies the dominant voice in Black autobiography as that of the 'mass', exemplified in the works of the male autobiographers whose texts are discussed in individual chapters. Significantly fewer in number are the published autobiographies by Black women, with whom he deals collectively in one chapter, in which he comments that they were forging their own separate tradition in this genre. This is where we can locate Hurston, for her autobiography is so blatant a celebration of the self as unique, is such an overt denial of her position as soldier in the struggle for racial equality, that even her admirer Alice Walker describes *Dust Tracks on a Road* as 'the most unfortunate' thing she ever wrote.[6] The disparity between the freshness and the originality of her other writing and the evasive ambivalence of this text cannot be explained simply as evidence of a failing talent. It is more feasible, however, that the irritating circumspection of the work springs from a struggle at self-definition in a society that had already labelled her as 'Black'. Hurston's lifewriting is not in the male tradition identified by Butterfield, one framed to arouse anger and indignation as a spur to collective action. Instead, she writes in a tradition associated increasingly with Black women autobiographers; one that draws form and tone from the oral tradition of the Blues, a mode associated with self-expression and discovery. Experiential reality in the Blues is subjective, allowing the singer to meander a road and record the emotional tensions of the journey. Clearly, Hurston's autobiography, the very title of which embodies a vision of life as a journey, is in this tradition, and the tracks made in the dust are unique to herself.

Her resistance to a definition of self based on race supports Gerda Lerner's comment in *The Female Experience* that

The periods in which basic changes occur in society and which historians commonly regard as turning points are not necessarily the same for men and women. . . . The traditional political and military chronology is largely irrelevant to the history of women.[7]

In her introduction to *Women's Autobiography*, Jelinek attempts to identify differences in method and content that distinguish male from female autobiography. She claims that those by men tend to be success stories charting professional and intellectual progress, in which family is diminished in importance, whereas those by women maintain a balance in concern for family and career. She adds that men tend to heroicise their lives, whilst women wish to examine experience to extract understanding and meaning. Our reading of these texts did not fully vindicate these comments, and we wondered if this could be evidence of a difference between Black and White autobiographies. Support for this assumption is found in Butterfield's comment that 'Black writers offer a model of the self which is different from white models, created in response to a different perception of history and revealing divergent, often completely opposite meanings to human actions'.[8]

The perception of history shared by Hurston and Emecheta was one of political oppression. Hurston's self-definition was shaped by her people's American enslavement, Emecheta's by British imperialism in Africa. Hurston was positioned inside a society whose values excluded her, Emecheta within a tribal community during childhood that was largely unaffected by White intrusion, until she won a scholarship to the Methodist High School in Lagos. Although these writers were born into culturally different communities, historical accident meant for both a cultural displacement. Hurston was born in a unique all-Negro town in which she exhibits great pride; but there is an uneasy tension in her assertion that White Maitland and Black Eatonville lived side by side in perfect harmony, for she never addresses why such separation was deemed necessary. Similarly the reader is aware of the cultural rape that occurred every time Emecheta was given a bad mark, or fined whenever she spoke in her own Ibo language at school. Neither writer dwells on cultural oppression but awareness might account for Hurston's reference to the Harlem Renaissance as 'so-called', as she was aware of White appropriation of this movement, and Emecheta's reference to 'so-called Western education' and that was a benefit of the 'so-called civilised world'. Scholastic achievement gave Emecheta admittance to a world from which her parents were excluded, but she remarks of her people that this did not take into account that 'in communal caring and mutual sharing, and language and gestures and music-making, they are unsurpassable in sheer sophistication'.[9]

Clearly, both writers feel the need to defend their own cultural heritage. Hurston's anthropological research focused on the collection and preserving of the rich oral folklore of her people in America, which she subtly weaves into everything she writes. Similarly Emecheta stresses her rich Ibo culture, of which the women are the keepers. Both had to make the difficult transcription into the written tradition of the dominant culture. In so doing, Hurston 'aimed to show what Beauty and appeal there was in *genuine* Negro material',[10] and Emecheta remarks that life in England meant she had to write, despite the fact 'All I ever wanted was to tell my stories from my own home, just like my mother Nwakaluzo used to tell her stories in her very own compound with her back leaning against the ukwa tree'.[11]

Although both writers have an African cultural identity, Emecheta took for granted what Hurston was bent upon preserving. Hurston's writing embodies Black American delight in word-play and story-telling that was part of rural Black life. The living reality of such culture in Emecheta's African homeland shows that there the power of the word is vested in a woman, a tribal 'Aunt' who sat and 'studied her stick, lying between her legs like a rod of life'.[12] The phallic rod is here transformed and given to a woman. It is interesting to note that in their enslavement in America the African women seem to have surrendered this power to the men, for in Hurston's writing it is men who figure most prominently as the spell-binders on Joe Clark's porch.

The importance of understanding the cultural roots of an autobiographer was the first lesson we learned in our study. It was fatuous to assume that because both writers were Black they would perceive life in a similar way. Their experience of being Black and female was initially shaped by where they stood in relation to the society within whose culture they were operating. In spite of Hurston's denial of feelings of inferiority to Whites, her father's reminder that 'You ain't white' (p. 38), and his warnings that her ambitions were such that 'The white folks were not going to stand for it' (p. 21) reflect the reality of racial politics. The oppression was real, pervasive and violent, in a country where a child could be threatened even in jest with a 'posse'. In Emecheta's childhood world, British power was absolute and the United Kingdom was envisaged as the Kingdom of Heaven. She heard that the ways of white people were strange, but within her tribal community she was protected from their perversity. Only when she came to England and confronted 'Sorry no Coloured' signs in her search for accommodation was racial discrimination a reality for her. Although she and her children have established themselves firmly in England, she refers to Nigeria as 'home' and views British society from the outside, safe in the knowledge of her racial identity. The various jobs she took to support her children and her writing she describes as 'affording me the kind of opportunity I needed to see at first hand the way many of my own race and people lived' (p. 169). She defines herself as observer, a watcher, inherently protected from a racism from which her African upbringing had distanced her. Hurston was less fortunate. Her devaluation by the society into which she was born must have occasioned her the same sense of hurt as that felt by the British children of West Indian parents, described by Emecheta in the 'Seventies' youth club.

Hurston and Emecheta had family histories that inculcated in them very different senses of responsibility. In Hurston's case this was diminished by the untimely death of her mother and the consequent dispersion of the eight Hurston children. She gives little space to her siblings. We learn of one brother who exploited her as a domestic drudge, and a favoured sister whose expulsion from the family home on her father's early remarriage is dismissed in a seemingly offhand way: 'So Sarah just married and went down on the Manater River to live. She took Everett with her. She probably left more behind her than she took away.'[13] The terse restraint of this statement is at variance with Hurston's normal ebullience and suggests an understated pain. Throughout *Dust Tracks* there are other equally distressing episodes in her life that she passes over with 'Too much went on to take the task of telling it' (p. 113). This is no disguise for a pain she carries with her on her single journey through life. The reader senses a deep loneliness in this writer who regards the admission of hurt as a sign of weakness, and perhaps explains why contemporaries thought of her as possessing an overbearing desire for self-aggrandisement. She certainly accepts responsibility for no person or thing beyond herself. Emecheta, on the other hand, never suffered such a similar severance from her own family, with whom contact was maintained in spite of the thousands of miles that separated her from them. The ties of kinship stretched across conti-

nents when the family gathered in London to discuss the estrange-
ment in her marriage. An ill-fated reconciliation was made with the
announcement '*Our* wife has forgiven her husband.'[14] The reluctant
Emecheta had bowed in this arrangement to the weight of a cultural
pressure she could not ignore. She summed up her sense of familial
responsibility in an interview she gave in America in 1985:

> In the West, educated women are free and only have themselves
> to look after. In my country your responsibility increases with
> your education and wealth. An educated woman has a responsi-
> bility to her own family, her husband and even her own children,
> who are normally supported by her husband. If I earn a lot of
> money, I also pay for the education of children who do not form
> part of my immediate family.[15]

Such an extended sense of responsibility was never felt by the childless Hurston.

The cultural divide between these writers is echoed in their
autobiographic impulse. More than once Emecheta confesses that
the exercise was therapeutic, 'Writing can be therapeutic and autobiographical writing even more so, as it offers a kaleidoscopic view
of life' (p. 3). She imposes order and logic on to her memories, that
are arranged into chronological episodes, in which she exposes painful
emotions. It is possible that *Head Above Water* provided a release for
Emecheta from the anguish she felt on the death of her daughter, to
whose memory the book is dedicated, Hurston's autobiography was
undertaken for very different reasons. She was impoverished, out of
favour and fashion as a writer, and was trying to capitalise on her
previous reputation. She was a reluctant autobiographer; this may
account for the ambivalence of the tone and her hesitancy to expose
her emotional life. Where Emecheta invites the reader into her
emotional world, Hurston draws a veil. Yet both women began their
careers as writers as the direct result of academic research. Hurston's
anthropological work involved collecting Black oral folk-tales that
she published with the encouragement of her professor as *Mules and
Men*.[16] Similarly Emecheta was persuaded to put her research into a
novel 'instead of a research piece which would be read by just a
handful of academics.'[17] Established success as novelists enabled them
to anticipate a receptive readership for their life-writing.

The question of perceived readership opened up some interesting
issues. Do women autobiographers write for other women? Do Black

women write for Black women? In Hurston's case, it became evident that her work was directed towards a white public on whose patronage she depended. Explanatory footnotes decipher for white readers Black idiomatic language; 'That is a Negro saying that means . . .' (p. 38); 'The word nigger in this sense does not mean . . .' (p. 41). Describing her research methods she says, 'We held two lying contests, story-telling to *you*' (p. 189, my emphasis). Awareness of White opinion and the power of the publishers produce an irritating circumspection. We know that the published version of *Dust Tracks* was sanitised for publication by the removal of her outspoken comments on American imperialistic ambitions. Pearl Harbor would have rendered these unpalatable though no less true. She was undoubtedly hemmed in by a fear of rejection by those in whose economic power she was held. There is a pathetic plea for acceptance in the final paragraph where she offers 'you all my right hand of fellowship and love, and hope for the same from you. In my eyesight, you lose nothing by not looking just like me' (p. 286). In spite of the attempt at a wryly humourous inversion of racist attitudes in this statement, we know her hand was offered to a white readership. No such need for circumspection is found in Emecheta's text. Indeed she confesses amazement that anyone should want to hear the outpourings of a woman who 'put down all my woes. I must say that many a time I convinced myself that nobody was going to read them anyway, so I put down the whole truth, my truths as I saw them' (p. 62).

Whereas Emecheta willingly accepted editorial help in the preparation of her first novel, Hurston was subject to editorial censorship. Emecheta admits to hounding publishers she considered tardy in progressing publication of her work, but Hurston trod carefully to avoid giving offence. The power of the publishers is openly discussed by Emecheta as an irritation, but is only implicitly expressed by Hurston in her guarded ambivalence. We concluded that in avowedly writing for and out of herself, Emecheta recreated a female experience that was recognisable by women irrespective of their colour.

The envisaged therapeutic benefits of autobiography are fulfilled in the assuaging of Emecheta's guilt about a mother who regarded her ambitious daughter as 'difficult'. She dismisses the rumour of her mother's dying curse with the comforting thought that if she did not understand the 'untalked-of agonies' of that 'laughing and doubly culturally-enslaved woman who gave me life, who else is there on this earth who will take the trouble to?' (p. 5). A similar guilt was engendered in Hurston when as a nine year old she was unable to carry out her mother's dying wishes, and blamed herself. She was 'to agonise over that moment for years to come' (p. 88), and the palpable sense of guilty was not diminished in the telling of it. Both writers exhibit a concern to establish a relationship with their dead mothers and give accounts of how their mothers had given birth to them, as retailed to them in hearsay from either the mother or aunts. Emecheta's birth was welcomed in the belief that she had 'cleared the way' for a boy, whilst Hurston's father seemed indifferent to the birth of yet another child. It was to her mother's urgings to 'jump at the sun' that Hurston listened, rather than her father's less sanguine comments that smacked of an acceptance of white supremacy, similar to Emecheta's father's worship of Whites. Indeed the acknowledged influence of these writers' mothers refuted Jelinek's assertion that female autobiographers generally stress their fathers as shaping forces in their development. We considered whether or not the fracturing of family that occurred during slavery, and the supposed establishment of Afro-American matriarchy identified in the Moynihan Report, influenced the depiction of Hurston's mother. We concluded that if Moynihan's analysis of Black American society was correct, then the matriarchy was a powerless one. Hurston's mother, isolated from parents who thought she had married beneath her, led a life of toil, while her handsome, charismatic, philandering husband pursued his own interests. Her mother's pattern of isolation is a perversion of the supportive network of females, accorded the title of 'Mother' described by Emecheta, who says that for the details of her own birth 'I had to rely on the different versions told to me by my mothers' (p. 6). Possibly the envisaged matriarchy of Moynihan was simply evidence of a cultural time-warp, which allowed Afro-Americans to preserve a sense of communal mothering in spite of their cultural dislocation. A dislocation of a similar kind was experienced by Emecheta, whose self-definition as a single parent would not have applied had she lived in her tribal compound, where such a concept was meaningless.

Clearly, another concept new to Emecheta was the Western one of class that had no relevance in her childhood community, where hierarchical authority was vested in the elders. Life in England was soon to alert her to the rigid social stratification that labelled her as a second-class citizen because she was a Black single parent with little money. Living in 'The Ditch', as she described life in London, entailed community with impoverished Whites, whose roughness and ignorance would have shocked her Ibo relatives, but with whom she formed friendships founded on a shared experience of poverty that was grim for 'all Adahs, white or black' (p. 110). The poverty trap is one that any woman 'black or white, with many children would find herself in unless she came from rich parents or her husband supported her' (p. 95). Although African life had taught her that the British presumed a superiority, she was unaware that her colour would be a social determinant of such a magnitude in England, where she realised that 'our colour which we had hitherto regarded as natural was repulsive to others and posed a problem' (p. 32). For Hurston this was no surprise, who as a child was warned by a white man not to be a nigger. A footnote explains that 'The word Nigger used in this sense does not mean race. It means a weak, contemptible person of any race' (p. 41). Why Hurston does not question the obvious racism in this advice is difficult to comprehend and it would be easy to attribute this to a time-serving servility, if it was not denied by articles she wrote for the Black press on such things as the Jim Crow laws. The placatory tone of *Dust Tracks* is explicable only as a measure of her fear of white publishers, who could silence and further impoverish her and 'There is something about poverty that smells like death' (p. 116). Her constant companion was a poverty only relieved by the patronage of rich Whites. This is matched by Emecheta's, whose financial struggle was to keep her head above water as 'the breadwinner, the mother, the father, the counsellor, the comforter' (p. 167) to her five children.

To climb out of second-class citizenship, both women took a typical working-class view that an education would provide the needed ladder. Hurston was dependent on the patronage of white friends and employers to pay her tuition fees, so there might be some truth in the claims of some of her contemporaries that to do this, Hurston 'played the Darkie'. If so, it was a calculated survival strategy in her campaign to achieve the place in the sun advocated by her mother. However we glimpse a defiance of Whites in her pride in her academic progress: 'I did not resolve to be a grind, however, to show the white folks that I had brains. I took for granted that they knew that. Else why was I at Barnard?' (p. 171).

Academic honours meant a lot to Hurston who quoted the dictum of Booker T. Washington that people should be judged not by the height of their achievement but the depth of their starting point, thus implying that education brought with it an upward social mobility.

Hurston's education began in the Eatonville school with books do-
nated by white Maitland; Emecheta's as a scholarship girl in the
Lagos school where, significantly, Black teachers were employed
only as teachers of domestic subjects. There Emecheta encountered
the hostility of a white teacher of English who resented the
presumptuous ambition of the young Emecheta to be a writer. Yet
she became not only a writer but a graduate in sociology. Neither,
she tells us, was achieved without struggle. Success depended on
her mastery of the language of her imperialist educators, a fact of
existence she accepted just as she did the burden of motherhood. No
obstacle was insurmountable for a woman who says, 'One way to set
my mind on achieving something was for another person to tell me
that I could not do it' (p. 49). The juggling of time between domestic
chores and study is one familiar to mature married students and is
the inevitable consequence of a self-definition as a student. It is also
accompanied by a nagging guilt that time given to study has been
stolen from the husband and children, in relation to whom women
are traditionally defined. In my experience of teaching in an institution
of higher education, where mature students fill a significant number
of places, this sense of guilt is transformed into an anxiety about
performance. Married mothers tend to compensate for their perceived
defection from the home by being extra vigilant about home and
child-care. They certainly strive for high standards in their academic
studies. What they tend to miss out on, inevitably, is the social life
enjoyed by their younger, unattached fellow students. Above all,
these mature students have a formidable commitment to their study
and a determination to succeed, to make up for 'lost' time in their
youth. Emecheta's determination to graduate was strengthened by
naïve belief in the equation between an education and financial
security. In the event, improvement in her financial position rested
not on her degree but on her success as a writer. The same is true of
Hurston, whose recognition did not spring from her study of an-
thropology. For both, the acquisition of an education was regarded
with pride, as evidence of progress, described by Hurston as 'a long
step for a waif from Eatonville' (p. 172), echoed in Emecheta's 'I had
come a long way' (p. 76).

In their determination to find self-definition through education,
both were challenging stereotypical social expectations. As a poor
rural Black American woman, Hurston's life might have been one of
domestic service, whilst Emecheta's status as the mother of young
children normally meant confinement within the domestic sphere.

Both were born into cultures that defined them as potential wives and mothers. In particular, Emecheta's society only took a woman seriously when she became a mother, so her determination to come to England for further education was a complete break with traditional gender roles. Her life-goals, like Hurston's, were in defiance of her society's assumptions regarding gender, class and the intellectual capacities of Blacks. Hurston's anthropological research directed her towards disproving the self-justifying white myth of the intellectual inferiority of Blacks, and Emecheta's sociological training allowed her to analyse the social reasons underlying the deprivation of her people in England. On the education of Africans by colonials Emecheta says that it 'helped to perpetuate the myth that blacks are low in intelligence while they themselves made sure that the myth held true' (p. 145). In disproving this myth both suffered a social dislocation. As a young woman Hurston had fought her hated stepmother with primeval violence and certain relish, yet when doing fieldwork in the Florida lumber camps, her education, her car, her easy familiarity with the men alienated her from some of the women, one of whom tried to kill her. The jealousy generated by the disadvantaged who succeed in spite of oppression is summed up thus:

> What the educated Negro knows further is that he can do very little towards imposing his own viewpoint on the lowlier members of his race. Class and culture stand between. The humble Negro has a built-in antagonism to the 'Big Nigger'. It is a curious thing that he does not resent a white man looking down on him. But he resents any lines between himself and the wealthy and educated of his own race.

Any suggestion that the educated should offer themselves as new role-models to the uneducated is clearly not welcomed. Hurston's admission that her people were only human, and so harboured less-than-admirable emotions, is borne out by Emecheta's reception in her job as a social worker for which her degree in sociology had qualified her. Fired with noble enthusiasm to improve the aspirations of Afro-Caribbean youths in London, she is soon disillusioned, rejected and physically assaulted;

> I was not aware then that I stood for the very type of black image they felt emphasised their failures. They knew that blacks like me who could claim to have made it were a pain to the masses of

blacks who could never make it. They also knew that my type of black suffered from a kind of false consciousness. We think that we have been successful in achieving equality with white middle-class intellectuals because we say to ourselves, have we not been to their universities, have we not gone through the same degree of socialisation via the educational system?[19]

She learns that, although education had helped lift her out of the 'Ditch', it does not bring automatic inclusion into the white middle class. Significantly she talks of belonging to a Black middle class, implying a separate hierarchical structure.

In both texts, dominant white society is viewed from a Black perspective that produces discomfort in a White reader. Seminar students underwent an uneasy process of self-examination when confronted by the enormity of an inescapable racism that had contributed to the self-definition of these writers and themselves. Within the seminar group there were two women of West Indian descent whose perception of difference from each other emphasised the falseness of labels. One, who had been born in Manchester, claimed complete immersion in the dominant culture; the other, whose childhood had been spent in the West Indies, confessed to her sense of alienation. Yet another student, whose 'Blackness' had been determined by an Arab father, said that having suffered racist discrimination in the West Country where she had been brought up, she had deliberately and consciously chosen a Black definition for herself. The description of racist attacks upon Emecheta from neighbouring White council tenants was particularly embarrassing to White students, as it forced a confrontation with endemic racism from which they could not claim immunity. They recognised the resentment of people who questioned her entitlement to council housing, and the familiar cry that neighbours 'had waited for years for the new flats to be built and did not understand why [Emecheta] should be given a brand new one just like them' (p. 47). England was not the promised land imagined by her father, but a hateful ghetto that she analyses with a commendable degree of objectivity. Ghettoisation, such as is endured by Black Americans and Black British immigrants alike, she sees as the inevitable product of the suppressed guilt of the dominant social group. She asks:

What then occurs in a society which is multi-racial, and you happen to belong to a minority, the hated and scapegoatable group? Education, then, could never be your sole agent for both social and economic mobility.[20]

She also denies that all Black immigrants share the same social aims. Discriminatory housing policies were not the province of Whites alone. As an African she was spurned by West Indian landlords, and as an Ibo by Nigerian. The diversity, complexity and irrationality of racism is not simply a matter of skin colour. Her castigation of the 'unrealistic' expectations of West Indian youths aroused the anger of some Afro-Caribbean students, highlighting the fact that any attempt to categorise people on any grounds other than humanity is a de-humanising process, that blinds the moral eye to the value of the individual.

Hurston steadfastly refuses a self-definition based on colour. She is determined to celebrate the diversity and beauty of her people and accepts no definition of them or herself as simply 'victims'. She points out that 'our lives are so diversified, internal attitudes so varied, appearances and capabilities so different, that there is no possible classification so catholic that it will cover us all' (p. 237).

The whole of this autobiography is a perplexing mixture of pride in, and contempt for, her people, and reflects her own inner conflict between her desire to be recognised as a writer rather than a 'Black', and her ambiguous attitude towards the race leaders of her time, who urged that a Black American was 'supposed to write about race problems' of which she confesses to being 'thoroughly sick' (p. 164). Her pursuit of a fully realised self that transcends racial considerations is no less laudable than Emecheta's, but her particular historical placing in the America of the 1920s to the 1940s has inevitably given rise to attack from literary critics, who devalued her work because it was not overtly political. What is often ignored is the double bind of gender and race in which she was held, and the fact that in spite of this she was one of the few Black women who became a published writer. Her resistance to being labelled and dismissed as nothing more than 'Black' generated a sexist hostility of the sort noticed by Emecheta, who comments that 'The world, especially the African world, still regards serious writing as a male preserve' (p. 66).

Early socialisation into the gender roles assigned in a patriarchal society was a shaping force that both writers initially imbibed then rebelled against. Emecheta's girlhood expectations of married bliss were soon dispelled, but Hurston seems to have found immense difficulty in ridding herself of the notion of romantic love as an ideal to be striven for. Consequently she glamourises her parents' life by aggrandising patriarchal double standards about fidelity. She pays homage to the idea of manhood as being defined in 'cussing and fighting and drinking as becomes a man' (p. 45.) She describes with some warmth the Saturday night gatherings on Joe Clarke's porch where women formed an admiring audience for the men. Yet there is an unresolved tension between what she seems to admire and what she will endure in her own life. Relationships foundered because she could not hide her intellectual strengths, although she knew that 'it is a griping thing to be a man and not to be able to whip his woman mentally' (p. 93). Her marriage failed because she could not sacrifice her career for it. Similarly Emecheta's long standing relationship with Chidi came to grief when she decided to research for a PhD. Chidi could tolerate her writing, 'but the Ibo man still thinks that taking on a serious project like a PhD should be for men only' (p. 236). This scenario was recognised by many students whose own relationships have suffered because their men have felt threatened by the women's expanded horizons. As women, we have become accustomed to dealing with sexual harassment, 'men at the old game of stealing a feel' (p. 144), as Hurston expresses it, but the hostility of the man who feels his intellectual sphere is being invaded presents a bewildering problem.

Sexism is exposed much more positively by Emecheta than by Hurston, partly because of the accumulated consciousness-raising that occurred in the years that separate their lives, partly because of their different life-experiences. Hurston admits that the impetus for her novel *Their Eyes Were Watching God*[21] was a love affair, but there is an old fashioned coyness in her statement that 'Ladies do not kiss and tell any more than men do' (p. 249). Childless, Hurston was far freer than Emecheta to enter into and discard relationships. Emecheta had the courage to leave a husband who abused her physically and mentally, but she could not abandon his children. Yet despite the logic of her separation, she was nagged by feelings of guilt that *she* had broken her marriage vows. The injustice inherent in patriarchical attitudes was felt most keenly when she agreed to the ill-fated reconciliation with her husband, whom she knew would be given the credit for the attempt, because 'he was the *man*. No one would like to offend him, because with me to work and boost his ego, he could one day be very powerful. Mine was to be the reflected glory. But then, is that not the lot of most women?' (p. 91). An added constraint on Emecheta in her search for self-definition was the fact of her position as mother to the children of a man who had even denied his paternity to avoid financial responsibility.

The burdens of motherhood as well as its joys provide an emotional framework for *Head above Water*, in which the concept of mothering is defined as a caring, self-denying process. Emecheta's life was dominated by her determination to fulfil the needs of her children, for whom she worked and planned. Sometimes she chafed under the injustice of the seeming ingratitude of her adolescent children, recorded in one stormy episode when she and Chiedu quarrelled. Her despair and self-questioning are agonising as she thinks,

> This was going to be my lot. I was going to give all I had to my children, only for them to spit in my face and tell me I was a bad mother and then leave and run to a father who had never in all his life bought them a pair of pants.   (p. 233)

The most telling phrase is the reference to being a 'bad mother', an insight into the guilt shared by all women who subject themselves to self-examination about the quality of their 'mothering'. She exposes as a myth the notion that biological parenting automatically brings with it instinctive wisdom or unquestioning self-denial; raising five children single-handed was an exhausting, complex, sometimes unrewarding experience. Yet in spite of her awareness of sexist oppression – 'To think we raise all these men who later suppress us' (p. 98) – Emecheta's social conditioning was such that for many years she felt guilt at the supposed incompleteness of a life without a man. The ideal to which she and Hurston aspired was a socially constructed one that embraced the illusion of undying romantic love and a permanent pair bonding on which stable nuclear families were supposed to rest. That 'ideal', society stipulated, was to be found in a monogamous marriage that lasted until death.

Although many feminists identify marriage as the site of women's oppression, it is an idea that still holds sway in Western society, and will continue to do so as long as it is associated in the mind with religious observance. Religion as a shaping force is apparent in both autobiographies. For Emecheta it is always present although she does not stress religious experience. She makes an early and never-amplified reference to Christianity that is described as tightening the knot of enslavement of her mother, and ends with an equally unexplained comment that she herself had a new appraisal of that religion. What this new appraisal might have entailed was perhaps a less puritanical view of marriage and a rejection of its supposed sanctity. One senses that, for her, Christianity provided a moral framework that she intelligently adapted in the light of experience, as it was a sensible code by which to live. In Hurston's life religion was a much more dominant force. The subversion of the enslavers' religion by her slave ancestors had acted as a cohesive force, allowing Black identification with the Jewish experience of diaspora and deliverance. Religion, even one that was forced upon a captive people, was a unifying element for American Blacks, especially as racial aggregation had led to the development of a separate Black church. As the daughter of a preacher, Hurston was brought up in a vibrant church, full of music and singing, and one where the oratorical beauty of sermons provided high drama in the behaviour of repentant sinners. Religious experience was for her people a cathartic one, engaging mind and body (very unlike, we imagine, the disciplined church-going of Emecheta at the Methodist High School). Hurston took obvious delight in the beauty of the language and music of her church, although the informing philosophy did not go unquestioned by her, and as a research student she claims to have been initiated into Hoodoo, the powers of which she does not question. Indeed, her own religious yearnings seem to be much nearer to African animism than are those of the African Emecheta. She is quite cynical about the urge to pray to a God to whom Emecheta makes frequent appeal, and suggest that 'people need religion because the great masses fear life and its consequences' (p. 277). It is in keeping with Hurston's philosophy of life that she rejects identification with the masses, and considers prayer to a personal God as a weakness; as she tells us, 'I do not choose to admit weakness' (p. 278). She has no faith in the notion of a Divine Being who will intervene in human affairs already directed by the exercise of will-power. Personal salvation is something in which she professes no belief, but she anticipates that death will mean a return to the infinity of Creation, and claims: 'I know that I shall be part and parcel of the world. I was part before the sun rolled into shape and burst forth in the glory of change' (p. 279).

Yet Christianity is an all-pervasive influence in *Dust Tracks*, in the flavour and structure of much of her language. The sonorous cadences, the stately dignity of some of her images, testify to a more than passing acquaintance with the Bible. Sermonical echoes abound, and she can accommodate these together with African anthropomorphism, as she does in the description of her mother's death:

Just then, Death finished his prowling through the house on his padded feet and entered the room. He bowed to Mamma in his way, and she made her manners and left us to act out our ceremonies over unimportant things. (p. 88)

It was in our evaluation of these autobiographies as literature that Hurston's linguistic flexibility caught our attention. We noticed that biblical phrases blended with the richness of Black idiom like 'Hitting a straight lick with a crooked stick' (p. 3); that dialogue was conducted when appropriate in a transcription of Black language, 'Oh, dat's one of dem niggers from over the creek, one of dem Hurstons' (p. 13). There were examples of Black linguistic inventiveness in words like 'bodacious' and 'vominates', and the vivification of language achieved by the use of double adjectival qualification, which Hurston identifies as being characteristic of Black American language. She describes the language of her people as being full of simile and invective, so that an enemy can be described as 'mule-eared' or 'hog-nosed'. The richness of this language she attributes to their having been denied access to books, so that their images were drawn straight from the barnyard. Perhaps because Emecheta *was* given access at school to books that emanated from a dominant culture that had replaced her own, there is a flatness in her style. English was not her mother-tongue so she uses it with the formality and exactness of someone who has learned a second language and is very conscious of its structure. Consequently her language is remarkably free of colloquialisms in *Head above Water*. Her language, like the text, is self-consciously structured, ordered and logical. Indeed, we were struck by the curious fact that she captured so much of female experience in a language that bore the hallmark of the masculine. Even the perception of her life as an academic success story seemed to place her within the male autobiographic tradition identified by Jelinek. This is not surprising in view of the fact that the literary models offered to Emecheta as a schoolgirl would undoubtedly emanate from the pens of men. Consequently, there are no passages in her text that match the lyrical beauty of those in Hurston's, like her description of Polk County. But Emecheta's flatness of style is at least consistent, whereas Hurston's voice fluctuates between restrained understatement and graphic fluency.

The unevenness of Hurston's style in which her own recorded voice is sometimes Black, sometimes that of an educated woman, is matched by the uneven tone of the whole text. The opening chapters are spontaneous, fresh, inviting, promising a structure based upon a series of 'visions' that is not fulfilled. Her freest and most natural language is in those early chapters that deal with her childhood, but later chapters which are a haphazard rag-bag of snippets from her other published writings, lack coherence and sincerity. When she describes her adult life we sense the deliberate adoption of a protective mask behind which she hides from public scrutiny. Sometimes she justifies this as respect for others: 'There was much, but my brother is dead and I do not wish even to risk being unjust to his memory' (p. 129); sometimes she is almost flippant, as in the comment on her marriage, dismissed in four paragraphs with the same question: 'Who had cancelled the well-advertised tour of the moon? Somebody had turned a hose on the sun' (p. 251). When she talks of a man she claims to have loved deeply, she deliberately avoids self-revelation with: 'And even if I did know all, I am supposed to have some private business to myself. Whatever I do know, I have no intention of putting so much in the public ears' (p. 261). This is a surprising comment to find in an autobiography, and is a far cry from the honest outpourings of Emecheta, who does not hesitate to explore her inner life in her novels and her official autobiography.

Our study of these two texts had opened up for discussion many issues, not least of which was: what are the expectations of a reader of autobiography? Does the reader look for secrets to be disclosed? Does the reader have the right to expect to 'know all'? Can she expect total honesty in a literature which inevitably involves the writer in a process of self-definition, in the course of which she recreates a former self? If it is apparent, soul-bearing honesty that the reader seeks, then *Head Above Water* will be more appealing than *Dust Tracks*. Yet we can deduce as much about Hurston from her silences as from her confessions. She tellingly points to every autobiographer's problem when recreating a past self when she says: 'so the difficulty lies in trying to transpose last night's moments to a day which has no knowledge of it' (p. 264). Perhaps all we can really expect of an autobiography is emotional integrity from the writers, whose subjectivity in their self-appointed efforts at self-definition has to be accepted. That the literary artefact recognised as autobiography is subject to as much constraint as the subject's life was in the living of it, was an important lesson for us. The study of these particular texts afforded us insight into the creative process involved in composition, the constraints imposed by audience and publishers, the courage and tenacity needed to succeed, as well as evidence of white racism in two entirely different multiracial societies. Above all, we learned something about self-definition. Emecheta and Hurston began the process by rejecting labels that had been attached to them by others and replacing them with some they chose for themselves. Initial labelling was a product of culture, race, class and gender, and autobiography was their attempt to redefine themselves in defiance of these shaping forces that govern all our lives.

NOTES

1. Z. N. Hurston, *Dust Tracks on a Road* (London: Virago, 1986).
2. B. Emecheta, *Head above Water* (London: Fontana, 1986).
3. S. Butterfield, *Black Autobiography in America* (Amherst, Mass.: University of Massachusetts Press, 1974).
4. E. C. Jelinek (ed.), *Women's Autobiography: Essays in Criticism* (Bloomington, Ind., and London: Indiana University Press, 1980).
5. Butterfield, *Black Autobiography in America*, p. 3.
6. A. Walker, *In Search of Our Mothers' Gardens* (London: The Women's Press, 1984) p. 91.
7. Quoted in Jelinek (ed.), *Women's Autobiography*, p. 6.
8. Butterfield, *Black Autobiography in America*, p. 3.
9. Emecheta, *Head above Water*, p. 18.
10. Hurston, *Dust Tracks on a Road*, p. 196 (my emphasis).
11. Emecheta, *Head above Water*, p. 242.
12. Ibid., p. 7.
13. Hurston, *Dust Tracks on a Road*, p. 97.
14. Emecheta, *Head above Water*, p. 89 (emphasis added).
15. Special edition on 'Women as Writers', *Sage*, vol. 2, no. 1 (Spring, 1985).
16. Z. N. Hurston, *Mules and Men* (Bloomington, Ind.: Indiana University Press, 1978).
17. Emecheta, *Head above Water*, p. 156.
18. Hurston, *Dust Tracks on a Road*, p. 216.
19. Emecheta, *Head above Water*, p. 141.
20. Ibid., p. 131.
21. Z. N. Hurston, *Their Eyes Were Watching God* (USA: 1937; London: Virago, 1980).

9

Reading from a Distance: Ama Ata Aidoo's *Our Sister Killjoy*

SARA CHETIN

But how can I help being so serious? Eh, my Love, what positive is there to be, when I cannot give voice to my soul and still have her heard? Since so far, I have only been able to use a language that enslaved me, and therefore, the messengers of my mind always come shackled?[1]

A modern dilemma tale – directed at an African man but written in the form of a letter that never gets sent. The Western-educated African woman has so 'great a need to communicate' that it leads her to attempt to engage her African male counterparts despite knowing, from experience, that it will be misconstrued, laughed at or silenced. An open dialogue aborted, Ama Ata Aidoo closes her novel *Our Sister Killjoy* with the heroine alone, flying back to Africa from Europe, reflecting on the difficulty of finding an authentic female voice that will be heard by her African brothers, but also a voice that will not be appropriated by a Western audience:

So you see, My Precious Something, all that I was saying about language is that I wish you and I could share our hopes, fears and our fantasies, without feeling inhibited because we suspect that someone is listening. As it is, we cannot write to one another, or speak across the talking cables or converse as we travel on a bus or a train or anywhere, but we are sure they are listening, listening, listening. (p. 115)

An African woman writer's dilemma tale – directed at an African audience but written within a Western structure that deviates from the conventional, unified shape of the novel. A product of a Western education, the modern African woman writer creates a fragmented

146

voice that reflects the alienated experiences of an African woman who is in search of a new language, a new way of conceptualising these experiences that ultimately aim to synthesise the fragmented consciousness of an uprooted people, her people:

> This is why, above all, we have to have our secret language. We must create this language. It is high time we did. We are too old a people not to. We can. We must. So that we shall make love with words and not fear of being overheard.   (p. 116)

This secret language that Ama Ata Aidoo searches for in *Our Sister Killjoy* highlights the complex issue of the writer's relationship to her audience. The novel, both structurally and thematically, resists identification with Western male literary traditions, but Aidoo also appears to be implicitly questioning the ways in which the First World feminist reader can enter African female-centred realities and interpret the unfamiliar codes produced by the text. We are attracted to a story about an 'African New Woman' whose journey into Europe's 'heart of darkness' turns the exotic, reified image of womanhood on its head and explores the growing consciousness of a woman coming to terms with her own identity and means of self-fulfilment. But does this signal a common terrain for female identification? As non-Africans, we are reminded that our 'listening-in' is intrusive and prevents Aidoo from speaking directly to her own people. Like other African women writers, such as Bessie Head and Buchi Emecheta, Aidoo purposely wants to keep her 'outsider' audience at a self-conscious distance – a political and literary device that makes the First World feminist reader all the more aware of her limited vision and need to resist universalising female experience and expectations which are not only culturally specific but politically charged.

In *Our Sister Killjoy* Ama Ata Aidoo makes a forceful plea to her African compatriots who are transplanted on a spiritually barren foreign soil to return home. Their moral and cultural values are misdirected and fragmented, and her adoption of the modern 'novel' form reflects these Western concerns. But Aidoo, in an attempt to articulate the modern dilemmas facing her people, has combined both poetry and prose as a means of juxtaposing the political against the personal. A satirical, political voice serves as a backdrop to highlight the personal adventures and inner feelings, narrated in the third person, of the main character, Sissie, as she goes to Europe and experiences what it means to be a Black woman in an alien environment. The naïve Sissie embarks on a journey of self-discovery and returns home to Africa a much stronger, more independent and self-assured woman who realises, despite the pain and bitterness it causes, what her responsibility to her people – and ultimately herself – entails. As Sissie's consciousness develops, Aidoo weaves in poetry that resembles the form of a song with its chorus-like structure and variations on a theme. The poetry/song is echoing Sissie's individual experiences on a wider more generalised landscape. The poetry parts of the novel resemble the function and structure of the epic tale which, originally based on oral improvisation and connected to preliterate cultures, has a cyclical structure that evokes a journey motif. Aidoo's African epic, tragic in character and moral in tone, has an impersonal, dignified narrative style which is more remote and objective than Sissie's personal narrative but is none the less closely connected as Aidoo weaves a fine line between subjective and objective responses, between personal dilemmas and political concerns. In this novel Sissie emerges as the female version of the epic hero who wants to fight for the honour and survival of her people.

So why does Aidoo end her novel with a letter? After two plays and several short stories[2] that draw on the tradition of oral story-telling, is Aidoo now ominously warning of the death of communal art, of her own art? Despite her intention to engage her audience, is 'our sister' so disillusioned that she is gloomily forecasting, in true 'killjoy' fashion, the end of her role as a storyteller? Or is Aidoo hinting at another type of closure that wants to leave behind, to exclude all those who do not share her African female-centred consciousness, a consciousness turned in on itself as a means of resisting attempts to appropriate an image of African womanhood for needs other than the writer's own?

Perhaps the answers lie in the epic form itself: the opening lines of the novel point to the cyclical nature of Sissy's voyage where she sets off alone to rescue her people and returns home alone, the tragedy being that her people wanted to be left behind. But her own needs become visible as she refuses to compromise with both her African brothers and Western demands. The woman warrior retains a sense of her integrity as she searches for a language that cannot betray her, a language that rejects 'so much of the softness and meekness . . . all the brothers expect of me and the sisters . . . which is really western' (p. 117), as well as a language that would affirm her own self worth and is more honourable than a compromise with a 'private white audience for whom [the superior monkey] performs his superior tricks' (p. 130). Nameless to others, the archetypal Sissie names a new African female identity that does not merely define itself in relation to others, but an identity which values its relationship to itself.

The opening five pages of *Our Sister Killjoy* indicate the way Aidoo envisions the relationship between form and content. The irony of the opening lines: 'Things are working out / towards their dazzling conclusions' which are placed on the stark background of two otherwise empty pages, emphasise both the irrelevancy of the 'ticky-tackies' that 'surround', 'block' and 'clutter' lives/pages and the frightening prophecy that 'things are working out', seemingly against one's control. But Aidoo's carefully controlled language attacks that very premise that 'talks of universal truth, universal literature and the Gross National Product' (p. 6). These are the ideas that have made her people lose touch with their sense of history, a history that evokes 'the massive walls of slave forts standing along our beaches' (p. 5). The empty opening pages symbolise both the loss of language and the uselessness of a false language as spoken by the 'moderate' and 'academic-pseudo-intellectual' Africans who, like dogs, chase the 'latest crumbs' being thrown at them by defending interests that 'are not even [their] own'. Aidoo's novel is addressed primarily to her African 'brothers' who, not wanting to confront their victimisation, are only perpetuating it, unaware of how they are hurting their own people. As an educated African, Aidoo shares some of her brothers' experiences and thus understands their dilemmas abroad; but as a woman, her experiences have placed her outside of their reality as well.

The full title of the novel, *Our Sister Killjoy, or Reflections from a Black-Eyed Squint*, establishes Sissy's perception of her brothers – or rather their ironic view of her – as well as her attitude to the world in general. Whose 'sister' is she? Obviously her fellow Africans recognise her as one of them, as 'belonging to the elite, whatever that is' (p. 107), as one of the 'migrant birds of the world'. But through her use of irony, Sissy clearly indicates she is buying no part of their dreams, a true killjoy who recognises that 'migrations are part of the general illusion of how well an unfree population think they can do for themselves' (p. 89). Her criticisms and anger directed at her own people leave them defensive and her full of despair. Despite the numerous references to her own naïveté, the self-conscious Sissy, 'from knowledge gained since', is able to see the world more clearly through her black-eyed squint. What she sees is neither joyful nor hopeful, for until her brothers realise how much they are needed at home, Sissy will distinctly remain a lost sister and a lost lover – her need for Africa greater than her need for romance.

After the initial five pages of the novel, Sissy leads us 'into a bad dream' where she journeys into that unreal, foreign territory of nightmarish Europe. The opening chapter serves as a type of chorus, a prologue which frames the action of the rest of the novel. The recurring symbols like food, archetypal 'Sammys' and consumer goods are juxtaposed against feelings of distaste, distress and powerlessness as Sissy begins to gain a self-conscious awareness about 'where', 'when' and 'how' her people lost control of their own lives and found themselves without a language to fill the blank spaces on the page. Her sarcasm and satire reveal a political awareness that doesn't uphold the supremacy of Western values, an awareness which essentially mocks the hypocrisy of those who want 'to make good again'. Sissy had been chosen to go to Europe, something that 'her fellow countryman' had seen as a kind of 'dress rehearsal for a journey to paradise' (p. 9). This man, whose real name she was never to discover, was referred to by her European hosts as 'Sammy'. His enthusiasm, eagerness to please and familiarity with them 'made her feel uneasy' and her distaste would never disappear as 'Time was to bring her many many more Sammys. And they always affected her in the same way' (p. 6).

Sissy's journey of self-development continues when she is made conscious of her Blackness, ironically by someone speaking a language she barely understands, and 'for the rest of her life, she was to regret this moment when she was made to notice the difference in human colouring'. The harsh reality of 'Power, Child, Power' is a nightmare from which Sissy can't escape as she 'came to know that someone somewhere would always see in any kind of difference, an excuse to be mean' (p. 13). The episode ends with a kind of epic simile that evokes the relationship between power and exploitation, between 'any number of plums' and the suffering of the powerless.

The second and longest chapter, 'The Plums', recounts Sissy's personal experiences as a Black woman working with an international youth group planting Christmas trees in southern Germany. The absurdity of the Bavarian widows who were attempting to purge their guilt and fill in the gaps of their own lives left damaged by a war they wanted to forget was not lost to the black-eyed squint. Against this background Sissy meets a German woman, Marija, who comes to symbolise everything that was unnatural and tragic about the isolation of life in Europe. Marija is in a sense also a widow, a victim of a society that had destroyed bonds between people. Forced into a stultifying existence where looking after her son was her one pleasure, Marija lives her life through her son, hoping her Little Adolph would make it, 'would go to university, travel and come back to tell her all about his journeys' (p. 60). Forced to think about her own mother, the African Mother, Sissy reflects on the universal loneliness of motherhood and the contradictions women are faced with when they are denied lives of their own but feel guilty when they desire 'to be alone. . . . Just for a very little time . . . may be?':

> It is
> Heresy
>
> In Africa
> Europe,
> Everywhere.
>
> This is
> Not a statement to come from a
> Good mother's lips –
>
>   . . .
>
> Yet
> Who also said that
> Being alone is not like
> Being
> Alone?
>
>   (p. 49)

These lines, like the other poetic passages in the novel, although not part of the action, reflect Aidoo's internal comments which are triggered off by the action in the story. The poetry attempts to place the personal conflicts in a broader context to illustrate that suffering and powerlessness are not isolated, individual problems but part of a whole system that continues to survive by feeding off individual misery. The poetic voice is more Aidoo than Sissy, but in the last chapter, as Sissy returns home, the separation between poetry and prose disappears. Sissy's and Aidoo's voices merge to reconstruct

'that secret language', the only hope left for their people. Marija is
distinctly excluded from this language, although her life epitomises
what it means to be a woman anywhere in the world:

> Any good woman
> In her senses
> With her choices
> Would say the
> Same
>
> In Asia
> Europe
> Anywhere:
>
> For
> Here under the sun,
> Being a woman
> Has not
> Is not
> Cannot
> Never will be a
> Child's game
>
> From knowledge gained since
> So why wish a curse on you child
> Desiring her to be a female
> ?
> Beside, my sister
> The ranks of the wretched are
> Full,
> Are full.

(p. 51)

Although in theory Aidoo speaks of a shared sisterhood, Sissy,
the woman warrior, believes that her first priority is to honour her
own people. Her interactions with Marija force her to examine her
own life and she comes to learn that a shared loneliness does not
create a sustaining life-force: Sissy has much empathy for Marija's
fate but their world views and cultural differences artificially bring
them together and naturally pull them apart. Aidoo explores the
cultural differences through the use of food and the women's

misreadings of each other's concept of hospitality. Food, that universal symbol of sharing and nourishment, is also a symbol of hospitality turned sterile and unnatural.

The symbolic significance of food emergences in 'The Plums' chapter as Aidoo establishes not only the relationship between women and food production, as represented by Marija's generous sharing of food and Sissy's 'The Bringer-of-Goodies-After-Lights-Out' role, but also depicts the obscenity of food surplus in the West where people stuff themselves in an attempt to satisfy other unfulfilled desires. This is symbolised through the depiction of Marija's sexual frustrations and the hypocrisy of foreign aid and the Third World rulers who feed themselves 'intravenously' with riches, oblivious to the poverty in their own peoples' lives. Against Aidoo's angry poetic voice we see Sissy and her companions 'benefiting' from Western hospitality as they 'were required to be there, eating, laughing, singing, sleeping and eating. Above all eating,' Their function was purely symbolic: why should they worry about anything, 'even if the world is rough, it's still fine to get paid to have an orgasm . . . or isn't it?' (p. 35).

The tinned, synthetic, unnatural food represents Europe itself where those who embrace it end up up ghosts of their former slaves:

> Brother
> The internal logic is super-cool:
> The only way to end up a cultural
> Vulture
> Is to feed on carrion all the way . . .
> (p. 39)

Sissy is initially seduced by the overabundance and the novelty of the food, particularly the plums, which represent her desire to experience a new world. But 'in knowledge gained since', Sissy is able to reflect back on the nature of Marija's hospitality which placed Sissy in the dangerous position of being the object of someone else's dreams and desires.

Marija's preoccupation with feeding Sissy reveals the frustrated, unnatural life Marija is forced to live where she is deprived of a community of human activity. Her life-giving past, which reminds Sissy of her own background, makes a sharp contrast to her sterile present:

They grew in her mother's garden. The black currants did. Plenty,

plenty. And every summer since she was little, her one pleasure had been preserving black currants – making its jam, bottling its juices. And she still went home to help. Or rather, she went to avail herself of the pleasure, the beauty, the happiness at harvest time: of being with many people, the family. Working with a group. If they had met earlier, she could have taken Sissy home for that year's harvest.   (p. 50)

The 'plenty, plenty' of her childhood community is now a nostalgic memory that she tries to reproduce by giving all of herself to Sissy who represents everything the German woman lacks in her own life. Though flattered, Sissy recognises that Marija's loss of her sense of self is born out of a 'kind of loneliness overseas which is truly bad', a disease like 'the cold loneliness of death' which is slowly killing Aidoo's own people whom she fears will also become ghosts of their former selves.

As well as using Marija as a vehicle for forcing Sissy to examine her own life, Aidoo also uses the relationship between the two women to explore gender roles and note specific contrasts between Western women's and African women's lives. When she arrives on foreign soil, Sissy detects that it is not at all 'normal' 'for a young / Hausfrau to / Like / Two Indians / who work in / supermarkets' (p. 23), and realises that Marija 'was too warm for Bavaria, Germany' where prying neighbours thought that a friendship between a Black woman and a white woman who didn't even speak the same language was something perverse: 'SOMEONE MUST TELL HER HUSBAND' (p. 44). Despite Sissy sensing 'a certain strangeness about Marija', she had no reason to question whether ulterior motives lay behind her hospitality. When Marija makes sexual advances, the surprised Sissy is able to empathise with Marija's tear-shaped

L
O
N
E
L
I
N
E
S
S

'like a rain cloud over the chimneys of Europe' (p. 65), that has forced her into the alienated position of sexually desiring other women. In this context, Aidoo appears to perceive lesbianism as a reaction against a culturally specific type of isolation but does not accept it as an alternative for a better world: it remains a symptom of a woman's pain in an unhealthy society where individuals' sexually repressed desires force them into extreme behavior patterns. 'How then does one / Comfort her / Who weeps for / A collective loss?' (p. 67).

Before Sissy is confronted with Marija's motives (whether Marija herself is conscious or unconscious of a sexual longing remains ambiguous), she plays with the idea of being a man and imagines 'what a delicious love affair she and Marija would have had if one of them had been a man':

> Especially if she, Sisie had been a man. She had imagined and savoured her tears, their anguish at knowing that their love was doomed. But they would make promises to each other which of course would not stand a chance of getting fulfilled. She could see Marija's tears . . . . (p. 61)

Although only a 'game', this type of gender-role-playing lets Aidoo explore male/female relationships and question why Black men become involved with European women when it is clear 'The Guest Shall Not Eat Palm-Nut Soup'. Despite the exceptional 'successes' of such relationships, most end up leaving the black men 'lost', 'Changed into elephant-grey corpses . . . . Their penises cut.' (p. 62). Racist societies have no compassion and Sissy is determined not to forget this. But later, when Marija hears of Sissy's imminent departure, Sissy finds herself enjoying the pain she was causing the German woman:

> It hit her like a stone, the knowledge that there is pleasure in hurting. A strong three-dimensional pleasure, an exclusive masculine delight that is exhilarating beyond all measure. And this too is God's gift to man? She wondered. (p. 76)

Aidoo is attempting to make a parallel between racial and sexual exploitation. Sissy is able to exploit Marija as long as Marija continues to be the masochistic female just as the white man is able to exploit the Black man as long as the Black man continues to play the scapegoat. Sissy in many ways becomes impatient with Marija's 'femaleness', but having the humanity and insight due to her own recognised vulnerability. Sissy reflects : 'Whoever created us gave us too much capacity for sorrow' (p. 68). It is the socially constructed systems that force people into unhealthy behaviour patterns, and Aidoo makes it clear that gender divisions, like racial divisions, must be exposed for their absurd and frightening distortion of human potential. The intolerant and incompassionate environment of the cold European nightmare affects all people in different ways, and as Sissy leaves Marija, taking with her memories of the tragedies of wasted possibilities in the form of some plums, Aidoo's poetic voice can be heard echoing through layers of Sissy's consciousness:

> We are the victims of our History and our Present. They place too many obstacles in the Way of Love. And we cannot enjoy even our Differences in peace.   (p. 29)

In the third chapter, Our Sister shifts her ground to explore the alienation of her own people living in the 'cold strange land where dogs and cats eat better than many children' (p. 99). Having sympathetically understood the isolation of Western women's lives, the African Sissy does not need the rallying cry 'Sisterhood is powerful' : her own experiences and history force her to see 'group survival' from another angle. Arriving in England, she is astonished at the number of wretched Black people and 'wondered why they stayed'. She remarks that the women were especially pitifully dressed in tattered, cheap clothes and knows that 'in a cold land, poverty shows as nowhere else'. But she begins to articulate her anguish at hearing the feeble excuses and outrageous lies her people have invented in order to justify their betrayal of their own families: 'We have all fallen victim, / Sometime or / Other' (p. 90).

As Sissy dismisses the ignorance of those non-Africans she meets who think the thing that 'binds the Germans, the Irish and the African – in that order naturally – together' is 'OPPRESSION' (p. 93), she is forced to examine the attitudes of her own people and realises 'every minute, every day . . . Ghana opened a dance of the masquerades called Independence, for Africa' (p. 95). The consciousness that shapes the African experience abroad takes the form of Kunle in this chapter, another 'Sammy' who defends 'science' without grasping a moral sense of his own history as witnessed by his justification of the Christian doctor who used a South African Black man's heart to save a white man:

Yet she had to confess she still had not managed to come round to seeing Kunle's point: that cleaning the bassa's chest of its rotten heart and plugging in a brand-new, palpitatingly warm kaffirheart, is in the surest way to usher in the Kaffirmillennium.   (p. 101)

Kunle ends up 'killed by the car for which he had waited for so long', and Sissy mourns for him and all the others who symbolically are killed by false Western promises and tricked into embracing the 'security' offered by their ex-colonial masters:

> although the insurance policy had been absolutely comprehen-
> sive, the insurance people had insisted it did not cover a chauffeur
> driving at 80 M.P.H. on the high road. . . . He had taken out
> his policy with a very reliable insurance company . . . Foreign,
> British, terribly old and solid, with the original branch in London
> and cousins in Ottawa, Sydney, Salisbury and Johannesburg . . . .
> (p. 108)

The novel ends with Sissy's letter – to that one special brother, to all her African brothers, but ultimately to herself. It speaks about the importance of language, of group survival and of reconstructing the future. It celebrates Sissy's strength as a woman but mourns what she has lost as a result of her newly defined womanhood. The letter is full of pain and compassion and to me is one of the most moving personal statements found in African literature today.

Aidoo's and Sissy's voices merge to explain how language still remains a collective creation that can only have value if people recognise what Sissy's 'killjoy' function serves:

> Of course, we are different. No, we are not better than anybody
> else. But somewhere down the years, we let the more relaxed part
> of us get too strong. So that the question was never that of changing
> into something that we have never been. No, we only need to
> make a small effort to update the stronger, the harder, the more
> insensitive part of ourselves. (p. 116)

Sissy recognises the dialectic between the past and the present, between the 'loss of perspective' and the language that will recap-ture it: 'the question is not just the past or the present, but which factors out of both the past and the present represent for us the most dynamic forces for the future'. Sissy empathises with her people who 'have been caught at the confluence of history and that has made ignorant victims of some of us' (p. 118), but condemns her people for remaining 'past masters for fishing out death', for staying in Europe where all they have learned is 'how to die':

> To come all this way just to learn how to die from a people whose own survival instincts have not failed them once yet. . . . I do not laugh enough . . . I remember how my old friends and I used to scream with mirth at home, looking at how we were all busy making fools of ourselves. . . . Maybe it was the sun and the ordinary pleasure of standing on our own soil. . . . Our beautiful land? One wonders whether it is still ours. And how much longer it will continue to be . . . .
> A curse on all those who steal continents!   (p. 120)

By attempting to reconstruct a new language in the hope of communicating with her people, Sissy also reclaims her lost identity as an African woman. Yet she can only do this by not sending the letter: her initial intention in writing the letter was to tell her brother how much she missed him, how much she needed and loved him, 'whatever that means'. But she gives up romance in favour of her own dignity and self-integrity. Aidoo's closure, which appears to destroy the communal function of language, really marks the birth of a new female African identity that has rejected its 'otherness' and returned home, the letter being an affirmation of how much Sissy is worth to herself.

As Aidoo's fictional character returns to its source, the difficult journey of the African woman writer continues. Ama Ata Aidoo speaks openly about the hardships she encounters in her own patriarchal culture that ignores or silences women's voices, voices that want, above all, to be heard at home, from their own centre:

> I am convinced that if *Killjoy* or anything like it had been written by a man, as we say in these parts, no one would have been able to sleep a wink these last couple of years, for all the noise that would have been made about it. If *Killjoy* has received recognition elsewhere, it is gratifying. But that is no slave for the hurt received because my own house has put a freeze on it.'[3]

Aidoo goes on to recount the story of how one of her own colleagues at an African university appeared to dismiss women's literature as not being of importance in Africa:

Dialogue, January 1980: My head of department (a good friend and a well-known writer himself) and I are discussing the latest edition of the book which had just then come out in New York. We are both going on about how well laid out it is, the beautiful type used, etc. Then I remark that unfortunately my impression is that the publishers don't seem to care much whether they sell it or not.

'What a shame,' says he, 'because there are all these women's-studies programs springing up in universities all over the United States. Surely *they* would be interested in it . . . '

And I bled internally. Because although the protagonist of the story is a young woman, anyone who read the book would realize that her concerns are only partially feminist, if at all. In any case, what if they are? Feminism is about half of the human inhabitants of this earth![4]

At First World feminists, we 'listen-in' from an unprivileged position[5] in an attempt to understand the kind of parameters that determine African women's writing, parameters that highlight the political difficulties of deconstructing feminism in an international context.

NOTES

1. Ama Ata Aidoo, *Our Sister Killjoy* (Harlow, Essex: Longman Drumbeat, 1981) p. 112. All page references are to this edition.
2. Aidoo has written *The Dilemma of a Ghost* (1965), *Anowa* (1970), *No Sweetness Here* (1970), all published by Longman Drumbeat. She has also published a collection of her poetry entitled *Someone Talking to Sometime* (Harare, Zimbabwe: College Press, 1985).
3. Ama Ata Aidoo, 'Ghana: To be a Woman' in *Sisterhood is Global*, ed. Robin Morgan (New York: Anchor Press/Doubleday, 1984) p. 262.
4. Ibid.
5. Gayatri Spivak speaks in an essay: 'In order to learn enough about Third World women and to develop a different readership, the immense heterogeneity of the field must be appreciated, and the First World feminist must learn to stop feeling privileged *as a woman*' (Gayatri Spivak (ed.), *In Other Worlds* (London: Methuen, 1987). p. 136).

10

Reconstructing the Past, Shaping the Future: Bessie Head and the Question of Feminism in a New South Africa

DOROTHY DRIVER

> Black women have long operated at a disadvantage. Now you as the storyteller are going to shape the future.
>
> Bessie Head[1]

Given Bessie Head's vehement feminist claim in *The Collector of Treasurers* (1977) that in Botswanan society women are 'of no account' or are treated like 'dogs',[2] her story 'Snapshots of a Wedding' seems surprisingly muted. Its subject is the marriage between a young man and a school-educated woman, called Neo for 'new'. After an idyllic opening – the wedding takes place at the 'haunting, magical hour of early dawn' (p. 76) – the story begins to establish the specific voices which make up the community. 'This is going to be a modern wedding' (p. 76), says one of the relatives of the groom. One of the bride's relatives responds: 'Oh, we all have our own ways. . . . If the times are changing, we keep up with them' (pp. 76–7). Uneasy about the marriage, the female members of the community instruct Neo in her duties: 'Daughter, you must carry water for your husband. Beware, that at all times, he is the owner of the house and must be obeyed. Do not mind if he stops now and then and talks to other ladies. Let him feel free to come and go as he likes' (p. 79).

At such a point, the story may seem to be less about the community's desire to 'keep up with' women like Neo than about forms of control. Even though she will be keeping her job as a secretary, rather than being 'the kind of wife who went to the lands to plough' (p. 80), Neo adjusts in other ways to community demands, becoming less aloof and more engaged in the life of the village. The community

160

despises Neo for her 'conceit and pride' (p. 77) and appreciates the 'natural' Mathata, who is 'smiling and happy' (p. 78) despite her impregnation and abandonment by the man whom Neo is going to marry. This opposition – whereby the educated woman is conceited and the uneducated woman content – is one of the givens of the story.

There *are* suggestions of an ironic stance being taken in the text towards this rural community's construction of a dutiful wife: the phrase 'we all have our ways' may seem sinister to some readers, and so may the manner in which the relatives 'nod their heads in that fatal way, with predictions that one day life would bring [Neo] down' (p. 77). The reference to the sacrificial ox – 'unaware of his sudden and impending end as meat for the wedding feast' (p. 76) – offers itself as a veiled allusion to the bride about to be sacrificed, and the fact that the marriage takes place at the police camp adds to the coercive undertones.

But these hints of the sinister or coercive can in the end only be part of the repressed of the text. The community of women exhort Neo to obedience in terms of the idyllic, which is in itself a marker of authorial sympathy – even yearning – in Head's writing: 'The hoe, the mat, the shawl, the kerchief, the beautiful flute-like ululating of the women seemed in itself a blessing on the marriage' (p. 80). Moreover, the final command 'Be a good wife! Be a good wife!' (p. 80), given by the aunt, is placed in the context of ritual and habitual gesture which form so important a part of Head's presented world. The aunt pounds the ground in a gesture symbolic of the act of pounding the newly-laid floor of the young couple's dwelling and, just before this, an old woman dashes towards Neo and chops at the ground with a hoe, symbolising the agricultural work which traditionally falls to women. Such acts – pounding floors, smearing walls, thatching roofs – contribute throughout Head's collection of stories to a harmonious village atmosphere, for they belong to a life made up of group activities and the sharing of tasks. The very congruence in this story between the aunt's gestures of pounding, the old woman's gestures of hoeing and the words themselves might add to the atmosphere of coercion lurking in the story's subtext. However, in the story's smooth return to the opening atmosphere of idyll, the village women deny the possibility of the existence of 'new' women who are other than 'good' wives.

Head expressed her attitude to the subjection of women in strong terms:

In the old days a woman was regarded as sacred only if she knew her place, which was in her yard with her mother-in-law and children. A number of oppressive traditions, however, completely obliterated her as a thinking, feeling, human being and she was exploited in all sort of ways. So heavy is the toll of centuries on the women of Botswana, that even with present-day political independence for the country, one finds that the few highly literate women of the country talk in uncertain terms of their lives and fear to assert themselves.[3]

This would seem to invite an ironic reading of 'Snapshots of a Wedding', with the narrator characterised as a 'village narrator', as Sara Chetin suggests, morally quite distinct from the writer herself.[4] There are no formal indications, however, that the third-person narrator is intradiegetic, and the very covertness of the narrative position suggests 'reliability'.[5] The motive behind an ironic reading is presumably the need to account for the sharp reference on the part of the primary narrator to Neo's 'conceit and pride'. In my own reading, however, the narrative voice is intricately structured around the writer's personal and political anxieties and desires.

The 'new' woman appears in expanded form under the name Life, in the short story of that name. The way she is depicted will help clarify Head's relation to modern women and the community, as well as to feminism. Life, who returns to her village from Johannesburg after an absence of many years, represents the world of urban capitalism, its commercial ethic particularly evident in the contamination of sex by money. In the rural world, sex flows freely ('People's attitude to sex was broad and generous' – (p. 39); in the world introduced by Life, money flows freely and sex becomes unfree – paid for by the men, and then paid for, in a different way, by Life. When she marries Lesego, he demands fidelity, and kills her when she disobeys.

This might have been a story about a 'new' woman coming into a world which is characterised by male ownership of the female body, and trying to insist – within a tradition of feminism – that her body is her own. But this is not, quite, the story Head writes, although in one important respect a feminist judgement *is* being made: the brief prison sentence Lesego is given for killing an unfaithful wife stands in obvious and sharp contrast to the death sentence delivered on Dikeledi in 'The Collector of Treasures' for killing the husband who abuses her and leaves her to feed, clothe and rear their children alone. Life is associated with the beer-brewers, 'a gay and lovable crowd who had emancipated themselves some time ago' (p. 39). The term 'emancipated' puts them in their place: it is offered with as much sharp disfavour as the term 'hysterical' (p. 42), used in relation to Life's behaviour. Life exhibits 'the bold, free joy of a woman who had broken all the social taboos' (p. 40); the gaiety of the beer-brewing women is similarly out of bounds. They may have emancipated themselves from the commands 'Do this! Do that!' (which echo the commands under which Neo has been told to live) but this leaves them with 'a language all their own' (p. 39), divorced from the codes, gestures and rituals by which a culture knows itself.

Thus 'Life', like 'Snapshots', seems to become a vehicle for the rejection of all that Head takes women's emancipation to be. Yet both stories are more complex than this, for in their refusal of contemporary models of emancipation (as Head chooses to represent them) another possibility is opened up.

In 'Snapshots of a Wedding' the 'new' woman is drawn back into a community by means of a series of gestures which make up the community's way of constructing a world. The exhortation to hoeing is 'only a formality' (p. 79) (the women know that Neo already has a secretarial job, and do not expect her to hoe). This reference to 'formality' suggests that the words 'Be a good wife! Be a good wife!' themselves be placed in the context of what Head called, elsewhere, the 'courtesies' of community life.[6]

In 'Life' the direction of Head's thinking in this regard becomes clearer. The villagers recall a world of communality – the task-sharing marks a barter economy – but they are also caught in a world of barely flourishing peripheral capitalism, whose figure is the set of anaemic calves owned by Lesego. Even before Life's arrival 'the men hung around, lived on the resources of the women' (p. 39). The farmers and housewives, a group of women set apart from the beer-brewers, and called 'the intensely conservative hard-core of village life' (p. 39), admire Life's independence, for they live in a world where only men 'built up their own, individual reputations' (p. 41). But they turn away from her when she becomes a prostitute, in a moment important in the story as a whole, not least because it prefigures one of the story's closing moments. This is a comment made to Lesego by Sianana: 'Why did you kill that fuck-about? You had legs to walk away' (p. 46). Like Sianana, the 'conservative' women are marginal to the plot, whose focus falls on a drama enacted between the 'new' woman and characters not fully repre-

sentative of rural society, as Head sees it – Life as against Lesego, not
Sianana; in accord with the beer-brewers, not the farmers and housewives. But their response, as we shall see, is crucial.

The final word on the drama between Life and Lesego takes the
form of a drunken song sung by the beer-brewing women about two
worlds colliding. The worlds they refer to are the worlds we have
seen in conflict: contemporary South Africa (Life) and contemporary
Botswana (Lesego). The words they sing come from a song sung by
Jim Reeves, a cowboy-type, like Lesego, as well as a voice from a
corrupt world. There is no consolation to be drawn from either
world; neither can offer the writer the future she wants. Her solution
is to go the world represented by the marginal characters, which
functions as a sign of the past. It becomes the writer's business to
reconstruct this past, and to depict it more fully, in subsequent
stories. 'Snapshots of a Wedding' also alludes to this project, pointing
to the way the 'past' tries to *contain* the educated woman. The
complexity of the concept of *containment*, suggesting incorporation
and expansion as well as limitation and control, precisely reflects the
precariousness of Head's literary–political project.

Head is under no illusion regarding the position of women in pre-
industrial, pre-colonial Southern Africa. Any nostalgic indication of
a conservative past is not intended to revive an old world where
women were systematically marginalised, but to reject a new world
– 'Johannesburg', in this story – where individualism flourishes, but
where neither men nor women can rely on having importance as
individuals, where a section of the population lives a privileged
existence, but where whole groups of people can be consigned to a
life of material and psychological wretchedness, and where Life's
apparently carefree slogan – 'live fast, die young, and have a good-
looking corpse' (p. 40) – is both in itself the sign of entrapment in a
world fundamentally hostile to women, and the heritage of a capitalist consumer culture, 'glaring paltry trash'.[7] 'Life' may be read, then,
as a justification of Head's refusal to accept models of emancipation
from the modern world. She wants not to see choice in terms of what
is offered by two versions of the present, but to cut another route,
taking the past as point of departure.

It is of course true that the text's use of the term 'hysterical' itself
recalls the hysterical anxiety on the part of patriarchal culture towards women who have managed to break free of its rule; the
congruence set up in the text between emancipation and sexual
immorality or prostitution also betrays this hysterical response.

Moreover, the conflation of 'feminism' and 'Johannesburg' or the world dominated by 'white' South Africa has its own political dangers: rebellious Black South African women are often slapped down as 'white'.[8] Nevertheless, it is worth taking seriously Head's desire to circumvent the package offered by the present, not only because the particular ways in which her writing returns to the past reveal a version of feminism other than that represented by the 'new' woman, not only because it is true that European models have often been hostile to Africa, but also because the route through the past corresponds, *mutatis mutandis*, to the direction being taken by other contemporary South African writers. Ellen Kuzwayo, for instance, has said that Black thinking on women would have developed differently were it not for the stultifying effect of laws entrenching 'ethnicity', many of which artificially elevate male authority over women: in this regard she constructs a certain version of the past in order to *inform*, like Head, the present and the future.[9]

Head's particular strategy is also symptomatic of the 'double allegiance' of African women writers to liberation from neo-colonialism on the one hand and to a feminist consciousness on the other.[10] One kind of reading may simply insist that this 'double allegiance' manifests itself in ambivalence and contradiction, but another kind of reading may see an altogether different shape emerging, finding its own precarious balance in a way which refuses the false polarity of national struggle and feminist struggle. Looking at some of the choices Head made through her writing career, and focusing particularly on the construction of the relation between women and community in some of the stories in *The Collector of Treasures*, her last published fiction, I intend in this essay to point to a certain feminism which, albeit by another name, is in the process of being forged in Black Southern Africa.

COMMUNITY, ORALITY AND THE QUESTION OF WOMEN

Speaking of her early life in apartheid South Africa, Head says:

> Twenty-seven years of my life was lived in South Africa but I have been unable to record this experience in any direct way, as a writer. . . . It is as though, with all those divisions and signs, you end up with no people at all. The environment completely

defeated me, as a writer. I just want people to be people, so I had no way of welding all the people together into a cohesive whole.[11]

Using writing as 'some kind of shrine to go to – some means of spiritual survival',[12] Head made a home for herself out of what she saw as Botswana's potential to be a 'cohesive whole'. Her ideal community is characterised above all by continuity: temporal continuity, where the past is recalled in the present, with the sense of a continuing and secure future; continuity between people, where neighbours are truly neighbours and not identified and thus separated in terms of class and race; and continuity between economic existence and natural surroundings, or, in Marxist terms, between the individual and the mode of production. The need to idealise certain aspects of the Botswanan community is a personal *and* political need which does not prevent her from recognising that real-life Botswana falls short of this ideal, but does lead her to optimistic conclusions in the novels that precede *The Collector of Treasures*.

Her first novel, *When Rain Clouds Gather* (1969),[13] finds its main fictional dynamic in an abuse of chiefly power, and its resolution in rural resilience and co-operation on the part of the people. The next novel, *Maru* (1971),[14] presents the racist attitudes in Setswana society towards the Basarwa (the San, once called 'Bushmen' in white South African discourse) whom the text identifies as 'the slaves and downtrodden dogs of the Batswana' (p. 18). Resolution is provided through romantic love – the chief offers an example to his people by marrying Margaret, a Masarwa – and the implication that a new community is in the making. The marriage gives hope to the Basarwa: 'a door silently opened on the small, dark airless room in which their souls had been shut for a long time. The wind of freedom . . . turned and flowed into the room' (p. 126).

In Head's first two novels the main focus is on feudal class relations in the first novel and tribal or race relations in the second: the question of gender is subordinated to the question of relations between chiefly authority, community leaders, and people. However, *When Rain Clouds Gather* does allude to problems regarding the patriarchal objectification and marginalisation of women, and offers as a model a particular male/female relationship which is not marked by neglect or abuse. It is worth looking at this novel and the next in some detail, as they reveal crucial problems and issues in Head's specifically feminist concerns.

The question of gender in *When Rain Clouds Gather* is addressed in the context of the breakdown of family structure under the system of migrant labour, with the text suggesting that the development of family feeling in men, and specifically romantic love, might help reinstate family life. This proposition is buttressed by the possibility of material improvement: the agricultural work that the women perform (under male direction) will eventually restore fertility to an overgrazed land and thus relieve the country of poverty. Head sees the need for men to develop feeling towards both family and community: the harmony of the second depends on the harmony of the first. Interestingly, only part of the necessary consciousness is rooted in the past (old tribal customs forced Makhaya 'to care about children' – p. 119) and so it needs to combine with a newer strain, the capacity for romantic, monogamous attachment: 'In this way Makhaya differed from all African men' (p. 172). Makhaya is also uncharacteristic in treating women as his equals, and in his non-tribalism. He is a man of the future, who has made a specific break with the past: 'It was only once his father died that he was able to come forward with his own strange Makhaya smiles and originality of mind' (p. 124).

At one point in the text, after a comment about women who are 'dead' because of their habitual abjection, the narrator suggests that 'even if a door opened somewhere' most women would not be able to grasp their freedom (p. 126). Only Paulina offers the hint of an exception; Maria, a woman composed of two selves, subordinates her feminist self to a self 'soft', 'meditative' and obedient (pp. 101, 103). In *Maru* a door is opened, but not on the question of gender. This is to say that the 'wind of freedom' which blows through the door is directed only at the Basarwa. The wind that Margaret feels, as woman, is a 'strong wind' (p. 103) blowing, as it were, in the opposite direction: towards a vision of romantic love which materialises in a marriage which promises to be the site of domestic subjection.

This signals, of course, a subtextual interest in gender. Yet, in a fascinating textual and ideological complication, Margaret's (like Dikeledi's) subordination within the ideology of romantic love cannot be addressed for fear of disturbing the function romantic love plays in the novel. Romantic love sets the world in motion in *Maru*, on both the realistic and allegorical planes of the story: Moleka is urged into monogamy, which heralds a new existence for women, and Maru is given an occasion for solving racism. Love also sets in motion the power of creativity which surges through the text in various forms: in the creation myth with its neo-Lawrentian sun/moon/earth symbolism, and (to speak of compassion rather than romantic love) in the artistic vision of Margaret Cadmore II, which differs from the coldly scientific vision of the first Margaret Cadmore. It is true that the women characters in *Maru* escape the deathly docility of oppressed women referred to in the earlier novel: they are both teachers, Margaret is also an artist, and in certain respects they know how to speak and think for themselves. Yet, even with the particular status given Dikeledi and Margaret within the framework of romantic love and monogamous marriage, which means that they are not consigned to 'some back room' (*When Rain Clouds Gather*, p. 124), the novel cannot help but give a sense of their subordination: Margaret because of the shift from financial and psychological independence, and Dikeledi because of the pain of loving more than she is loved. While this inequality is in an interesting way balanced by Margaret's ability to look away from Maru, for she also loves Moleka, the text keeps such meanings submerged, along with the whole question of gender. Some of them emerge in *A Question of Power* (1974),[15] Head's third novel, where humiliation, dependence and pain become the major topic. This makes all the more imperative the careful definition of romantic love that will take place in *The Collector of Treasures* if Head's social vision of family and community is to be possible.

But the particular anguish of *A Question of Power* goes deeper than this, for it records what Head has pointed to as a growing and finally devastating recognition that cruelty and lack of compassion could exist as readily in Botswana as in South Africa, and could, equally, be a part of her own psyche: 'there is a line that forms the title of the book – if the things of the soul are really a question of power then anyone in possession of the power of the spirit could be Lucifer'.[16] The particular forms taken by the 'madness' of the narrative self in this novel dramatise the artificial divisions or splits at war in the racist, sexist social order. The text's affirmative ending – which reads more like an act of will than an organically conceived resolution – is again constructed around the sense of community, which (appropriately to Head's general project) is emphatically placed as vision rather than reality: '[falling asleep, Margaret] placed one soft hand over her land. It was a gesture of belonging.'[17]

After this novel of personal breakdown, Head moved away for a while from fiction, with its particular inward-turning, and began to collect oral tradition, as if needing by this means to bring community and communality once again to the foreground. She collected and transcribed the set of oral accounts that would make up *Serowe: Village of the Rain Wind* (1981);[18] some of these would later provide the germs for the short stories in *The Collector of Treasures*.[19] (Though published later, *Serowe* precedes *The Collector of Treasures*.)

Despite these close links, the books differ from each other in two major ways, both of them of import for the argument being developed in this essay. One difference is the writer's insertion of women into the presented world. With the exception of the anecdote that produces 'Heaven is not Closed', the oral accounts give virtually no sense of women's presence. The other difference concerns the question of orality. Even as the record of oral accounts, *Serowe* retains little connection with orality, since the performative element is missing: the gestures, expressions and movements of the oral tale-teller are silenced in the literal transcription. In *The Collector of Treasures*, however, Head strives, as writer, to recreate that sense of performance. We need to look at this process first, before we turn to the textual incorporation of women.

As part of their artistic reconstruction of the oral tradition, Head's texts incorporate into the ontology of the presented world both storyteller and audience, setting up one or more subordinate narrators – distinct from the authorial narrator – as well as a group of listeners. Through these devices the reader is invited to adopt a spatio-temporal perspective within that world, becoming part of the community. This is a common device in regional literature which intends to seduce the outside metropolitan reader into its world, and is employed by writers as diverse as William Faulkner and Ama Ata Aidoo. Head's stories often reconstruct the gestures around the act of storytelling, referring to the postures, positions and physical responses of both storyteller and audience, and thus continue to reinforce the sense of a community gathering together to tell and to hear a tale.

In a slightly different way, Head's writing recalls the oral tradition by incorporating into the collection: (a) genealogy, or epic history; (b) proverbs and sayings; and (c) gossip and community responses to events and people. These three devices draw attention to the continuing presence and contemporary reconstruction of community voice and community values, reminding the reader that in a culture with no written history, no codified legal system, no written text books, it is word-of-mouth accounts, passed from generation to generation, in a process of frequent debate, which provide history, entertainment, education and law. For the first story in the collection the narrator draws on community memory in order to present the genealogy of the Taloate people, who broke away from the Monamapee people, thus placing the written text within the oral tradition, that 'ancient stream of holiness' (*Collector of Treasures*, p. 11) referred to in her story 'Heaven is not Closed'.

Head also sometimes incorporates proverbs and sayings into her narrative, in a way comparable to, although considerably less often and less explicitly than, Chinua Achebe in *Things Fall Apart*, where the male speakers deploy the proverb in order to reach back to traditional wisdom for their authority. In 'Jacob: the Story of a Faith-Healing Priest', Head has a woman speaker reach back for her authority. Johannah needs to justify herself in the face of accusations from her relatives about having entered a number of sexual relationships: 'At last Johannah was allowed to speak. She raised her hand proudly and quoted an old proverb: "I agree with all that has been said about me. . . . But I am a real woman and as the saying goes the children of a real woman do not get lean or die"' (p. 30). And she later repeats: 'the children of a real woman cannot fall into the fire' (p. 31).[20]

Probably the most noticeable example of orality in Head's texts is the constant use of 'they said', 'they exclaimed' and so on, which give the impression of everyone talking, having their say: a community of volubility. The standard trajectory of Head's stories is to open with a wide-angle focus on the community, to close in on individuals within that community, and to end with a focus on community again, so that the individual voice typically emerges from and then slips back into communality. The voice of the (impersonal, virtually invisible) authorial narrator is generally taken over by one or more voices within the community, or what I call here a community voice. Only in two stories is the primary narrator placed explicitly apart from the community; but in 'The Special One' she is represented as a visitor being drawn into the village community, despite her initial remoteness and confusion, and in 'Jacob: the Story of a Faith-Healing Priest' as the one gathering together the voices that will make up the full (written) story.

The implicit disjunction between literary and oral voice notwithstanding, there is as little reminder as possible in the stories generally of the literary as opposed to the oral, for Head's representation of the storyteller and storytelling involves a refusal both of the authorial authority and the authorial creative function that typically mark the literary text (I refer to the general realist tradition, within which Head writes). The shift is of course not to a modernist disappearance of the author and her replacement by the individual subject, but to an impression of communal creativity and communal response. In this regard there is a marked similarity between Head and other Black South African writers, although the particular strategies are very different: Noni Jabavu, for instance, whose project in *The Ochre People*[21] is virtually to repress the individual by means of the communal, and Ellen Kuzwayo, whose *Call Me Woman*[22] flips back and forth between the voice of the autobiographical subject and the voices, or lives, of other South African women.

One consequence of the authorial limitation of authority and the focus on community response is an invitation to the reader to share in the dramatic conflict around which the story pivots. Michael Thorpe, who also looks at Head's constructed kinship with the village storyteller of the oral tradition, attempts to come to terms with the various contradictions in Head's stories by arguing that 'the [authorial] narrator seems often to be telling the story as an exploration, as a way to develop or even question her own understanding'.[23] It is hard to say whether she *is* developing her own understanding by dramatising community responses, but certainly through this dramatisation Head reveals a desire not to construct the stories as an expression of moral judgement, and thus, I suggest, refuse to cast herself as outsider, as part of the world of missionaries, colonial legislators and judges and what she on one occasion calls the 'lily-white artist'.[24]

But even if Head as author of the literary text disappears behind the voice of the community and its varying and often uncertain intellectual and emotional responses, this does not mean that we do not periodically hear an authorial attitude at odds with the patriarchal communal voice. The opening story of the collection, 'The Deep River', heralds the concern with gender evident in many of the stories. Tracing the emergence of individual desire from the single 'face' (p. 1) of the people, the story represents the individual as specifically anti-patriarchal: young Sebembele falls in love with the woman possessed but not loved by his father. This picks up the father-son difference referred to earlier in relation to *When Rain Clouds Gather*, confirms that the concept of community has all too easily referred to a *patriarchal* community whose idea of cohesiveness depends on the subjection of women, and suggests that the idea of community will be differently defined.

Often the authorial attitude is explicit. Some of the critical statements regarding the community's treatment of women were mentioned at the start of the essay. 'The Collector of Treasurers', the title story, provides the most extended feminist statement, commenting on both pre-colonial and post-colonial times. Correspondingly, then, in view of her overall project, we shall see Head taking particular pains in this story to close the distance between feminist writer and oral community. In the collection as a whole she takes pains to represent the voices of women, and often 'hears' in these voices the origins of her own feminist voice.

THE VOICES OF WOMEN: RECONSTRUCTING COMMUNITY

The feminist intervention in 'The Collector of Treasures' reads as follows. In the pre-colonial African world women were regarded 'in a congenital sense, as being an inferior form of human life' (p. 92). By diminishing customary paternal authority, colonialism has also neutralised paternal responsibility, and in the process has helped entrench anti-female behaviour:

> The colonial era and the period of migratory mining labour to South Africa was a further affliction. . . . It broke the hold of the ancestors. It broke the old, traditional form of family life. . . . [The man] became 'the boy' of the white man. . . . Men and women, in order to survive, had to turn inwards to their own resources. It was the man who arrived at this turning point, a broken wreck with no inner resources at all. . . . [I]n an effort to flee his own inner emptiness, he spun away from himself in a dizzy kind of death dance of wild destruction and dissipation.   (p. 92)

In general, Head's solution to the problems posed for women in such a community is to reconstruct patriarchalism by inserting or re-inserting women into oral tradition, and thus both giving women a central moral place in communal life and creating a different kind of community. This process of reconstruction will also involve, as we shall see towards the end of this chapter, the creation of a different kind of male figure, who modifies the nature of the patriarchal community.

'The Wind and a Boy' concerns itself, particularly poignantly, with the idea of a woman trying to take charge of a story. The grandmother artfully incorporates into her storytelling that British novel which marks the start of the novelistic tradition, for she tells a wonderful story about Robinson Crusoe as a hunter who serves the community by killing an elephant. The grandmother, Sejosenye, is the Black and female Daniel Defoe; her grandson's name Friedman marks him as an emancipated version of the enslaved Friday. However, Friedman is killed within the ambit of an altogether uglier story: by 'progress' (p. 75) in the form of a 'small green truck' (p. 74) driven by a man with 'neither brakes on his car nor a driving licence' (p. 75): 'And thus progress, development, and a pre-occupation with status and living-standards first announced themselves to the village. It looked like being an ugly story with many decapitated bodies on the main road' (p. 75). When she learns of his death Sejosenye says, 'Can't you return those words back?' (p. 74), and spends the rest of her life feverishly singing and talking to herself, as if still desperately hoping to substitute her own story for someone else's version of progress.

In 'Kgotla' the focus is on people having their say, with the woman's moral authority voiced at the end of the story. Women were traditionally not allowed into the *kgotla*, the seat of tribal administration or council where court activities traditionally take place and, after the establishment of colonial rule with its magistrate's court, the 'people's place' (p. 62), where 'people could make their anguish and disputes heard' (ibid.). Under the leadership of Khama (Kgama III: 1875–1923) women were allowed for the first time to come to court to lodge a complaint personally rather than through a male sponsor.[25] Head observed that Khama gave women a 'feeling . . . that they could talk for themselves'.[26] Women are still excluded from being judges, but since, as the male judges admit, 'we can never settle cases at kgotla' (p. 68), it is noteworthy that the woman called Rose, who has had an unfair informal judgment passed on her by the community, is now in a formal setting able to produce her own words of generosity and commitment to the well-being of the community, thus providing a settlement accessible neither to the male judges nor her extended family nor the 'bureaucratic world' (p. 62) bequeathed by British rule, which had 'no time to listen' (p. 61).

In 'The Deep River' the oral account produced by the old men at the end of the story characterises the whole story as a piece of genealogy, or epic history. As the Africanist historian Basil Davidson notes, 'There is scarcely a modern African people without a more or less vivid tradition that speaks of movement from another place. Younger sons of paramount chief would hive off with their followers, and become paramount themselves in a new land.'[27] Epic history such as this is typically narrated by men.[28] Head, as woman writer, thus takes over the epic, inserting women into a tradition which has excluded them. (Head later added *A Bewitched Crossroad*[29] to her historical *oeuvre*.)

What difference does the woman's voice make? At the very least, its presence invites one to take a critical perspective on patriarchalism. Within the general community the different values given to 'woman' become the sign of the community's internal differences: the new community is defined as one in which women are valued for more than their reproductive capacities. Nevertheless, the fact that difference speaks itself in the following way – some say 'A man who is influenced by a woman is no ruler. he is like one who listens to the advice of a child' (p. 3), others say 'Let him keep her' (ibid.), as if women were in some sense still like dogs – betrays the marks of *the same*: the romantic resolution continues to place woman as object rather than subject.

The ending of the story offers comment on the romantic resolution. Echoing Moleka's insistence in *Maru* that '[attractive] women like you are the cause of all the trouble in the world' (p. 83), this story ends:

> The old men there keep on giving confused and contradictory accounts of their origins, but they say they lost their place of birth over a woman. They shake their heads and say that women have always caused a lot of trouble in the world.   (p. 6)

As the men see it, the story is thus one of loss rather than reparation, and the 'account' with which women are now credited is simply one of *blame*, the inverse of the romantic idealisation of women (in both moves they are the objects against which men define themselves and towards which they yearn). In this way 'The Deep River' puts under scrutiny its own romantic ending as well as, by implication, those of the earlier novels to which it indirectly alludes.

The resolution of the plot is provided by the marriage and the establishment of a new community, with the closure of the story represented as a patriarchal account. This juxtaposition (again) casts doubt on whether attitudes to women in the new community differ at all from the old. But, as I have suggested, only in one sense *is* this the story's last word: the story is ultimately *written* not by the old men but by the writer, a woman, who presides over all the tale-telling in the text, gathering, shaping, invisibly narrating, occasionally commenting, and taking to print. A gap thus opens up in 'The Collector of Treasures' between the oral account, defined here as a patriarchal account, and the written account which questions it, with the act of representation – the representation of women, and of romantic love – posing itself as an issue straddling that gap.

The writer's interest in elevating the voices of women, which she does in many of the subsequent stories, is in part an interest in reconstructing a male-dominated community. In this way Head heralds the current interest in South African literary and political life in hearing the voices of women. But the problem of the relation between men and women remains, even if women become more vocal, if the representation of women does not change: if, in other words, women still define women in terms of the patriarchal symbolic system, thus confirming themselves as the signs of the feminine as it is patriarchally conceived, however much the presence of women's voices seems otherwise to contradict such conceptions. The pressure on women in terms of the liberation struggle has been and still is enormous: men have spoken out publicly about the need for women to 're-encourage' them rather than to deflate or 'castrate' them, as if continuing the damage done by white racist rule.[30] Head's contribution in the face of this difficulty *is* to define masculinity in different terms, but at the same time to find the roots for this new masculinity in the past itself, as discussion of her 'new man', generally called her 'great man', will show.

THE 'GREAT MAN'/THE 'NEW MAN'

The period of reading and research in between writing *A Question of Power* and *The Collector of Treasures,* a period during which Head makes a turn from personal to community focus and also attends more carefully and explicitly to the position of women in the community, is also marked by Head's developing respect for Khama the Great, in whom she found qualities which cohered with what she had already been dreaming of in a figure like Makhaya. In a lengthy interview Head gave in 1983, there are fascinating links to be detected between what Head sees as the contribution of Khama the Great and the processes of her own creativity. Most obviously, Head's strong

response to what she called Khama's 'balancing act'[31] offers itself as
a model for her own literary project as it unfolds in *The Collector of
Treasures*. In her view, Khama adopted a number of new practices
from the 'West' without disrupting the continuity of traditional life,
and managed to resist what Cecil Rhodes was planning for Botswana,
thus saving the country 'from what happened to South Africa'.[32]
More subtly, Khama functions as the god-like figure who replaces
the 'Lucifer' referred to in relation to *A Question of Power*, affirming
Head's vision of god-on-earth, and turning the author's potentiality
for destructiveness on to the path of creativity and good.[33]

The great man, for Head, is one who is able to reform custom and
tradition without losing the customary 'courtesies'. By this Head
means more than ritual or social gesture; 'courtesies' refers above all
to a consciousness of the community which expresses itself in
community service and personal responsibility to family as well.
The observance of such 'courtesies' helps forge in people an awareness
of their own continuity, which involves an awareness of history,
accessible through Botswana rather than South Africa, where the
history is primarily one of 'land-grabbing wars and diamond- and
gold-rushes', with 'whole breaks' instead of a 'beautiful pattern' of
human coexistence.[34]

Besides being primarily concerned with the welfare and dignity
of others, men and women alike, Head's great man has a 'broader
view of life' which is the gift of the literary artist, too, who has 'the
biggest view possible';[35] this view enables both man and writer to
stand against racism, she says, and against sexism, as her fiction
implies. Interestingly, Head suggests that this 'broader view' is developed from influences outside Botswana, even from South Africa,
which 'with all its horrors, creates international sorts of people. They
identify with the problems of mankind in general, rather than their
own.'[36] She also says, 'It's not so much a question of being black as of
having got control of life's learning.' All this, in her view, accounts
for her literary contribution: the 'broader view' brought in from
outside, along with her own freedom from particular customs and
traditions, given the specific dislocations of her childhood as well as
her foreignness in Botswana: 'I shape the future with this cool stance.'[37]

What Head means by 'life's learning' is not explicitly clarified, but
– in view of her literary and other references – I conclude that it
implies an interest in ideas, what she once called a 'life of the mind',[38]
as well as book-learning of a particular kind: the agricultural
knowledge that Gilbert brings to Botswana is the obvious example

here. Head's alignment with the figure of the 'great man' who can solve Botswana's social problems is evident in her first novel, in the figure of Makhaya, a man from South Africa, de-tribalised and in search of a better world. Some contribution is made through his links with the communal past, to which he can make certain crucial adjustments of his own, given his 'broader [external] view'; other contributions are made through his absorption of Gilbert's university education and agricultural research.

But if Head is herself her own 'great man', she is also his creator. She makes clear that when these great men do not exist in reality they must be produced. Speaking of *Maru* she says: 'A Botswana chief is not going to marry a Masarwa and publicly make it a huge thing like that. But he was created to do it. . . . We don't walk around with gods in our heart. We have to have a character like that to solve racialism.' And speaking of the anecdote from which she wrote 'The Collector of Treasures', she says, 'that's why the basic plot I borrowed from life. Now, when I actually wrote that story I mentioned all these things. I borrowed it exactly more or less as it happened, but there's a huge, majestic man that moves into the story – now he's going to solve all the problems.' The writer clearly distinguishes between the collected story and the invented story, the original taken from the reality that the oral tradition offers (a story from the community), with her version adding what reality fails to provide: 'you've got to solve a problem. . . . [Paul Thebolo] is juxtaposed against a man who has low animal tendencies – but the problem is it is all too much of a reality in the society, and the story wasn't entirely invented in my own head.'[39]

The language here bears out the terms with which *Maru* was discussed, Head in both cases distinguishing between reality and literary invention. Perhaps fancifully, but in tune I think with the unconscious logic of Head's thinking, my imagination has been caught by the use of her own surname in the phrase 'in my own head', whose juxtaposition against 'all too much of a reality' emphasises – her projected image as a writer who invents what is not provided by the oral and experienced material offered her in her village community, and who is engaged in the detached judgement that the word 'shaping' must imply. At the same time Head is anxious not to be seen as the 'lily-white artist' removed from communal life and its oral tradition. The 'writing of books', Head claimed, is like 'baking bread and peeling potatoes'.[40] Thus adjusting at least some of her references to 'life's learning', her stories take pains to reintegrate writing into such everyday acts, to make the figure of the artist a part of communal action and communal expression, and thus to make her fictional resolutions seem organic to the community rather than brought out of the 'head' of a remote outsider.

This is one of the contributions of *The Collector of Treasures*, offered, I think, as a kind of propitiation for her outsider status, and her learning, and – in the title story of the collection – as a screen for the radical way in which she rewrites the community.

'THE COLLECTOR OF TREASURES'

'The Collector of Treasures' focuses on the work done by women's hands: Dikeledi, for instance, is good at knitting, sewing, weaving baskets and thatching. Then the text focuses, too, on the hands themselves, the beautiful hands of this creative woman: 'she had soft, caressing, almost boneless, hands of strange power – work of a beautiful design grew from those hands' (p. 90). With these hands, she says, she 'fed and reared [her] children' (p. 90). And with these hands, 'with the precision and skill of her hard-working hands' (p. 103) Dikeledi castrates her husband.

Given the implicit connections between creativity and the work that hands do, castration here signifies the creative and constructive rather than the destructive act. Dikeledi has another skill: 'she had always found gold amidst the ash, deep loves that had joined her heart to the hearts of others. . . . She was the collector of such treasures' (p. 91). That 'The Collector of Treasures' is the title for the collection as a whole extends the referent of that phrase, even as it is used in this story, to the figure of the author herself: also a 'collector of treasures', whose heart has been 'joined' through her writing to the 'hearts of others', and who has also found gold amidst the ash. If Dikeledi is admired for 'the pattern she had invented in her own head' (p. 90), so now is the writer.

The connection between writer and creative character makes its conscious or semi-conscious emergence when Head speaks about first hearing the anecdote that provides the source for the story: 'it was so shocking to me, it was actually the first time I had ever heard of a man dying like that. When the relative told me, the first thing that I felt was the knife going through me. I even put my hand out.'[41] Initially, her response suggests an identification with the corrupted male figure who is being destroyed, himself destroyer of family life. But she also says that she puts her hand out, as if to take hold of that knife, which suggests an identification with Dikeledi. And, in fact, character and writer are linked, for the writer's characterisation of Paul Thebolo carries hints of metaphorical castration. Just after Garesego has been literally castrated, Thebolo steps 'out of the dark' (p. 103), with 'a tortured expression' (ibid.) on his face, and for a moment words fail him. Of course in the full metaphorical meaning of the term he is not 'castrated': the writer associates him throughout the story with power, in the positive sense, and even specifically with the power of virility (he is man enough for two women, the text tells us, but also man enough not to have to prove himself in that way). But, given the representation of Thebolo as kind, gentle and compassionate, a man who is not afraid to bind himself romantically to a single woman and who does not define his masculinity in a way that leaves mothering to women, Thebolo functions in the story as a 'feminised' hero, something like Makhaya in *When Rain Clouds Gather*.

Dikeledi stands as a figure for the author, then, and the castrating act is to be seen here as an equivalent of the writerly act. Or, to put it another way, the writerly act camouflages itself as a community act, as just one of the expressive acts women perform in a world that comes to the writer through the oral tradition. Having represented herself as the male god-like figure associated in her mind with Khama the Great, as I suggested earlier, Head takes this link further: 'what was beautiful about the man was that he would slice any harmful . . . eliminate . . . but keep'. The lexical choices here recall and extend the word 'slice' used for Garesego's genitals; the horror of that act still remains, as the hesitancy of expression suggests (the ellipses mark the hiatuses in Head's original speech).[42]

Why am I labouring this connection between Head and Dikeledi, and Head and the 'great man' curative figure, the social healer who comes in with elements from an imagined world which are the products to some extent of the Botswanan past and to some extent of an outsider's experience and detachment? There are two reasons: one to do with understanding the precariousness of Head's literary project as a 'balancing act', and the other to do with the question of feminism in South Africa today; the route that it tends to take through the African past, rather than the corrupted present; the oblique, courteous manner in which it takes up its feminist voice; the merging of the individual voice with the voice of the community; and the continual elevation of communality. Like 'Life' and 'Snapshots of a Wedding', 'The Collector of Treasures' is a tale about the modern world which has lost the values of the communal world. But here the modern world is represented not by 'conceited' or 'hysterical' women, but by the way Dikeledi's life has been ruined by Garesego. Moreover, in this world, neighbours shun Dikeledi, which means that (apart from her idyllic relations with Thebolo and Kenalepe) she does not live in communality.

Then it is also about an ideal world, which the writer has constructed as a vision of the (reconstructed) past. The relationship between Dikeledi, Kenalepe and Paul is built on barter, neighbourliness and task-sharing, with paternal responsibility and romantic love put forward as the two major components of Head's feminist vision. We even almost shift back into a world of polygyny, for Kenalepe suggests that Dikeledi become Thebolo's unofficial second wife, taking over the conjugal duties that Kenalepe, pregnant, does not wish to perform, and experiencing a sexual pleasure Dikeledi's husband was too brutish to make possible. Kenalepe *offers* her husband to Dikeledi, proposing (in small) a kinship system where women are the negotiators rather than the objects of exchange. Nevertheless, this textual direction into the (idealised and redirected) polygynous pest is deflected, and the nuclear family, bound by monogamous romantic love and paternal responsibility, is maintained as one of the elements of Head's idyll.

Within these two tales there are two acts: literal castration and feminisation. The act of castration is the solution of a group of women *in the world*. Given to Head through the oral tradition, it may thus be placed in a communal world; moreover, all the women in the prison have killed their husbands. But it keeps them imprisoned: if they form a happy community of women within the wider community, they are also set apart, kept in a space characterised by high walls and an anxious male warder who insists that the women stand with their hands at their sides: 'He does not mind anything but that. He is mad about that' (p. 90). The act of feminisation is the solution offered by the literary artist, pointing to a new world premised on what Head sees as the best of the old (task-sharing, barter, communal cohesion) and the best of the new (romantic love, nuclear family, monogamy, greater value and voice for women, men stripped of their phallic egos). Although the act of writing is not referred to, it becomes associated, through the association of feminisation with castration, with the other creative acts I have mentioned, and thus characterised as a communal act, where writing is linked to thatching and knitting and weaving, the acts women perform in their construction of home and community. Thus the writer defines herself not as a *writer* who stands outside the community, but as a figure within. However much the act of writing may look like an extraneous act – for it produces what is not produced by a rural, predominantly pre-literate community – it becomes, in this story, part of the oral/ communal act. And so it is that the writer places herself within a community, reconstructed in terms of a feminism whose origins are now not outside, but inside.

In 'The Special One' the first-person narrator makes its only extended appearance,[43] and in certain ways the device functions to blur the separation made in this essay, largely on the basis of Head's own statements, between the literary, individual and feminist voice and the oral, communal and patriarchal voice. It is not, at first, the narrator but one of the rural characters who says 'women are just dogs in this society' (p. 81). Marked as an outsider to the community, the peripheral narrator comes to take that belief as her own, as if she has been educated by this woman's story. In this way Head establishes a feminist voice as organic to the community, which is now – in general terms – largely defined by the voices and judgements of women.

The question of representation is raised, as I have said, in 'The Deep River'. Women are viewed by one section of the male population in terms of their reproductive functions, and then by another section as the objects of romantic love, which simply leads to their being finally placed in the patriarchal shuttle between praise and blame. Head's incorporation of women's voices and women's views means that women can no longer be considered 'of no account'. Conservative her project certainly remains, for although it expands and adjusts the nature of community and family to make a more hospitable space for women, it also calls upon the feminine in its conventional idealised associations: in 'Kgotla', for instance, Rose is valued for her self-sacrifice to the larger good of the extended family, and in 'Jacob' the proverb Johanna brings forward from the past defines her as 'real woman' precisely through her motherhood.

Yet such moments of representation need to be seen in the context of Head's careful redefinition of masculinity in precisely the terms accorded the feminine: generosity, compassion, self-sacrifice and motherliness. These are the community 'courtesies' being demanded of both men and women. Head's new men in *The Collector of Treas-*

ures eschew greed and power, and are characterised by generosity and humility, like Tholo in 'Hunting' and Thebolo in 'The Collector of Treasures' in their realised forms, and like Sianana in 'Life' and Friedman in 'The Wind and a Boy' in their potential. For specific textual indications that Head's characterisation of such men is to be read as a feminising act, beyond the subtle metaphor set up in 'The Collector of Treasures', we may go to the story 'Hunting', where one of the villagers says of Tholo: 'I don't know whether he is a girl or what' (p. 105). And, reversing the conventional literary situation where men are the poets and women the poems, Thebolo in 'The Collector of Treasures' is 'a poem of tenderness' (p. 93).

Thinking again of the construction of community in 'Snapshots of a Wedding', any authorial correction that might await this community would involve Neo's husband, in the terms offered by 'The Collector of Treasures' and 'Hunting'. Neo herself has been defined as 'good wife', and the story makes clear that this function is to be seen in communal rather than simply familial terms. Life, in 'Life', cannot be contained by the community in this way, for she lacks – like Head's damaged modern men – the resources to see village life as anything but a 'big, gaping yawn' (p. 43). Head's feminism directs itself away from any tendency in middle-class feminist practice to take male access to power and independence as its model; individualism is defined as 'conceit', unacceptable in both women and men. Given Head's *de facto* relation with the Botswanan community, this approach must involve repressing – or containing – certain aspects of herself.

Noni Jabavu, also writing about the problem posed to the community by modern manners in men and women (in the Eastern Cape rather than Botswana) refers to the 'chasms [that] yawned before you' if your personal inclinations and habits' of privacy 'tended against the principle' of sociability, which she glosses as an 'exposure to the public gaze'.[44] The topic is slightly different, and the points of departure and destination are too, for throughout *The Ochre People* Jabavu represents herself as obedient to patriarchal rules about women. Yet what binds Head and Jabavu, and Kuzwayo as well, is their recognition of the risk people take when they separate themselves from the demands made in the name of community, for this leaves them without a social structure by which to know themselves. Although Head and Jabavu accept the cost of this communal incorporation, the word 'yawn' in both cases betrays a semi-conscious resistance, and briefly points to the gap that necessarily exists between modern, cosmopolitan, highly educated writer and rural, conservative, pre-literate community.

To what extent are Head's women freed from the grip of patriarchal ideology? Even in 'The Collector of Treasures', within the idealised world created between Dikeledi, Kenalepe and Paul, Dikeledi and Kenalepe still sit 'on the edge' (p. 95) of male political debate about colonialism and independence, listening but never participating, although they go over the discussions themselves the next day. Perhaps at this moment, despite the idealised representation in other respects, Head feels herself limited by social reality. As Miriam Tlali has explained regarding her own writing, her women characters play a supportive role to their husbands not because she thinks women ought to, but because in reality they are not allowed to come to the forefront.[45] However much Head's women characters *are* brought to the forefront, their voices preside over rural communal and familial concerns, and do not extend into the politics of modern life.

The main project of this essay has been to *listen* to the contribution being made by Head to the question of feminism, and to recognise some aspects of the personal and political desire that lies behind some of her textual decisions and strategies. But it must also be said that an ideological gap keeps opening up between Head as writer (that is, the position formulated in her texts) and myself as (white, urban, post-Lacanian) critic, precisely over the representation of women as mothers and wives, over the ideological place of family and community, and over the definition of feminism itself, to say nothing of the difficulty of translating Head's vision into an urban environment and making it speak in the face of contemporary political realities, however much I yearn, like her, to find a place in Africa no longer marked by 'all those divisions and signs'.

NOTES

1. 'Bessie Head: Interviewed by Michelle Adler, Susan Gardner, Tobeka Mda and Patricia Sandler', in C. MacKenzie and C. Clayton (eds), *Between the Lines* (Grahamstown, S. Africa: National English Literary Museum, 1989) p. 11.
2. Bessie Head, *The Collector of Treasures and Other Botswanan Village Tales* (London: Heinemann Educational, 1977) pp. 3, 83.

3. Bessie Head, 'Despite Broken Bondage, Botswana Women are Still Unloved', *The Times*, 13 August 1975, p. 5.
4. While Chetin's analysis of *The Collector of Treasures* is interesting and useful, her desire to read Head's narrator as a 'village narrator' and her general focus on myth ('around which all our lives are constructed') mean that she is not engaged with the specificities of the writer's relation with the village community, which I need to look at as part of a political debate. Another difference between Chetin's approach and mine is that she is interested in the 'distinctly ambiguous, unresolved tone' in Head's writing, whereas my interest lies in tonal precariousness, which again involves political intentions (S. Chetin, 'Myth, Exile and the Female Condition: Bessie Head's *The Collector of Treasures*', *Journal of Commonwealth Literature*, Vol. 24, no. 1 (1989) pp. 132, 115, 114).
5. S. Rimmon-Kenan, *Narrative Fiction: Contemporary Poetics* (London: Methuen, 1983) p. 103.
6. 'There were so many things in African custom and tradition that are good. You had to offer life certain courtesies' (MacKenzie and Clayton (eds), *Between the Lines*, p. 16).
7. 'The cheap, glaring paltry trash of a people who are living it up for themselves alone dominates everything' (Bessie Head, 'African Story', *Listener*, vol. 88, no. 2279 (1972) p. 736).
8. Kirsten Holt Peterson quotes a South African woman speaking as follows:

> In South Africa the question of Western feminism, encroaching into the minds of the African women is a very, very sensitive question, particularly for the African man. Anytime you ask him to do something, to go and fetch the child today, or something like that he says: 'Look, you are already a feminist. You are a white woman and a feminist.' It is thrown into your face in the same way in which Communist is thrown into the face of the blacks in South Africa.
> K. H. Peterson (ed.), *Criticism and Ideology: Second African Writers' Conference, Stockholm 1986* (Uppsala: Scandinavian Institute of African Studies, 1988) p. 185.

> Like most other South African (and African) women writers, Head did not call herself a feminist. But this was not for fear of being called 'white': 'I do not have to be a feminist. The world of the intellect is impersonal, sexless. . . . I have worked outside all political and other ideologies, bowing to life here and there and absorbing all that I felt to be relevant, but always fighting for space and air. I needed this freedom and independence, in order that my sympathies remain fluent and responsive to any given situation in life' ('Writing out of Southern Africa', *New Statesman*, 16 August 1985, p. 22).

9. Ellen Kuzwayo has spoken of the way the South African government has capitalised on the traditions and customs of Black South Africans in an interview with Beata Lipman (B. Lipman, *We Make Freedom* (London: Pandora Press, 1984) p. 18). For further discussion of Kuzwayo's

feminism, in relation to Black Consciousness, see D. Driver, 'M'a-Ngoana O Tsoare Thipa ka Bohaleng – The Child's Mother Grabs the Sharp End of the Knife: Women as Mothers, Women as Writers', in M. Trump (ed.), *Rendering Things Visible: Essays on South African Literary Culture* (Johannesburg: Ravan Press, 1990) pp. 225–55.

10. See C. B. Davies, 'Introduction: Feminist Consciousness and African Literary Criticism', in C. B. Davies and A. A. Graves (eds), *Ngambika: Studies of Women in African Literature* (Trenton, N. J.: Africa World Press, 1986) p. 1.

11. B. Head, 'Some Notes on Novel Writing', *New Classic*, vol. 5 (1978) p. 30.

12. Quoted in J. Marquard, 'Bessie Head: Exile and Community in Southern Africa', *London Magazine*, vol. 18, nos. 9 and 10 (1978) p. 54.

13. B. Head, *When Rain Clouds Gather* (London: Heinemann Educational Books, 1987). Page references to this novel are given n the essay itself.

14. B. Head, *Maru* (London: Heinemann Educational Books, 1972). Page references to this novel are given in the essay itself.

15. B. Head, *A Question of Power* (London: Heinemann Educational Books, 1974).

16. Quoted in Marquard, 'Bessie Head', p. 53. In 'Some Notes on Novel Writing', Head says 'I found myself in a situation where there was no guarantee against the possibility that I could be evil too' (p. 31).

17. Head, *A Question of Power*, p. 206. Head noted that she balanced the 'inward turning' of the book by incorporating 'an everyday world where a little village gets on with its everyday affairs and is interested in progress and development' (Bessie Head', in L. Nichols (ed.), *Conversations with African Writers* (Washington, D.C.: Voice of America, 1981) p. 54).

18. B. Head, *Serowe: Village of the Rain Wind* (London: Heinemann Educational Books, 1981).

19. See Craig MacKenzie, 'Short Fiction in the Making: the Case of Bessie Head', *English in Africa* (Grahamstown), vol. 15, no. 1 (1988) pp. 17–28.

20. Bessie Head gives formal acknowledgement to C. L. S. Nyembezi, *Zulu Proverbs* (Johannesburg: Witwatersrand University Press, 1954), which draws attention to the frequent incorporation of proverbs in her writing, but I am referring here to the self-conscious use of proverbs by characters in dialogue. In 'Life' Head presents a saying in the making: 'I'm not like Lesego with money in the bank' (*Collector of Treasures*, p. 41).

21. N. Jabavu, *The Ochre People* (London: John Murray, 1963).

22. E. Kuzwayo, *Call Me Woman* (Johannesburg: Raven Press, 1985).

23. M. Thorpe et al., *Essays in African Literature* (Mysore, India: Center for Commonwealth Literature and Research, University of Mysore, 1978) p. 414.

24. MacKenzie and Clayton (eds), *Between the Lines*, p. 24.

25. For a discussion of Khama's revisions regarding the *kgotla* see I. Schapera, *Tribal Innovators: Tswana Chiefs and Social Change, 1795-1940* (London: University of London, The Athlone Press, 1970) p. 93. Schapera also discusses Khama's abolition of *bogadi* (p. 93) and his revision of the laws of inheritance for women (pp. 144–5). Head refers to these changes in

'Bessie Head', in MacKenzie and Clayton (eds), *Between the Lines*, p. 16. Schapera is probably her source.

26. MacKenzie and Clayton (eds), *Between the Lines*, p. 16.
27. Quoted in Thorpe, p. 416, n. 71.
28. Research by Harold Scheub and A. C. Jordan shows a gender division in the oral tradition: epic history is typically narrated by men, generally as part of public performance, whereas the narrative fictional tale is the domain of women, and told in a domestic setting. See A. C. Jordan, *Tales from Southern Africa* (Berkeley, Cal.: California University Press, 1973) pp. 1–2; H. Scheub, *The Xhosa Ntsomi* (London: Oxford University Press, 1975) pp. 5-6, 12. The division is not rigid, except in the obviously significant case of public performance. Elizabeth Gunner confirms that although women do participate in the genre of the praise poem, closely linked to the epic, their recital-performances are conducted in the company of women. See E. Gunner, 'Songs of Innocence and Experience: Women as Composers and Performers of *Izibongo*, Zulu Praise Poetry', in C. Clayton (ed.), *Women and Writing in South Africa: A Critical Anthology* (Johannesburg: Heinemann, 1989) pp. 13, 16.
29. B. Head, *A Bewitched Crossroad* (New York: Paragon House, 1986).
30. The term 're-encourage' comes from V. February in conference discussion, November 1986: 'South African Literature: Liberation and the Art of Writing' Special Issue of *Dokumente Texte und Tendenzen* ,vol. 7 (1987) p. 79. A similar point has been made by the psychologist N. C. Manganyi, *Being-Black-in-the-World*(Johannesburg: Spro-cas/Ravan, 1973) pp. 10–11. This desire for support is what lies behind the accusations of 'white-ism' referred to earlier.
31. MacKenzie and Clayton (eds), *Between the Lines*, p. 16.
32. B. Fradkin, 'Conversation with Bessie', *World Literature Written in English* (*WLWE*), vol. 17, no. 2 (1987) p. 432.
33. Bessie Head wrote:

> I have used the word God in a practical way in my books. I cannot find a substitute word for all that is most holy but I have tried to deflect people's attention into offering to each other what they offer to an Unseen Being in the sky. When people are holy to each other, war will end, human suffering will end. . . . I would propose that mankind will one day be ruled by men who are God and not greedy, power-hungry politicians. 'Writing out of Southern Africa', p. 23).

34. MacKenzie and Clayton (eds), *Between the Lines*, p. 11.
35. Ibid., p. 13.
36. Fradkin, 'Conversations with Bessie', p. 429.
37. MacKenzie and Clayton (eds), *Between the Lines*, p. 13.
38. Quoted in Marquard, 'Bessie Head', p. 51. At various times in interviews and essays Head refers to reading Russian novelists and Indian philosophers, as well as historians and anthropologists of Southern Africa. Among the writers she singles out for mention and/or quotes from are Bertolt Brecht, Chinua Achebe, D. H. Lawrence, Gabriel Garcia Marquez

and Olive Schreiner. *When Rain Clouds Gather* shows her own keen interest in agricultural research.

39. See MacKenzie and Clayton (eds), *Between the Lines*, pp. 19, 14, 13. However, I have quoted from the original transcript of the taped interview, held at the National English Literary Museum (NELM), Grahamstown, since this is a slightly fuller and more faithful version. See pp. 17, 11, 10 of typescript held at NELM. In 'Writing out of Southern Africa' Head says, 'I would propose that mankind will one day be ruled by men who are God and not greedy, power-hungry politicians. . . . Only then can the resources of the earth be cared for and shared in an equitable way among all mankind' (p. 23).

40. Ibid., p. 24.

41. Ibid., p. 14.

42. I have again quoted from the original transcript of the taped interview (p. 13; See note 39 above). The published version edits the original to read, 'So he would eliminate, but keep' MacKenzie and Clayton (eds), p. 16).

43. It is one of the contentions of this essay that the first-person point of view lies behind the authorial narrative situation of all the stories in the particular sense that Head as writer has collected and shaped these tales. What I mean here is made clear in 'Jacob: the Story of a Faith-Healing Priest', although instead of using the first-person pronoun the text uses the word 'you', in order to camouflage the first-person relation with the story: 'There is a point in the story when you begin to doubt . . .'; 'you lean forward eagerly . . . [and] ask . . .'; 'So you say, almost violently . . . ' (p. 25).

44. Jabavu, *The Ochre People*, p. 132.

45. 'Miriam Tlali: Interviewed by Cecily Lockett', in MacKenzie and Clayton (eds), *Between the Lines*, p. 75.

Index